W9-CZO-489

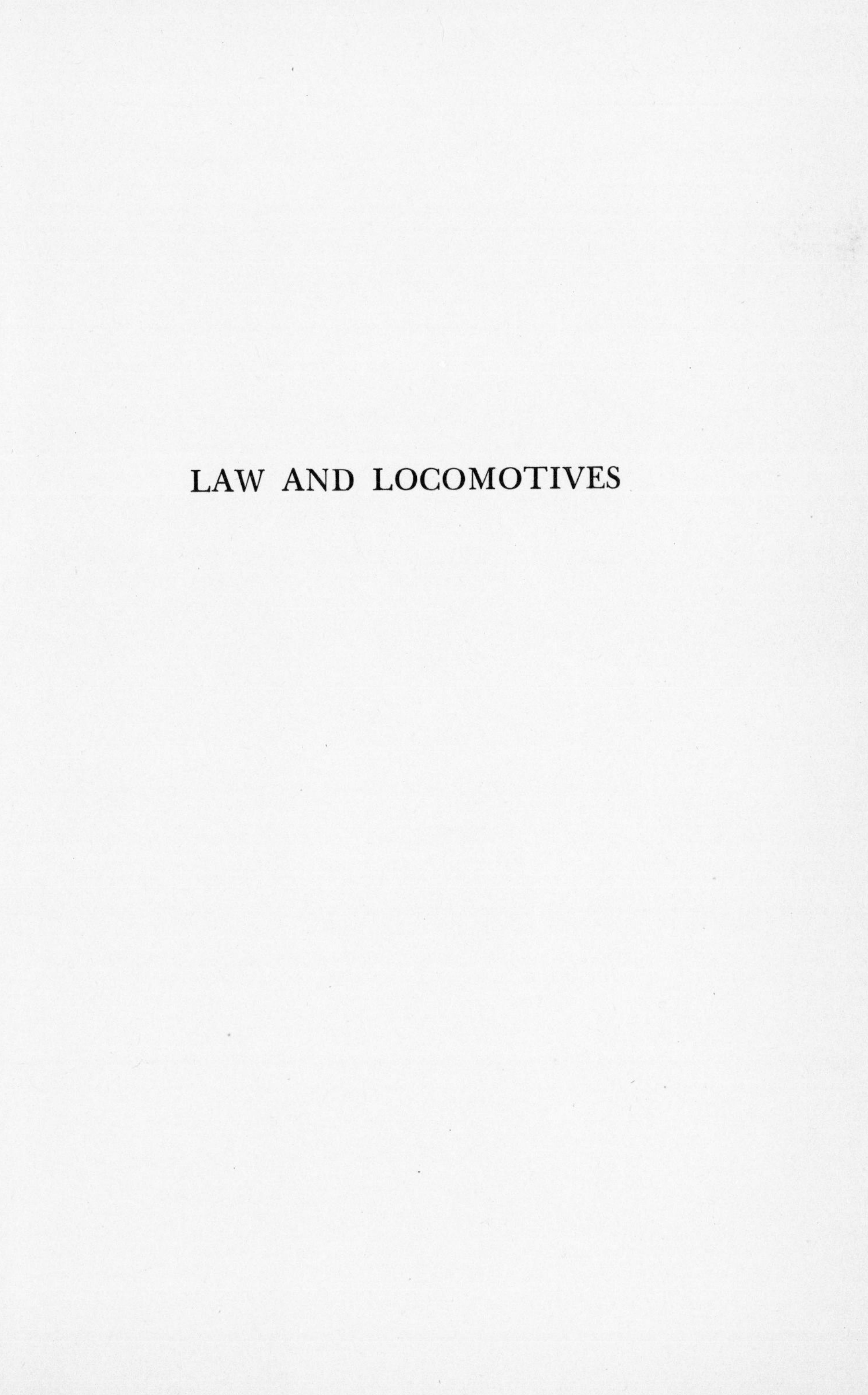

LAW AND LOCOMOTIVES

LAW AND LOCOMOTIVES

The Impact of the Railroad on Wisconsin Law in the Nineteenth Century

By ROBERT S. HUNT

THE STATE HISTORICAL SOCIETY OF WISCONSIN
MADISON, WISCONSIN

It should be the aim of a wise man neither to mock, nor to bewail, nor to denounce men's actions, but to understand them.—BARUCH DE SPINOZA, *Political Treatise.*

Preface

THIS book tries to show some of the problems presented to law in Wisconsin by the coming of the railroad. The emphasis is not on logical development of legal doctrine, but rather on function: What new jobs—or extensions of old jobs—did men of law and legal institutions have to do because the railroad came? What kinds of stress and strain did the entrance of a major new industry and the growth of a new center of non-official decision-making put upon legal concepts and organization in the Wisconsin community? And what general themes of United States legal history appear in this example of the interaction of law and economics in Wisconsin during the last half of the nineteenth century?

For raw materials I have used mainly law men's documents: statutes, court opinions, legislative journals and committee reports, executive documents and administrative reports. At certain critical points I have made first-hand examination of newspaper and manuscript sources, but on the whole I have relied on the work of other students—especially on the classic monograph by Frederick Merk, *The Economic History of Wisconsin during the Civil War Decade*—for insight furnished by contemporary newspapers.

Although I have used lawyers' materials, this is not, in the usual sense, a lawyer's book. I have paid only scant attention to matters that are, and must be, vital to practitioner, judge, and administrator. A lawyer will look in vain, for instance, for a study of the development of the law of vicarious liability or a definitive treatment of the law of eminent domain in Wisconsin during this period. If two or three sentences dispose of scores of cases dealing with accidents to railroad employees—as in Chapters III and V—without meticulous analyses of facts, attempts to distinguish holdings from dicta, or efforts to achieve a synthesis of doctrine, this is not to deny that these aspects of the cases are essential to advocate and counsellor. It is simply that the focus of this study is on other matters.

But in a larger sense this is a lawyer's book. If, perforce, a part of the lawyer's job involves policy and politics, if he is called on more and more to assess the role of official agencies of law in dealing with economic and social issues, and if he finds his traditional forum of the court being supplanted by administrative hearing and even legislative committee room, then perhaps in this study he may find something relevant to his career. For if United States legal history is to embrace the full scope of the law, it must recount in some meaningful way how society deals, through its legal system and organization, with the problems that events thrust upon it.

The story of the law and the railroad during these years is a mixture of melodrama and routine. In this it is typical of legal history in pointing up something at the heart of the working realities of law in men's social life: the problem of devising institutional means to cope, on the one hand, with long-range policy judgments and points of high tension accompanying them, and, on the other hand, with the essential day-to-day business of bringing policy alive through operations.

* * *

THIS study was made possible by a grant from the Rockefeller Foundation to the University of Wisconsin to finance a long-range project in Wisconsin legal-economic history under the direction of Professor Willard Hurst. As a recipient of a portion of that grant, I want to express my appreciation to the Foundation, the University, and Professor Hurst for the privilege of participating in this project.

To Professor Hurst I owe especial thanks. In the field of legal history he was and is my mentor. I had the good fortune to take his course in United States Legal History at the University of Wisconsin, and I have borrowed the frame of reference, and even some of the terminology, that he used in his pioneering work *The Growth of American Law: The Law Makers* and his later monograph *Law and the Conditions of Freedom in Nineteenth Century United States.* Thus the phrase "agency of law" as used in this book refers not to the Liquor Control Commission, for example, or the Bureau of Indian Affairs; rather it comprehends those general institutions which, in our country's history, have been responsible for shaping our substantive and adjective law: four agencies of official decision-making—the legislature, the courts, the constitution, and the executive—and one nonofficial but nonetheless significant agency—the bar.

I wish to thank the faculty of the University of Wisconsin Law School, and particularly Dean Oliver S. Rundell and Dean John Ritchie III, for making their facilities available to me on several occasions. To David Clark Everest, the donor of the prize awarded me for this book, I owe, of course, a special debt of thanks. To Clifford B. Lord and other members of the staff of the State Historical Society of Wisconsin—particularly to Alice E. Smith, its director of research, to Lillian Krueger, Margaret Gleason, Josephine Harper, and Ruth Davis—I wish to express my gratitude for extending me the full use of the facilities of the Society and its library. Unless otherwise noted, all illustrations were made from photographs and other prints in the collection of the Society. I owe more than I can possibly acknowledge to Livia Appel, my editor, who took me by the hand and led me through the wilderness of English syntax.

I wish to thank my partners, Messrs. Dallstream, Schiff, Hardin, Waite & Dorschel, and their office manager, Paul Draths, for allowing me to impose on the stenographic services that they command. And for their help at various stages I want to convey my thanks to Elaine Hess, John Stern, Nancy Gilson, and Frances Hurst for advice and counsel; to Eve Duggan for typing the entire manuscript submitted for the Everest Prize; to Aileen BeDell, Georgia Berry, Lolita Buonaguidi, Ruth Crum, Eleanor Feulner, Mary O'Leary, Adeline Sax, Patricia Snyder, and Nancy Walpole for typing various portions of the manuscript; and to Barbara Chancellor for designing the dust jacket.

ROBERT S. HUNT

Chicago, Illinois
January, 1958

Contents

Illustrations

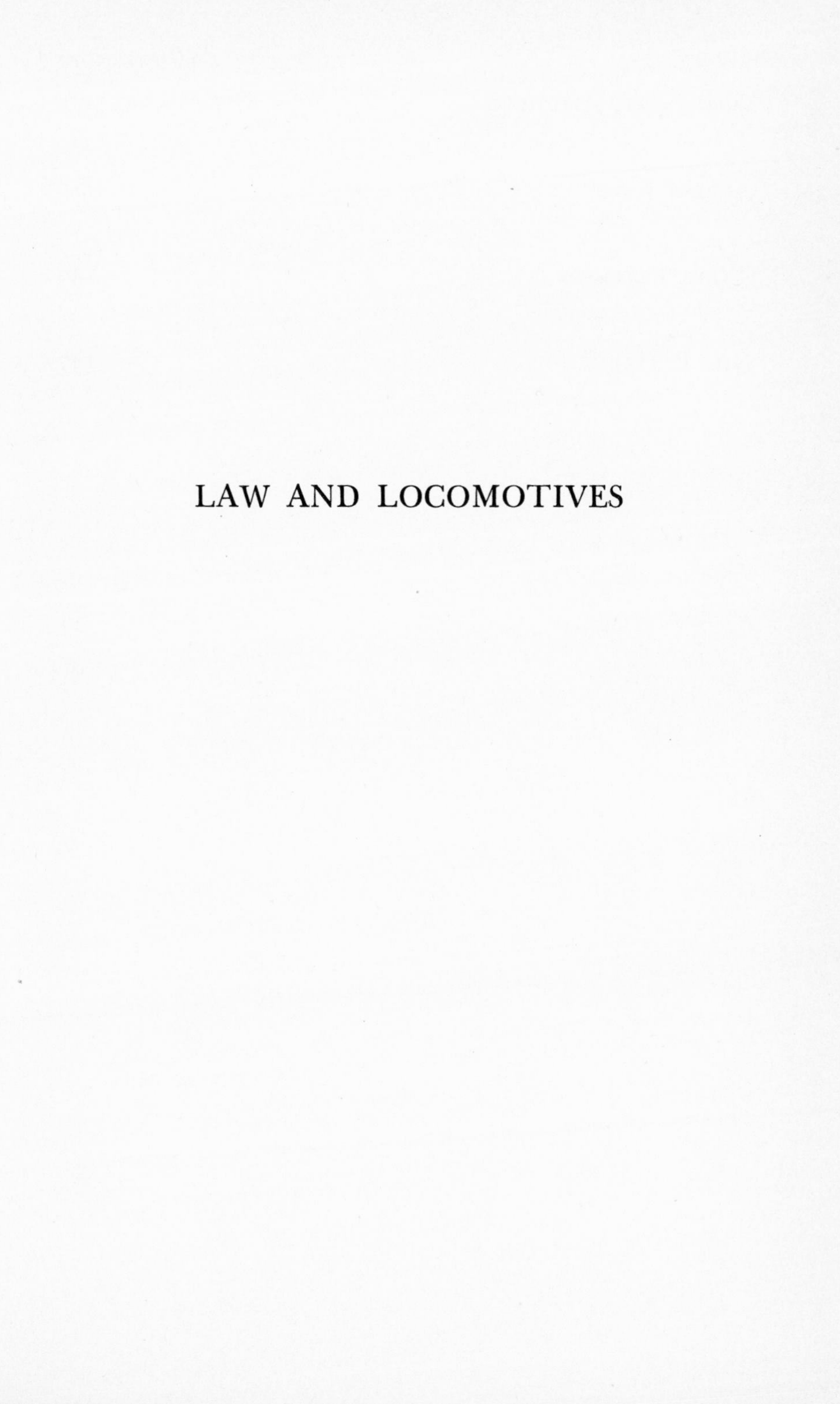

LAW AND LOCOMOTIVES

I. Wisconsin Purchase, 1856

By me kings reign and lawgivers decree just things.—Proverbs viii:15

A STREET and a park bear his name and once two cities did. But the "Route of the Hiawathas" from La Crosse to Milwaukee is his greatest monument. His immortality stems also from events that took place in a small hotel room off Capitol Square in Madison. For it was there, in 1856, that Byron Kilbourn of Kilbourntown had a rendezvous with Wisconsin law—no bashful maiden—and paid her well for her favors.

* * *

BY THE eighteen thirties the expanding economy of the Northwest Territory was in dire need of better transportation facilities to get its goods to market. In the area that became Wisconsin the demand was vociferous and unceasing. Strategically located as it was between two great inland waterways, it needed only access to them to ship its product to rich markets—to the East via the Great Lakes and Erie Canal and to St. Louis and New Orleans via the Mississippi River. Moreover, it could legitimately hope for a share of the trade between the Lakes and the River.[1]

In the beginning even plank roads were welcomed as a vast improvement over the unspeakably bad roads that were the only means of overland transportation. For a time canals seemed the answer to the problem, and during the thirties serious attempts were made to build one connecting the Fox and Wisconsin rivers and another linking the Mississippi with Milwaukee via the Rock River. Both projects were doomed by the financial scandals they engendered and by the advent of the railroads to the region. The period of plank-road construction lasted longer, but it too petered out when it became apparent that only the railroads could meet the need.[2]

By the late forties it was clear that the eastern route would ultimately replace the long haul down the Mississippi, and the wheat farmers took up the cry for cheap transportation that the lead miners in the southwest had initiated earlier. Agitation for a railroad from Lake Michigan to the Mississippi had begun as early as 1836, but canal and plank-road activity delayed positive action until 1847, when the legislature chartered the first line in Wisconsin, the Milwaukee and Waukesha Railway. After 1850 the question was no longer whether railroads should be built in the state but what routes they should follow. The legislature became a battle ground for competing charter-seekers, and more than one promising venture was stalled by sectional rivalry. Even so the legislatures of the fifties ground out one railroad charter after another.[3]

Actual construction, however, was another matter. The Milwaukee and Waukesha—after 1850 called the Milwaukee and Mississippi—reached Waukesha in 1851, but it did not reach Madison until 1854, and did not cross the state until three years later. The La Crosse and Milwaukee Railroad reached Beaver Dam, sixty miles northwest of Milwaukee, in 1855, and there for a time it stopped.[4]

Wisconsin, like all frontier communities, was short of capital, and capital in unprecedented amounts was what it needed. The promoters resorted to two expedients. The Wisconsin constitution prohibited the state from contracting debts to finance internal improvements, but it did not forbid the legislature to authorize cities and counties to buy railroad stock. This was the first device the promoters used. A second was to sell stock to individuals, mainly farmers, who usually made payment with notes secured by mortgages on their farms. The company converted the notes and mortgages into cash immediately by discounting them in the Eastern money market. Even these expedients, however, failed to produce enough capital, and the promoters began to eye covetously the only real source of capital Wisconsin had—the public lands within its borders.[5]

At first general sentiment was opposed to land grants for railroads. The sad experience of other states that had thus subsidized internal improvements, and the scandals born of the ill-fated Rock River Canal project, had soured many Wisconsin people. Of the same frame of mind were the settlers who poured into the area during the forties; they were opposed to the withdrawal of any lands from immediate occupation or any increase in price. But during the next decade opposition waned, and the legislature repeatedly memorialized Congress for a grant of lands in aid of railroad construction. The 31st and the 32d Congress both killed bills providing for such grants to Wisconsin, and once more—in 1854—the opposition waged a successful fight, but it was their last victory. When a similar bill came up in 1856—this time providing for a grant of a million acres and more—it passed both houses easily and was signed by President Pierce.[6]

Obviously the grant was the product not of disinterested analysis in Congress but of the pressures applied by forceful men who very much desired that railroads—their railroads—should cross the state. The giant among these early entrepreneurs was Byron Kilbourn; his figure intrudes upon every aspect of the acquisition and disposition of the grant.[7]

Kilbourn had a better education and wider experience than the average Westerner of his day. His father, a public figure in Ohio, was a man of great ability. He had been unable, however, to prevent the loss of his business during the panic of 1819, and his seventeen-year-old son had been forced to fend for himself.

After studying law for a brief space young Byron turned to engineering. He plunged into Ohio's internal-improvement program and acquired first-hand knowledge of the techniques of canal construction. In 1834 he decided to see what the Northwest had to offer and accepted a post as government surveyor in Michigan Territory, which still embraced the Wisconsin area. In the course of his work he spotted along the west bank of the Milwaukee River a tract of great potentiality, which he bought when it came on the market and promptly developed as a townsite. The transaction proved highly rewarding; Kilbourntown, of which he became "president" in 1837, rivaled the settlement of Juneau across the river until the two communities merged in 1839 to become the nucleus of Milwaukee.

From the first Kilbourn was active in local and territorial politics. In 1840 he ran, unsuccessfully, for delegate to Congress. Four years later he was elected to the territorial Assembly, and in 1847 he was a delegate to the second constitutional convention, where he served as chairman of the committee on general provisions and co-author of the "Declaration of Rights" that was embodied in the constitution as ratified. In the meantime he had twice been elected mayor of Milwaukee. In 1855 his cherished ambition to go to Washington suffered another setback when he lost the election for United States senator.

Chief among Kilbourn's early business ventures in Wisconsin was the promotion of the internal-improvement program that had begun so inauspiciously with the Rock River Canal fiasco. He himself had conceived that project and was partly responsible for the scandals that enveloped it. When the lands granted in aid of it were forfeited, he had tried, unsuccessfully, to get the territorial legislature to make them available for railroad construction. He was a member of the first board of directors of the Milwaukee and Waukesha and in 1849 became its president and chief engineer. When the first train pulled into Waukesha in 1851, Byron Kilbourn was in the cab. A few months later, however, his prestige was seriously jeopardized when the board of directors removed him from the presidency for the fraudulent issuance of stock to a New Yorker with whom he was conniving for control of the board.

Out of this set of circumstances was born the La Crosse and Milwaukee Railroad. Kilbourn was too daring and too astute a promoter to remain on the edge of a railroad boom. He decided to form a new company. To do this he must get a new charter; to get a new charter he must go to the legislature. He was no novice at extracting charters from the legislature, but at this particular moment it seemed expedient to entrust the job to someone else. The man he selected was his able and loyal lieutenant Moses M. Strong.

Moses Strong, educated at Dartmouth and Lichtfield Law School, had come to Mineral Point, in the southwestern part of Wisconsin Territory, in 1836. He was a government surveyor in 1837, United States district attorney during the next three years, member of the territorial legislature from 1841 to 1846, and delegate to the convention that framed the first constitution, which owed much to his influence. He was speaker of the state Assembly in 1850 and without peer in Wisconsin as an orator and debater. Being from the western part of the state, Strong also helped to rid Kilbourn's scheme of its Milwaukee coloration.[8]

Kilbourn summoned Strong to tell him of his plans for a railroad from Milwaukee to La Crosse. It was a project, he said, "worth a dozen of the Milwaukee and Mississippi," promising as it did the trade of the Minnesota country. The enterprise was presented to the public and to the legislature as a La Crosse rather than a Milwaukee project, and the incorporators—called "commissioners"—were selected with a view to broad geographical distribution. Strong lobbied the bill of incorporation through the legislature, and it became law on April 2, 1852.[9]

From the first, it seems clear, Kilbourn and Strong had a

grant of land in mind. Kilbourn had spearheaded a vigorous public discussion of the value of land grants for railroads, and the legislature included in the incorporation act a "sleeper" clause, later repealed, giving the La Crosse and Milwaukee a proportional share of any lands along its route that might thereafter be granted to Wisconsin for railroad construction.[10] After the legislature adjourned, Kilbourn sent Strong to Washington to "make a death struggle for a grant."[11]

In Washington, Strong met formidable competition. Other Wisconsin companies, notably the Milwaukee and Mississippi, the St. Croix and Lake Superior, and the Rock River Valley Union, also had emissaries in the capital. For four years they pitted their strength and political skill against one another, and when in 1856 a measure was ultimately enacted in the interest of railroad construction in Wisconsin, each of them took the credit for it.[12]

The act of 1856 provided for a grant of land to help finance the building of two railroad lines in the state: a northwestern line extending from Madison or Columbus by way of Portage to the St. Croix River and thence north to the west end of Lake Superior and to Bayfield; and a northeastern line running in a northerly direction from Fond du Lac on Lake Winnebago to the state boundary. In accordance with conventional patterns the law granted to the state alternate sections of land, for six sections on each side of the route, in aid of the construction of the two roads, and prescribed in detail the terms of its sale. The grant totaled more than a million acres adjacent to 503 miles of projected railroad: some 678,000 acres along 348 miles of the proposed route of the northwestern line and some 380,000 acres along 155 miles of the northeastern route. It was indeed a munificent bounty.[13]

The grant had been won, but that was only half the battle. How would the state dispose of these rich and fertile lands? If handled properly, the proceeds from their sale would more than finance the two projected lines. Would the same or different companies build them? Would an existent company or companies get the grants or would the state charter new ones? These would be the burning issues when the Wisconsin legislature met again. Able advocates would come before it to urge the cause of their respective companies.

Whatever the worth of their claims, it was clear that none of them would give up without a fight; the battle ground would simply shift from Washington to Madison. Governor Coles Bashford called a special session of the legislature for September of 1856, but the prospective recipients of the land subsidy did not wait for that. A week after President Pierce signed the bill a group of the state's leading citizens assembled in Milwaukee to formulate a plan for the disposition of the grant.

Kilbourn's design was to have the entire grant placed in the hands of a non-competing and tractable new company. In pursuance of this strategy Moses Strong presented at the Milwaukee meeting an ultimatum outlining the conditions that must be met to eliminate the La Crosse and Milwaukee as a competitor for the grant: the lands must not go to any road leading more directly to Chicago than to Milwaukee; no portion of them must go to any road competing with the La Crosse and Milwaukee; they must be disposed of in such a way as to promote the growth of Milwaukee, the "commercial emporium of the state"; and the route must be as prescribed by the La Crosse and Milwaukee and make convenient connection with it.[14]

The four conditions met with no dissent, and the meeting agreed upon the names of persons who should be asked to become members of an "association" that should seek incorporation as a new company or companies to build railroads along the routes designated by Congress. The group embraced virtually every important personage in Wisconsin, including many legislators, and was thus strong and representative enough to resist encroachments if it remained united on the four conditions it had subscribed to. The La Crosse and Milwaukee seemingly had little to fear.

Two months later another meeting was held to lay final plans. A definitive list of "association" members was agreed upon, sixty in all, and, most important, each was allotted the names of certain legislators whom he was to educate in the virtues of the plan. A committee, with Strong as chairman, would meantime draft a bill.

The scene now shifted to Madison. Kilbourn quartered himself in a suite in the Capital House to direct operations. It was not long, however, before he was forced by events that took place early in the legislative session to abandon his strategy for acquiring the entire federal grant for the company to be created by the recently formed "association," and to seek instead its division between two companies: the northwest portion for the La Crosse and Milwaukee, and the northeast portion for a new company to be organized under his control.[15] In his efforts to carry out this plan he ran into strong opposition.

In the first place, there was still considerable sentiment against land grants for internal improvements. There were those who viewed land subsidies to railroads as a potential source of corruption, an impediment to settlement, and an irresistable opportunity for speculation. Accordingly both houses entertained motions to decline the grant. These motions never really stood a chance of passage, but right up to the end eighteen members of the Assembly continued to vote against acceptance of the lands.[16] Governor Bashford himself felt—at least so he said—that great caution must be exercised in accepting such a grant; far better to reject it than to dispose of it unwisely.[17] The inference was that he would veto an "unwise disposition."

The La Crosse and Milwaukee also faced the competition of other Wisconsin railroads. The Milwaukee and Mississippi petitioned for the northwestern portion of the grant through a satellite, the Milwaukee and Watertown. The St. Croix and Lake

Superior insisted that the northern part of this tract should go to it, and the small Sugar River Valley Railroad also put in a request for some of the bounty. The strong contestant for the northeastern lands was the Chicago, St. Paul and Fond du Lac, successor to the Rock River Valley Union Road, which was dominated by Chicago interests.[18]

Finally, there was a vague but none the less real disapproval of Kilbourn throughout the state. People had not forgotten his connection with the Rock River Canal fiasco, and his dominating personality was not one to win friends.

Kilbourn's methods of overcoming the opposition he faced revealed keen perception and well-informed wariness. He was quick to realize that Strong, as a former assemblyman and a Westerner, was the man to work directly with the legislature. He must also line up a member of each house to take charge of parliamentary maneuvers. The two men he picked were Senator Jackson Hadley, a fellow Milwaukeean, and Assemblyman Thomas Falvey of Racine.

Kilbourn's keen appreciation of intrastate rivalries governed his whole course of action. He sought support from all sections and had groups from different areas memorialize the legislature in favor of the La Crosse and Milwaukee. He tried in every way possible to identify the La Crosse and Milwaukee as a Wisconsin rather than a Milwaukee enterprise and to present the issue as a conflict between Wisconsin and Chicago, which Wisconsin must win if she was not to be drained of her resources.[19]

Kilbourn had originally contended that for every conceivable reason the whole grant should go to a new company. When he was forced to abandon this objective he argued—apparently without embarrassment—that it would be folly to award the northwest portion to a new company when a going concern—that is, the La Crosse and Milwaukee—stood ready to accept it. But logic and persuasion were not enough; something more was needed to win over the legislature. So Kilbourn let it be understood that the LaCrosse and Wisconsin, should it obtain the northwestern tract, would deal "liberally" with the senators and assemblymen who voted for the bill. Each senator would get ten thousand dollars and each assemblyman five thousand dollars in La Crosse and Milwaukee first-mortgage construction bonds.[20]

In dealing with the competing railroads Kilbourn adopted the political axiom "If you can't lick 'em, jine 'em." The contest with the Milwaukee and Watertown had begun with a battle of words: the road's petition for the northwestern portion of the grant, countered by an answer from the La Crosse and Milwaukee, which in turn elicited a reply from the applicant. At this point Kilbourn confined his argument to the folly of giving the lands to the Milwaukee and Watertown, a satellite of the Milwaukee and Mississippi, rather than to a new company, since the La Crosse and Milwaukee had not yet entered the contest.[21] But when events forced him to modify his position and seek the northwestern tract for the latter road, he recognized the need for more concrete action than mere argument. He therefore negotiated a merger of the Milwaukee and Watertown into the La Crosse and Milwaukee. The cost was high, involving as it did substantial expenditures to satisfy competing officials, but by the merger the Milwaukee and Watertown was eliminated from the contest.[22]

The La Crosse and Milwaukee, however, did not want to build the northern section of the line along the northwest portion of the grant. The St. Croix and Lake Superior did, but unfortunately the congressional act contemplated that the entire northwest line be built by a single company. To circumvent this difficulty the two interested companies entered into a secret and complicated financial arrangement, which involved a conveyance of such doubtful validity that Kilbourn felt constrained to obtain an unofficial opinion from Supreme Court Judge Abram D. Smith.[23]

By persuasion and exercise of power Kilbourn finally succeeded in quieting the opposition to his company's receipt of the northwest tract. He was less successful in controlling the disposition of the northeast lands. After it had become clear, early in the legislative session of 1856, that there was no hope of getting both sections of the grant for the "association" he worked for its bestowal upon a new company not hostile to his interests —the Milwaukee and Superior Railway.[24] These proposals for the disposition of the two tracts—the northwest portion to the La Crosse and Milwaukee, the northeast to the Milwaukee and Superior—were incorporated in a bill which passed both houses but was vetoed by Governor Bashford, partly on the ground that it embraced more than one subject, in violation of the state constitution. In the light of Bashford's subseqent conduct it is hard to believe that the reasons he gave for his veto represented more than window dressing.[25]

When the legislature received the governor's veto it split the measure into two bills. In October of 1856 both houses—activated by Kilbourn's promises of pecuniary reward—passed with remarkable speed the bill disposing of the northwest portion of the grant, and Bashford signed it forthwith.[26] But the bill relating to the northeast lands again bogged down in his office. Before he finally approved it Bashford insisted, for reasons of his own, that two more members be added to the board of directors of the newly chartered Wisconsin and Superior Railway and that he should control their appointment. Both Kilbourn and William B. Ogden of Chicago, president of the Chicago, St. Paul and Fond du Lac Railroad wanted to control this board, and Bashford was astute enough to capitalize on his strategic position. Ultimately Ogden won out: most of the directors, including those appointed by Bashford, resigned in favor of Chicago men, and a year leater the Wisconsin and Superior was consolidated with the Chicago, St. Paul and Fond du Lac.[27] Thus Byron Kilbourn met his match, not in an incorruptible legislature, nor a public-spirited governor, nor a stiff-backed judge, but in a railroad entrepreneur of greater acumen, initiative, and ruthlessness.[28]

In the meantime there was the matter of the bonds that had been promised legislators who helped pass the desired legislation. The details of payment, which have intrigued all chroniclers of the incident, were designed to insure the payment of the proper amounts to the proper persons and at the same time to cloak the transaction in as much anonymity as possible.[29]

With eight exceptions—those who were to benefit in other ways—each legislator who voted for the bill received a package containing the promised amount of La Crosse and Milwaukee securities. A few who had rendered special services, such as Senator Hadley and Assemblyman Falvey, received more than their colleagues. In addition, the comptroller, the lieutenant-governor, the chief and assistant clerks of the Assembly, and the governor's private secretary also received five or ten thousand dollars in securities. Kilbourn had a package of ten thousand dollars worth of bonds prepared for Judge Abram D. Smith of the Supreme Court, and Governor Bashford got fifty thousand dollars worth. The two senators and twelve assemblymen who did not vote received no package. Six senators and seven assemblymen refused the bonds and voted against the bill. One of them, Senator Amasa Cobb of Iowa County, later made this statement:

Some five or six days before the final adjournment of the said adjourned session, Mr. William Pitt Dewey, who was then the assistant clerk of the Assembly, invited me to take a walk with him, and while walking around the capital [*sic*] square in the city of Madison, he (Dewey) introduced the subject of the bill granting the lands which had been granted to the State of Wisconsin to aid in the construction of certain railroads, to the La Crosse and Milwaukee Railroad company, and which bill was then pending before the Legislature. During said conversation he informed me that should said bill pass, he would get a quantity of bonds. He stated the amount that he was to receive, and to the best of the recollection of this deponent, it was ten thousand dollars. He asked me what amount would induce me to cease my opposition and support the bill, or come into the arrangement. I asked him why, or by what authority he made the inquiry? He replied that he had come right from Kilbourn and was authorized by him to say that I might make my own terms. . . . He further stated that "they were bound to carry it through any how, and that I might as well make something out of it, as the rest of them. . . . I asked him what was the amount of the capital stock of the company? He replied ten million dollars. I told him to say to Byron Kilbourn that if he would multiply the capital stock of the company by the number of leaves in the Capitol Park, and give me that amount in money, and then have himself, Moses Strong, and Mitchell *blacked,* and give me a clear title to them as servants for life, I would take the matter under consideration.[30]

Kilbourn did not limit his pecuniary rewards to men in official positions; gifts ranging from a thousand to twenty-five thousand dollars in construction bonds were made to newspapermen who had helped the cause in one way or another. Among them were Rufus King of the *Milwaukee Sentinel,* Moritz Schoeffler of Milwaukee's German-language *Wisconsin Banner,* and Samuel D. Carpenter of Madison's *Wisconsin Patriot.*

From this welter of gratuities, secret dealings, and power politics developed a situation that rapidly caught up the principal actors in their own machinations. The La Crosse and Milwaukee soon fell on evil days and presently found itself in a predicament from which it could hardly hope to escape with impunity. To procure the grant and to silence opposition the promoters had issued stocks and bonds in amounts that saddled the company with debts and claims on earnings it could not possibly meet. In addition, the road was also in difficulties with its two contractors, Newcomb Cleveland and Selah Chamberlain, both of whom had judgments for substantial claims against it.[31]

Rumblings of discontent and rumors of bribery grew apace in 1857. Only the intercession of former governor Leonard J. Farwell, presumably at Kilbourn's instance, dissuaded Horace A. Tenney, clerk of the Assembly, from publishing a savage review of the La Crosse and Milwaukee's annual report for 1856. Tales of fraud and mismanagement in Western railroads were so persistent in the East that Kilbourn sent for two hand-picked investigators to make a perfunctory examination and convince their fellow Easterners of the soundness of the La Crosse and Milwaukee Railroad.[32]

It was obvious that these rumors would not be ignored by the legislature when it met in the autumn of 1857. Kilbourn dispatched Strong and Henry L. Palmer, another attorney for the railroad, to Madison to ward off a possible legislative probe, and they succeeded in doing so; the bills calling for an investigation were reported out of committee adversely and were defeated in both houses. The committeemen—one of their number dissenting—justified their action on the ground that an investigation might impair the company's credit, delay construction, and possibly jeopardize the validity of the grants. The railroads would get built, they contended, if the companies were let alone.[33] It has never been established whether or not additional bribes helped suppress an investigation in 1857, but in any event they were probably not greatly needed. Many of the legislators were holdovers from the previous session, and the Bashford administration was still in office.[34]

One bit of legislation, not unrelated to the 1856 affair, did come out of the session: an act to punish fraudulent issue and transfer of stock certificates. The act made it a felony punishable by fine and imprisonment for a company officer to transfer stock certificates without express authorization to do so.[35] Whether this law was born of the La Crosse Company mélee is uncertain, but it is not unreasonable to suppose that it was.

The panic of 1857 clarified the situation. It placed the La

Crosse and Milwaukee in a predicament that could not possibly be worsened by any slander against its credit. Farm mortgagors, local governments, and minor entrepreneurs all saw that there was little hope of recovering their investments. There was no longer anything to be gained by averting an exposé, and the climate of opinion changed markedly. A new regime was voted into office: Alexander W. Randall replaced Bashford in the gubernatorial chair, and a new legislature assembled in January of 1858.[36]

The governor had the first word. The people of the state, he asserted, had the right to know whether their representatives could be "bought and sold like slaves in the market or like cattle in the shambels," and it was "time this clamor ceased, or the guilty parties were exposed and punished." The legislature did not delay. A few days after the session convened the Assembly committed the whole matter to a select committee of five men, who two days later recommended unanimously that a thorough investigation be made.[37]

The leading member of this committee, and later of the joint committee that conducted the investigation, was James H. Knowlton, assemblyman from Janesville. He dominated the entire proceedings, and all significant activity, accordingly, took place in the Assembly. Knowlton had been a member of the "association" formed during the summer of 1856 for the purpose of getting the grant. He had also been a member of the select committee of the legislature charged with recommending disposition of the lands and, according to Kilbourn and Strong, it was he who had blocked the plan of the "association" to form a single company and forced the shift in strategy. He was, finally, one of the assemblymen who had voted consistently against giving the northwest tract to the La Crosse and Milwaukee.[38] His handling of the investigation was consistent with his habitual role of tribune of the people, but he may also have been animated by personal dislike of Kilbourn, Strong, and their cohorts.[39]

However that may be, Knowlton ran the investigation with zeal, dispatch, and shrewdness. Three times the Assembly voted its confidence in the propriety of his serving on the committee, despite his membership in the infamous 1856 legislature.[40] He conducted the greater part of the interrogation himself and personally took charge of most of the parliamentary proceedings on the floor. The committee questioned forty witnesses, whose testimony ran to more than two hundred printed pages; it examined and set out over a hundred pages of documents; it issued five citations of contempt, enforced one citation with imprisonment, and argued successfully for affirmation of another in the Supreme Court.[41] It succeeded in bringing out most of the salient facts of the whole sordid affair, and it presented a fifty-page report embodying its findings and its recommendations for remedial legislation.[42]

Other departments of government, too, contributed to the collapse of Kilbourn's schemes. The governor called for action in his address to the legislature. But it is a question whether his exhortations contributed to the investigation. The episode was already of concern to the legislators and they undoubtedly would have conducted a probe without his call. On the other hand, the governor had a really effective weapon in his hands. The federal grant stipulated that transfer of title to blocks of sections was to be contingent on the governor's certification that twenty continuous miles of road had been completed. In the past, failure to submit such certification had usually been treated as an inadvertence, and hence some positive action was needed to forestall the transfer. Governor Randall and his successors therefore issued explicit statements of non-certification to the secretary of the interior; consequently only a small fraction of the lands passed into the hands of the La Crosse and Milwaukee.[43]

The courts, federal and state, also dealt with certain aspects of the affair. Newcomb Cleveland, one of the contractors of the

BYRON KILBOURN

From a painting in the possession of the Milwaukee County Historical Society

POLITICAL MARKET

CONSCIENTIOUS RAIL-ROAD PRESIDENT TO DEALER. *"Ah! let me see. I think I'll take this bunch of Legislators at $5000 a head. The Senators, at—what price did you say?"*

DEALER. *"Can't afford 'em less than $10,000 each."*

R. R. P. *"Well, hand them over. I suppose I'll have to take the lot."*

DEALER. *"Any thing else to-day? I have a lot of Editors, at various prices, from a Thousand down to Fifty Cents."*

R. R. P. *"No, nothing in that way, to-day. But I want a Governor very much indeed, and will stand $50,000 for him. Get me a Wisconsin one, if possible!"*

Cartoon published in Harper's Weekly *of June 12, 1858,*
at the time of the Land-Grant Investigation

La Crosse and Milwaukee, brought suit in the federal court in Milwaukee against the road and obtained a judgment in excess of a hundred thousand dollars for the company's breach of contract with him. His judgment lien on the company property represented a claim that could not be compromised, and eventually it had to be bought off by Selah Chamberlain, another contractor for the road.[44] A similar default on the company's contract with Chamberlain created a second judicial lien against the property. At first Chamberlain had taken a lease of the entire road from Kilbourn, mainly to immunize the property from other creditors. When he learned that this transaction could probably be invalidated, Chamberlain obtained a confession of judgment considerably in excess of the amount owing him but conditional on ascertainment of the actual indebtedness. When these dealings became known in the East, the firm of Vose, Livingston & Co., suppliers of iron to the La Crosse and Milwaukee, obtained an injunction restraining the company's New York financial agent from disposing of any more land-grant bonds. Subsequently the firm prayed for the appointment of a receiver to carry out the terms of the injunction.[45]

On the question of the constitutionality of the investigating committee, which had been challenged in the course of its proceedings, the Wisconsin Supreme Court handed down its opinion in 1858.[46] Kilbourn and Thomas Falvey, his lieutenant in the 1856 legislature, had both been subpoenaed by the committee; both had refused to appear and to answer certain prepared interrogatories. They were then taken into custody, arraigned before the Assembly, and cited for contempt. The Assembly denied Falvey's request to appear by counsel, and also held the written answers of the two men to be insufficient to purge them of contempt. Kilbourn and Falvey sued out writs of habeas corpus to the Supreme Court in which they challenged the constitutionality of the proceedings, the authority of the sergeant-at-arms to hold them in custody, and the procedures of the committee.[47] The issues involved also made it necessary for the court to pass on an act pertaining to witnesses that had been passed at the session.[48] Knowlton and two others argued the committee's case. Henry L. Palmer, attorney for the La Crosse and Milwaukee, George B. Smith, a leading attorney in Madison, and one other represented Falvey and Kilbourn.[49]

In re Falvey was the first case in which the legality of a legislative investigating committee was challenged in the state's highest tribunal.[50] By its decision and in its opinion the Wisconsin Supreme Court contributed to American law a leading case on the legislative power of investigation. The court held 1) that a legislature could lawfully investigate its predecessor if the subject of investigation was within an area of permissible legislation and 2) that it might conduct its investigation either with a committee of one house or a joint committee of both houses—such matters of procedure were within the discretion of the legislature; the court found no merit in the argument that a witness could not be in contempt of both houses at the same time, though in actual fact the witness was in contempt of the house that had issued the subpoena. 3) The committee could decide for itself whether a witness might appear by counsel or whether it would accept a witness' answer as satisfactory. 4) The act concerning witnesses was not constitutionally objectionable, although it might have been somewhat harsh in the penalties it imposed for failure to answer; considerations of state policy demanded that the legislature be given wider latitude in this respect than courts of justice. 5) A witness could not refuse to answer on the ground of self-incrimination, since the act contained an immunity clause. Conceivably there were some limitations which the court would put on the scope of legislative investigations—an inquiry into the conduct of an attorney, for instance—but none were before it here for decision.[51]

In its obiter concerning possible limits to the legislative power of investigation the court enunciated the typical American departure from British and colonial precedents. In affirming the committee's every contention, on the other hand, it displayed not only admirable judicial self-restraint but, presumably, a careful consideration of the "iliction returns." It obviated the threat of any serious challenge thereafter of the legality of legislative investigating committees.

If the Supreme Court's action gave judicial sanction to legislative investigations, and the law concerning witnesses gave them statutory authority, the procedure adopted by the committee for the investigation gave them also the weight of legislative practice. The procedural steps included a detailed resolution creating the committee and defining the subject matter of the investigation; a standard subpoena, endorsement, certification, and return; arraignment before the Assembly; issuance, by resolution, of the citation of contempt; and supplementary resolutions in pursuance of the main subject of investigation.[52] By present-day standards the procedure seems somewhat amateurish. The committee's examination of witnesses—both its prepared interrogatories and its oral questioning—was most formal, and frequently the prepared interrogatory was not supplemented by oral questioning at all. The result was that witnesses were able to withhold details which persistent probing would have uncovered, and astute witnesses like Kilbourn, for instance, were able to control the direction of the questioning.[53] And the committee was of course without the services of professional staff or counsel, though its guiding spirit, Knowlton, was himself an astute lawyer.

No legal sanctions except for procedures ancillary to the investigating committee's activities were invoked against either the donors or the recipients of the "pecuniary compliments." Criminal statutes were available for the punishment of both groups, but, as the dissenting committee member observed in 1857, everyone knew they would not be invoked. To many it seemed paradoxical that punishment should be limited to mere exposure of the conspirators, and some were disposed to view the whole investigation as a wasteful outlay of public funds.[54]

The more serious criticism may be that the committee did not air the matter thoroughly enough. Ready as it was to blacken ex-Governor Bashford and members of the 1856 legislature, it was reluctant to tar the judiciary with the same brush. On evidence quite as damaging as that used against many of the legislators, it reached a Scotch verdict with respect to Judge Abram Smith's guilt. It reported that it had no "satisfactory proof" of his receipt of bonds, though there was "enough of testimony to arouse suspicion."[55] But let the judge speak for himself:

> Some time in the latter part of 1856, or forepart of 1857, I think in January, 1857, but am not sure, I found one morning on my table, in my library in Milwaukee, a package containing ten bonds of the La Crosse and Milwaukee Railroad Company, payable five years from date, I think. From whom they came, I did not know; or for what purpose; but supposed most likely they were left there by the management or direction of the La Crosse Company, and I had no reason that I knew, or could think of, to believe or suspect that they were intended for any unworthy purpose. But although I stood in no official relation to the Company, I could perceive that such relation might arise. I could foresee other circumstances wherein I thought it would be my duty, in justice as well to myself as to the State, to retain those bonds, safely and securely within my control, to be produced as circumstances might require. I therefore replaced the bonds in the envelope, took them into the bank where I kept my account, and requested the Cashier to put his seal upon it, and deposited the package in the vault of the bank subject to my order, as a special deposit, and there they remain to this day.[56]

Nor did the committee's report do more than mention the subornation of the press.[57] Rufus King, editor of the *Milwaukee Sentinel,* had, at first, been an uncompromising critic of land grants to railroads.[58] Kilbourn had needed his support and, presumably, had bought it for ten thousand dollars in bonds.

There is evidence, too, that the persons advancing the cause of the Chicago, St. Paul and Fond du Lac Railroad were guilty of the same conduct as Kilbourn and his fellow supporters of the La Crosse and Milwaukee. The committee, however, cavalierly dismissed Kilbourn's testimony concerning the aggressive tactics that Ogden and Nelson Wheeler had employed at the 1856 session and in its report went so far as to justify the Chicago company's manipulation of the Wisconsin and Superior's board of directors.[59] It seemed bent, as Kilbourn and Strong charged, on whitewashing the conduct of the Chicago interests.

Ex-Governor Barstow, who was as deeply implicated as any, received lighter treatment than the other principals. The Assembly cited him for contempt as it did others, but permitted his discharge from custody on bail. Moreover, the committee never aired fully Barstow's machinations as president of the St. Croix and Superior.[60]

There is considerable doubt of Knowlton's innocence. Since he ran the investigation, it is not surprising that it disclosed nothing against him. The only testimony implicating him in any way was given by Strong and Falvey, who obviously had a motive for discrediting him. The fact remains, however, that Knowlton was almost unduly zealous in clearing his name. He questioned most of the witnesses himself, and at every opportunity sought to elicit from their testimony that they knew and had heard nothing linking him to the scandal. Twice the Assembly voted its confidence in the propriety of Knowlton's membership on any committee dealing with the land-grant matter. After Moses Strong had leveled a blast against him Knowlton received a final endorsement from the Assembly. On two occasions certain members of the legislature moved for an investigation of the conduct of Knowlton and others in the whole affair, but their motions were tabled.[61]

Both Kilbourn and Strong accused Knowlton of subservience to the Chicago, St. Paul and Fond du Lac and of receiving pay for services rendered in the Assembly in the company's behalf. Strong contended, both before the investigating committee and elsewhere, that Knowlton was the real villain in the piece. Kilbourn made the same charge outside the legislative inquiry, but he did not make it in his formal testimony. Was he avoiding any stronger clash with the chief investigator? Or did he fear that he could not substantiate the charge, that it would boomerang?[62]

After his release from the Dane County jail Strong plotted the indictment and prosecution of Knowlton.[63] Insisting that the legislative committee should be the preliminary forum, Kilbourn dissuaded Strong from pursuing this course, though he agreed that it would not be difficult to get testimony that Knowlton had bribed witnesses.[64] Most of the charges against Knowlton can probably be set down as calumny, born of a desire for revenge, but his extreme sensitiveness at the investigation and his eventual removal to Chicago raise at least a question whether he was altogether above suspicion.[65]

Be that as it may, the committee accomplished under Knowlton's leadership considerably more than mere muckraking of the past. The investigation had pointed up the helpless position of the small investor in the face of high-handed methods such as Kilbourn had been guilty of, and Governor Randall had called for legislation that would preclude a repetition of them. The legislature responded with a measure that prohibited any director or officer of a railroad company from having a direct pecuniary interest in company contracts, leases, or other agreements and from disposing of company securities for any purpose other than the "necessary and legitimate" purposes of the corporation. Stockholders representing ten per cent of all the subscribed stock might appoint a committee to examine the books and investigate the affairs of the corporation—a provision which may have been merely routine but which may likewise indicate the weakness of existing common-law right.[66]

The act required every railroad company in the state to make an annual report to its stockholders, a copy of which was to be filed with the secretary of state. The report was to state the length of road in operation and its total cost; the amount of capital stock subscribed for and the amount actually paid in; the amount and kind of its indebtedness; the number of passengers and amount of freight carried and the rates of carriage; total receipts from the transportation of passengers, property, and mails, and from all other sources; total expenses, broken down into categories; the number and causes of casualties and the losses resulting from them; and details pertaining to the payment of dividends.[67] Another section required every Wisconsin railroad corporation to keep its principal place of business and its books and records in a Wisconsin city along its line.[68] Finally, the act defined as a felony, punishable by one to five years' imprisonment, any wilful noncompliance with its provisions on the part of any director, officer, or employee of a railroad company.[69]

The measure had its deficiencies, but it was nevertheless a pioneering step in the development of Wisconsin corporation law and perhaps prepared the way for more effective regulation of railroads. Its provisions reflect the reactions of Wisconsin legislators to the frauds perpetrated in 1856 and the practices of Kilbourn and company.

The investigating committee made a second recommendation: that legislation be enacted to stamp out undesirable practices designed to influence legislation. The session of 1858 passed an anti-lobbying law which voided all contingent agreements for the payment of money in return for assistance in procuring legislation and declared the contracting parties guilty of a misdemeanor. It forbade any lobbyist interested in pending legislation to talk with any legislator without first disclosing the fact of that interest.[70] This was also an unsophisticated statute, almost impossible to enforce, but it was nevertheless a step forward, and subsequent legislation profited from its defects.

These were the immediate and concrete legislative results of the exposé. Equally important was the impact of the investigation on concepts and ideas current in the Wisconsin community and elsewhere and on the role of law in balancing private interests to effect the public good.

When the first rumors of fraud, bribery, and mismanagement reached the Eastern investment markets, La Crosse and Milwaukee securities plummeted precipitously, and throughout the nation investors for some time viewed Western railroads, and Wisconsin roads in particular, with great skepticism. It was grimly ironic that the abuses for which Kilbourn was responsible should, by virtue of depressing the value of the stock and causing the bonds to go into default, eventually have placed control of the road in the hands of Easterners, for it had been the vociferous claim that acquisition of a land grant would insure local control of the road.[71]

Throughout the East the Wisconsin legislature was in complete disgrace, but Wisconsin people seemed more disposed to vent their wrath on the company itself.[72] At first there was little hue and cry other than the wails of disappointed aspirants for the grant, highly partisan newspapers, and personal enemies of Kilbourn and his colleagues, but before long the affair began to lodge itself in the anti-monopoly philosophy of the day, and it helped lay the foundation for later agrarian radicalism in Wisconsin.

As regards its balance-of-power function the law was ambiguous in its reaction to the affairs of 1856 and 1858. The legislature of 1856 could scarcely have failed more completely to perform that function. The courts succeeded somewhat better; if they were not directly moved by considerations of the public interest, they did at least act on grounds of general principles, and not merely to satisfy the selfish desires of the parties involved, when they arbitrated conflicting interests by their decisions and transferred power from one private group (Kilbourn and the Western promoters) to another private group (the Eastern security holders and contractors).

Ultimately, if belatedly and inadequately, and spurred by public opinion, the legislative branch rose to its appointed task. Whatever the underlying motives of Knowlton and his committee, the action they took did serve to enlighten the public on a public matter. True, they did little more than expose the shabby affair to public view, refraining from imposing any penalties on its perpetrators. But this did not mean that the public interest was not vindicated. On the basis of the committee's findings the governor refused to make the certification that would have consummated the transfer of the land grant to the railroad companies. Part of the lands included in the grant were later used to help farmer-mortgagors who had lost their homesteads under foreclosures resulting from the same kind of corporate chicanery as provoked the investigation of 1858.[73]

The several legislative investigations of 1858—there were five of them in addition to the one conducted by Knowlton[74]—probably did much to enhance the power and prestige of the investigating committee as a recognized feature of legislative procedure. Under Knowlton's leadership the commiteee he headed proceeded with dispatch, making no compromises and giving no quarter. Its victory was complete with the court's pronouncement in the Falvey case, and its power was dramatically asserted once more when Moses Strong was cited for contempt after refusing to honor the committee's subpoena. In view of the opinion recently voiced by the Supreme Court it might have been wiser to refrain from challenging the committee's authority again, but Strong persisted, despite Kilbourn's obvious impatience with his obstinacy. Strong asked to be granted a few moments to explain his position, but the committee denied his request and on Knowlton's motion committed him to the sheriff, who locked him up in the Dane County jail. Two days later Strong yielded, ostensibly for the reason that the Assembly, in acting upon a petition of grievance he had submitted, had given him all the satisfaction he desired even though its action was adverse to him. The investigators won a clear victory here, and Strong and Kilbourn suffered a humiliating defeat.[75]

* * *

THE conditions that tended to foster corruption among the 1856 legislators were various, some more susceptible of control than others. The affair was in one sense a product of the pull and haul of federalism over the question of internal improvements. Whereas on the one hand Jackson's Maysville Road Veto of 1830 specifically, and the atmosphere of Jacksonian democracy generally, had for the moment precluded any possibility of federal monetary aid for internal improvements, the rush of events, on the other hand, had greatly weakened the argument of unconstitutionality which had been advanced by congressmen, mainly Southerners, opposed to land grants. Henceforth land grants to railroads were to be a matter of course; the last significant constitutional polemics had been exhausted in 1854.[76]

Such being the case, why could not the federal government, exclusive proprietor of the public domain, have made the Wisconsin grant directly to the railroads, thus eliminating the need for state action and, presumably, the opportunity for corruption? There were two objections to this procedure. First, its analogy to federal sponsorship of internal improvements, halted momentarily by the Maysville veto, was too patent to escape notice; secondly, it could be interpreted as an invasion of state sovereignty. Within a decade both these concepts were to capitulate to pressure for direct transfer of federal lands to railroads, but during the fifties they were still effective arguments.[77]

Moreover, it is questionable whether the federal government would have been more zealous than the state in formulating and executing a land-grant policy directed toward the public good. And certainly the federal government was no less responsive to private pressures. Indeed, the federal grant to Wisconsin, in the form it took, was itself the product of private pressures: Kilbourn and Strong pressed Congress for the northwestern lands, Ogden and his minions for the northeastern lands; their efforts almost certainly contributed to the passage of the land-grant act of 1856. It is hard to believe that federal in lieu of state control would have prevented the unsavory aspects of the disposition of the public domain.[78]

Another factor contributing to the breakdown of government over this particular land-grant matter was the nature of the incorporation procedure. This was the day of the special charter—that is, a separate legislative measure for each railroad incorporated; no general railroad incorporation law was enacted until 1872.[79] Although the Wisconsin constitution urged incorporation by general laws, and a general statute adequate for incorporation was on the books, promoters still regarded it as advantageous to be chartered by special act.[80]

In drafting special charters early Wisconsin legislatures borrowed indiscriminately from Eastern prototypes, which had in turn been modeled on English canal-company charters. Unfortunately the Wisconsin lawmakers did not borrow enough. Fewer than five per cent of their charters were complete in all respects, and many included fewer than a third of the essential elements.[81]

Most of the Wisconsin charters, moreover, lacked the declaration found in preambles of English acts that the charter was being issued in the public interest. Nor was any such underlying philosophy manifest in the legislature's procedures. Seldom was a request for a charter denied if its proponents employed the "proper methods"—that is, manipulated the situation as necessary to achieve their ends. Such conditions and limitations as were included in some charters seemed capricious, technical, and, in the main, unenforceable.[82]

The legislature's indifference to matters of substance in these special acts was accompanied by great concern for technical detail: the time and place of board meetings, the form of ballots for election of directors, the procedure to be followed for appraisal, arbitration, and review in condemnation proceedings. Each time the company wished to modify any of these details it had to ask the legislature to amend its charter.[83]

The eighteen fifties saw a great proliferation of railroad charters, and the legislature did not and could not give proper consideration to each and every application.[84] It did not inquire into the good faith of the applicant, nor even into the feasibility of the projected route. Normally only those legislators who were prospective incorporators gave serious attention to any given charter, and many wildcat proposals were enacted into law—a road from Milwaukee to Puget Sound, for instance, and another from Lake Michigan to the Bering Straits. The *cause celèbre* was the charter of the La Crosse and Milwaukee itself, which originally contained a clause donating to the road a proportional amount of any lands which Congress should thereafter grant to the state along its route. The bill—with the joker clause—passed both houses, was enrolled, signed by the governor, and published before the offensive section was finally eliminated by amendment.[85]

There were few prominent public men of the day who were not members of the governing board of at least one railroad company, and the temptation was great for key legislators to insist on such membership as the price of a charter's passage. This was exactly the difficulty over the charter for the recipient of the northeastern tract, the Wisconsin and Superior. Here the governor as well as the legislature used his position for private gain. Many legislators, moreover, were interested financially in the railroads applying for the grant. The stakes—public lands worth ten million dollars—were high enough to explain the victory of acquisitiveness over moral responsibility.[86]

Wisconsin newspapers of the time laid much stress on the lack of a general incorporation law. Eastern states had already passed such a law and in 1853 a bill patterned on a New York act of 1850 was reported favorably by committees of the two Wisconsin houses, but failed of passage. It is doubtful, however, whether such a law would in itself have helped very much. Making the grant of a corporate charter an administrative rather than a legislative act might have eliminated some of the jobbery among the legislators, but the real need was for an agency equipped to give mature consideration to each application.[87]

Less obvious and less commented upon at the time was the fact that the terms of the two acts—the act of Congress making the grant and the Wisconsin act accepting it—contributed to the fiasco of 1856. Under the federal grant conveyance of the lands and passage of title to the railroad companies was made contingent upon the completion of twenty miles of rail; by the terms of the Wisconsin act sale of the lands by the railroad was contingent on acquisition of title. Thus, so the framers thought, construction was bound to keep pace with sale of the lands. But no restriction was placed on the execution of mortgages. Accordingly, construction bonds secured by mortgages having conventional "after acquired" property clauses covering the entire grant were issued in prodigious numbers by Kilbourn and other railroad promoters whenever they felt that the joints needed oiling. On the legal distinction between sale and mortgage, therefore, were premised the practices that enabled Kilbourn to bribe the legislature. On the other hand, it must be granted that inability to issue bonds would have seriously impeded progress, for the land grant was the railroad's main source of capital.[88]

Another handicap was the clear implication in the grant that each of the two roads contemplated must be built by a single company. The prescribed length of the northwest route, however, was beyond the capacity of one company to build, and it was this fact that gave birth to the secret dealings with the St. Croix and Superior Railroad, the issuance of a million dollars worth of construction bonds, an *ultra vires* conveyance, a *douceur* to Judge Smith, and an authorization act lobbied through the 1857 legislature by Strong and H. L. Palmer.[89]

The La Crosse and Milwaukee affair, centered as it was in the legislative process, belied the claim commonly made for the superiority of the bicameral legislature. Not only did the existence of two chambers fail to insure proper scrutiny and consideration of the railroad charters submitted to them, but it also failed, apparently, to arrest the lobbyists in any way. It is hard to see how the work of Kilbourn and Strong could have been made any easier. The greater stability of the Senate is often cited as providing a necessary balance to the flux of the Assembly, but this factor can hardly be said to have been operative in the La Crosse and Milwaukee episode unless one equates the greater stability of the upper house at five thousand dollars per man. Because senators enjoyed the longer term—two years as compared with one year for assemblymen—they might have been expected to show greater wisdom in the ways of government, but in actual fact they seem to have been quite as responsive to Kilbourn's inducements as members of the Assembly.

The one-man geographic-district basis of representation had some initial significance: it tended at the outset to subject the land-grant legislation to an intrastate sectional battle. But the conflicting interests of different areas of the state tended to be submerged as the lines of battle were drawn, and what had begun as a contest between various legislative districts resolved itself into a struggle between two competing aspirants for the grant. Kilbourn was able to overcome the hostility that existed toward Milwaukee and enlist the support of most of the state for the La Crosse and Milwaukee Company. Only the representatives from the Winnebago Lake region apparently stood fast against his efforts to woo them away from Ogden and the the Chicago interests.[90]

The episode occurred at a moment in Wisconsin's history when party alignments were shifting and party discipline was weak. The Indian summer of the Whig Party had ended in 1854 with the passage of the Kansas-Nebraska Bill; the Republican Party was still little more than a loosely knit aggregation of the enemies of that Bill; and the Democratic Party, rent wide open on the slavery issue, found it hard to keep its disaffected wing in tow. The result was that party discipline was not strong enough to stiffen the legislature against the onslaughts of "pecuniary compliments."

It is a question which party really suffered disgrace. The Republican Party could not boast of any special virtue on the ground that it embraced almost all of the fifteen legislators who had refused Kilbourn's bonds; many of those who had succumbed to bribery were also members of the party, and it is not certain that even some of the fifteen had not been more effectively bribed by Ogden and the Chicago interests. The conduct of Bashford, first Republican governor of Wisconsin, did much to discredit the fledgling party in the state, but the legislature of 1856 was regarded as Democratic. Both Republicans and Democrats apologized for the incident in their platforms of subsequent years. The investigating legislature of 1858 was Republican, and the governor, Alexander Randall, was an anti-Nebraska Democrat who had run on the Republican ticket.[91]

In evaluating the collapse of the governmental machinery one must guard against judging the events of an earlier day in the light of a modern climate of opinion. It is easy, for instance, to ascribe the legislative corruption of 1856 to the absence of any effective regulation of lobbyists, but to do so is to ignore a more fundamental factor, namely the concept of government that prevailed in the mid-nineteenth century. Wisconsin people, like people elsewhere at the time, came to regard the state legislature as a counter over which private groups could acquire legal rights and privileges, without undue squeamishness about the methods employed by lobbyist or legislator. It was the era of the "old lobby" in Wisconsin; of "Monk's Hall" and the "forty thieves" and of "Barstow and the balance." When the promoters of the La Crosse and Milwaukee assigned to individual members of the "association" the names of legislators whom they were to persuade to vote right, they were following a well-defined technique.[92]

The explanation offered the investigating committee by the principals in the bribery scheme, obviously in all seriousness, reveals clearly the prevalent standards of conduct. Kilbourn's narration of his relations with Bashford best preserves the flavor:

> After the act was passed and a rumor was circulated that he had signed it, I called on him with a feeling of perfect freedom from restraint, which I had not previously felt, and being informed by him that he had approved the act, I expressed to him the deep sense of gratitude which I felt on behalf of the La Crosse company, for the liberal spirit manifested by him on that occasion, and stated to him frankly, that his veto, which so much disappointed us at the time, had resulted very greatly to our benefit, by separating the grants, and giving us a separate act, unconnected with and unincumbered by the voluminous provisions of the first bill relating to the Northeast grant which would have been very greatly in our way, and a serious incumbrance on our operations. I also took that occasion to express the friendly sentiments which we felt toward him personally, with the hope that we should enjoy his confidence so long as our official relations should bring us in contact; and alluding to the circumstances that in our operations, and the new and extended duties devolving on us in carrying out the objects of the grant, we should have to trouble him in various ways, and especially in our correspondence with the General Government, which would have to be conducted mainly through him, and that in consideration of the part and prospect of the future the company felt disposed to extend to him a pecuniary compliment, if he would feel at liberty to accept it. He said that with the views and purposes expressed by me he

should not feel at liberty to decline a compliment of the kind, and would accept of it cheerfully. I then stated that I would at an early day, place in his hands the bonds of the company to the amount of fifty thousand dollars, which would be payable in five years or convertible into stock at any time, and that if he desired it at any time the Company would convert them into money.... There was no corrupt intent in this transaction with Governor Bashford, nor was it prompted by any unworthy motive. Understanding that he was much disappointed in the direction which by force of circumstances the grant had taken, different from that which he and his immediate friends desired, I deemed it necessary to propitiate his feelings with reference to the future operations of our company by an act of such liberality as would reconcile him to the disappointment, and obliterate whatever feeling of hostility he may have entertained toward our company. Such were my only motives, distinctly stating to him at the time, that I wished this gratuity to have no influence upon any official act which it might hereafter devolve on him to perform. On his part I believe he accepted it for the reason that he thought the company could well afford to make such a donation without doing it any material damage while to him the sum was large enough to confer a real benefit.[93]

Prevailing ethical standards exacted no more exemplary conduct from the men holding positions of trust in a company than from public officials. A director of a corporation might very well expect a gratuity from a contractor to whom a construction job had been awarded. Selah Chamberlain and Newcomb Cleveland, both established railroad contractors, seemed to accept this as a perfectly normal practice; they balked only when the director's cut seemed exorbitant.[94] It was the fate of the La Crosse and Milwaukee to have a board of directors who kept so busy arranging side deals that they had no time to work for the company. Similarly, mass resignations engineered for the purpose of packing a new board of directors, a practice condemned by the investigating committee as a breach of fiduciary duty, were probably not unusual.[95] The trustee concept of corporate directorship had not yet found its way into the Wisconsin community, which seems to have tolerated many derelictions during these years: an alleged split of eighty thousand dollars among eight directors of the Milwaukee, Fond du Lac and Green Bay Railroad when it merged with the La Crosse and Milwaukee; a transfer of school lands to the La Crosse and Milwaukee at a price considerably in excess of their value and the bribery of a company officer to keep quiet; a shady transfer of land from the La Crosse and Milwaukee to a private individual for the benefit of a director.[96]

It is to this lax code of ethics rather than the absence of formal restraints that the 1856 affair may be attributed. Had it been otherwise, existing law could have been invoked against the perpetrators. There was already on the statute books a measure imposing fine and imprisonment for offering a gratuity to any member of the government for the purpose of influencing his official actions, and even greater penalties for the acceptance of such a gratuity by the public official. Granted that the statute did not provide the best way to control pressure groups, the fact remains that not one of the culprits in the 1856 affair was prosecuted under it. And the new anti-lobbying law that came out of the investigation, it is fair to say, represented little advance in scope or technique.[97]

In still another respect—the attitude toward natural resources—the climate of opinion was quite different from that of the present day. The mid-nineteenth century regarded the country's natural resources as virtually inexhaustible, and believed that unrestricted exploitation was the most promising way to develop America's economic potentialities.[98] These convictions were reflected in the popular attitude toward the public domain—the assumption that the public lands were a never-ending bounty to be parcelled out with a lavish hand; the only question was who should get them. When the time came for railroads to seek a share of the booty an even more palatable philosophy gained currency: the railroad did not seek lands merely for its own profit; it would also, by populating the countryside and hauling goods to market, contribute to the development of all the other natural resources, thus producing a hundredfold return on the value of the lands granted to it.

It was a philosophy that was particularly appealing to a young frontier community. Wisconsin had not yet completed a decade of statehood. Only twenty years before, Milwaukee had been a mere trading post, and even in the fifties there was not a city between Milwaukee and the Mississippi of more than thirty-five hundred population. With the tremendous immigration into the state during the forties and fifties, the railroad came to be regarded as the great deliverer, promising benefits to one and all alike. A spirit of optimism prevailed, to which hustling stock agents, orators, and newspaper panegyrists addressed their appeals. It is not surprising that the project for a railroad grant should have captured the enthusiasm and enlisted the support of virtually every important person in Wisconsin and that all of them—public servant and private citizen alike—wished to share in the exploitation.[99]

Who should carry on that exploitation was a question that had by this time been settled; neither the federal government nor the state government would do it directly. It would be delegated to private entrepreneurs. "The legislature," said the Supreme Court of Wisconsin in the Falvey case, "deeming it improper or unwise that the State itself should undertake to carry on these works, chartered certain railroad companies, and granted to those companies all the estate and interest of the State in the lands donated to it by Congress to be disposed by these companies, under certain limitations, and the proceeds exclusively applied to the construction of the roads."[100]

Such a delegation of the administrative power of the state was perhaps inevitable, for Wisconsin found itself in a historical dilemma. It could not do the job itself because the job to be done was far beyond the capacity of the state's civil service. By relinquishing its prerogative to private entrepreneurs, on the other hand, the state exposed itself to pressures which its public institutions were as yet little prepared to resist.[101] Having delegated its industrial development to private companies, the state was faced with the question whether that development should be supported with public moneys. The Wisconsin constitution had two answers to this question. Without qualification it prohibited the state from contracting debts for purposes of subsidy, but it expressly permitted grants of land in aid of internal improvements.[102]

It was doubtless wise to freeze this financial policy in constitutional form. The experience of other states with government-sponsored internal improvements—the Erie Canal being the sole exception—had ended disastrously. Nevertheless, by prohibiting direct aid the framers of the constitution made it inevitable that the quest for other sources of revenue would be the more assiduous and the lure of the land grant the more glittering. The incident of 1856 is only one example of the unfortunate effects that sometimes attended the application of this constitutional provision.[103]

There remained the question of what sort of control, if any, the state should retain over a grant of land made in aid of internal improvements. In other words, should public regulation go hand in hand with public subsidy? The supervisory provisions in the railroad charters were at best capricious, and the clauses in the land grants were intended only to insure that construction would get done and to outline the mechanics of transfer. Beyond that the state made little attempt to exercise any control over the companies it chartered. True, Bashford sonorously repeated the well-worn commonplace that "corporations of enormous wealth and great power are only to be tolerated by the necessities and wants of the state and shall be shorn of their power," and he urged that the grant be divided between two companies on the ground that "two roads running through nearly the entire state, owned and controlled by one corporation, would in time be cancerous to the legislation of the state." Leaders within and outside the state also voiced the warning that to confer a land grant on one railroad to the prejudice of others was an invitation to monopoly. But by and large the greater emphasis was on the fact that it would be unfair to do so, in view of the many rival railroad interests that deserved a part of the grant. The same point had been made by opponents of land grants in 1854 in Congress.[104]

The significant struggle, far from being a class conflict, was between various groups having substantially the same interests. There was a well-defined hostility to the East generally, and to Eastern capitalists specifically. Kilbourn found the sentiment useful; with ardent chauvinism he insisted that the La Crosse and Milwaukee—and the Milwaukee and Mississippi before it—would be a Wisconsin venture with ownership and control lodged in Wisconsin people. Such a slogan was indispensable for the promotion of the farm-mortgage financing scheme.[105] Within the state the struggle was at first a sectional one, which took two forms, not mutually exclusive: regional support of competing railroad interests, and the rivalry between Milwaukee and the rest of the state. Early in the 1856 session of the legislature several Wisconsin railroads petitioned for the grant, but as the situation developed, the smaller lines became absorbed in the major clash of interests. The sentiment against Milwaukee, likewise, was most manifest in the early days of the struggle: other lake cities fancied themselves as leading ports; western Wisconsin resented Milwaukee's dominance as a market; and southern cities flirted with Chicago.

But this conflict, too, was eclipsed when the battle lines formed for the major engagement—the bout between the cities of Chicago and Milwaukee, between the Chicago, St. Paul and Fond du Lac and the La Crosse and Milwaukee, between William B. Ogden and Byron Kilbourn. Rivalry between Chicago and Milwaukee, which dated from their earliest days, had been apparent in Congress in 1854 during a preliminary skirmish over a land grant for Wisconsin railroads. At that time the proposal was for a grant in aid of a line from Chicago north to Lake Superior, but not touching Milwaukee. The railroad that proponents of the grant had in mind was undoubtedly the Rock River Valley Union Railroad, predecessor of the Chicago, St. Paul and Fond du Lac. Milwaukee interests helped defeat the proposal, but many Wisconsin towns along the contemplated route had favored it because, by connecting them with Chicago, the line promised a readily accessible metropolitan market.[106]

In the main struggle between the two cities, which was staged in the legislature during the fall of 1856, the legislators themselves seemed almost like mere spectators watching the titans slug it out. Superficially appraised, the match ended in a draw: the La Crosse and Wisconsin got the northwestern tract and the Chicago, St. Paul and Fond du Lac—in fact—the northeastern one. Indeed, one might well wonder what the fight was about: Kilbourn had no interest in the northeast line, and Ogden said he did not want the northwest line. The real point was that the La Crosse and Milwaukee did not want the northeast lands to go to Ogden's company, and hence the disposition of this portion of the grant was the climax of the struggle. In the end Kilbourn lost the battle. Did Ogden bribe more effectively than Kilbourn? Did Bashford and the legislators from the Lake Winnebago area feel more closely tied economically to Chicago? The record is inconclusive, but the Wisconsin and Superior was under Ogden's thumb from the moment it was chartered.[107]

If the fledgling state of Wisconsin embarked upon railroad building with enthusiasm and high hopes, it soon learned that these were no substitute for knowledge. And knowledge was woefully lacking; there was little appreciation of the large initial investment required, the fixed charges that must be met regardless of revenues, and the related fact that railroads operated most profitably at full capacity. There was not even a premonition that unbridled competition might not achieve the most efficient system of railroad transportation. It took the panic of 1857, the Civil War, and numerous reorganizations to bring these lessons home.

To begin with, the Wisconsin economy was not ready for the large-scale financing required for railroad promotion and construction. The issuance of mortgage bonds secured by property and franchises had by this time become the established technique for raising funds. To accumulate the necessary capital promoters had to execute mortgages that would cover after-acquired property. So long as property was acquired regularly and in small increments in accordance with a definite plan, bonds were not issued too lavishly. But when the amount of potential company property suddenly increased tenfold, the temptation to mortgage it to the hilt was irresistible. Similarly, since most charters required only a token amount of paid-in shares as a condition of corporate existence, there was also a prodigious and unrestrained issuance of stock. The promoters' overoptimism regarding the earning capacity of the securities fostered fatal overextension and overcapitalization.

The contractors employed to build railroads during this era—men of competence and experience—permitted themselves no such overoptimism. They had to accept payment largely in corporation securities, but they did not do so with blind faith in the outcome. The astuteness of both Newcomb Cleveland and Selah Chamberlain in reducing their claims to judgments showed that they had a sophistication born of experience which Wisconsin security holders lacked.[108]

Although the concept of a corporation as a quasi-public institution was reflected in the jobs it had to do, it was not yet a part of the pattern of corporate management. The fiduciary character of the stockholder-director relationship was undeveloped, and the separation between ownership and management was already complete. The minutes of the board of directors and executive council of the La Crosse and Milwaukee testify to the rudimentary state of corporate management.[109]

If the Wisconsin economy was not sufficiently developed to meet the problems of railroad building, the state's legal institutions were still more unprepared. Not only the legislature and statute law but the courts, too, were unequipped to meet the new challenge. They had at hand only ill-adapted weapons from the armory of the common law. The law of private corporations was still wedded to agency, partnership, and joint-stock associations. There was no effective limitation on the flotation of securities; whenever they thought it expedient to do so, directors could simply vote another bond issue or another block of stock, and thus they built up obligations and liabilities from which there was no escape but repudiation. The small bondholder or minority stockholder had no effective recourse against gross mismanagement; the derivative suit was still years in the offing. The common law, of course, offered the remedies of foreclosure and sale, or judgment for damages, but these were less useful to the small investor than to parties in strong bargaining positions—the Eastern security holders, the contractors, and the supply firms. Many small farmer-investors found, when the time came for them to protect their homesteads, that the law had no practical remedy for them.[110]

Nor did the bar show much sensitivity to the problems posed by the new large-scale corporation. The lawyer-legislators—and there were a good many—were not educated to their task. They held the extreme sectional-interest theory of representative government which inevitably accompanies the geographic-district basis of representation.

Unfortunate as were the consequences of these legal and governmental deficiencies, it is hard to see what alternative there was within the framework of Wisconsin society in the mid-fifties for getting the railroad-building job done. Wisconsin was tied inextricably to Eastern capital for absorption of both the farm-mortgage notes and, most important, the land-grant construction bonds. Local government subsidies were inadequate; indeed it is doubtful whether sufficient capital could have been raised even if there had been no constitutional ban on state aid. The eventual flooding of the Eastern markets with La Crosse and Milwaukee securities selling far below par ultimately brought about the transfer of control from the West to the East.[111]

For the necessary skills, promotional techniques, and general know-how and for the needed equipment Wisconsin was equally dependent on these Eastern regions, which had been building railroads for a score of years. Newcomb Cleveland was a New Yorker who had acquired experience on Vermont railroad projects, and Selah Chamberlain had built railroads in Vermont, New York, and Ohio. The contractors of the day were in a sense actual entrepreneurs, who by virtue of their exclusive skills were able to call the turn in their dealings with Western promoters. Equally shrewd bargainers and formidable creditors were the suppliers of equipment, who again were almost without exception Eastern concerns.[112]

The legal techniques employed were likewise imported from the East, where lawyers had first developed tools to implement railroad finance: indenture and debenture bonds, deeds of trust, convertible stock, etc. Western entrepreneurs borrowed these devices lock, stock, and barrel, but they found that even Eastern experience had not been extensive enough to produce a settled body of principles to control and administer the financial structure of railroad systems.[113]

Thus in every particular of railroad building—liquid capital, promotional techniques, and economic and legal know-how—the Wisconsin community was tied to the East. It is not surprising that there should have been a vigorous struggle for the one item Wisconsin had to bargain with—the land itself—and that ethical niceties and basic public purposes should have been lost.

II. Embattled Farmers and a Common-Law Court

Tenacity of a taught legal tradition is much more significant in our legal history than the economic conditions of time and place.—ROSCOE POUND in *The Formative Era of American Law.*

AS PUBLIC clamor for railroads mounted during the eighteen fifties early Wisconsin enterpreneurs bent their efforts toward devising workable means of acquiring funds. They could not or would not take all the risk themselves, and the state had decided against making subsidies for internal improvements. After railroad promoters were denied a loan from the school fund they sought to get a land grant from Congress, but it was not until 1856 that their appeals were answered. In the meantime they had to rely upon local governments and private individuals to furnish the necessary capital. Villages and towns, panting for railroads, subscribed for stock and contracted large bonded debts. Farmers up and down the line who had to haul their produce forty or fifty miles were equally eager to have a railroad passing by. But the farmers had no cash, and cash was what the railroad companies needed. To resolve this impasse the Milwaukee and Mississippi Railroad devised a plan unique in the annals of railroad finance.[1]

Under this plan the farmer bought railroad stock by giving a ten-year negotiable note bearing eight per cent interest, secured by a mortgage on his farm. In return he received fully paid shares of stock carrying a dividend rate of ten per cent. Eight per cent, however, was reserved for the company to be applied against the interest on the note. By a separate agreement the farmer agreed to assign to the company so much of the remainder of his dividends—i.e., in most cases two per cent—as was sufficient to liquidate the principal of his note. In consideration of the relinquishment and assignment of his dividends the company agreed not to demand interest on his note and, in the event the note and mortgage were negotiated, to save him harmless from any obligation to pay interest. Finally, the farmer agreed that the undertaking of the company to forego interest and to save him harmless was not to constitute a defense on his part in a court action if the note and mortgage found their way into the hands of a third party. "Nevertheless," the agreement concluded, "the said railroad company agrees to pay said interest promptly."[2]

By this somewhat irregular transaction the farmer came into possession of fully paid shares of railroad stock without putting up a cent of cash and, apparently, without having to pay any interest on his note. The railroad company in turn acquired a set of documents that it could readily convert into cash in the Eastern money market. This it proceeded to do, not by endorsing the note and mortgage but by issuing a convertible bearer bond, with interest at eight per cent, to any willing investor. The bond, under the terms of its issuance, took the note and mortgage with it as security, and it was expressly stated that if the company should default on either principal or interest the holder might foreclose on the mortgage or avail himself of any other legal remedy against the mortgagor or company or both. Thus the company got cash for construction and the investor acquired a security backed by what seemed to be adequate collateral.

The plan caught on fast. Between 1850 and 1857 nearly six thousand farmers subscribed to almost five million dollars' worth of railroad stock, nearly half of which was issued by two companies—the La Crosse and Milwaukee and the Milwaukee and Mississippi. Railroad rallies up and down the land, a friendly press, and hustling stock salesmen convinced the farmer that this was an opportunity he could not afford to miss. But he did not need much convincing. The early fifties were years of lush prosperity—the 1853 and 1854 wheat crops were bumpers—and pessimism was not the frontier farmer's failing. He figured that at the end of ten years the accumulated two per cent dividends would cover a fifth of the principal debt and that he could wipe out the balance by selling some of his stock, which certainly would be worth many times what he had paid for it. Besides, when the railroad came through, the value of his farm would increase ten-fold.[3]

The day of reckoning was not far off. The railroads perpetrated frauds and corruption such as no one had dreamed of: some of them did not lay a foot of track; others used the proceeds of their bond sales to pay handsome sums to directors and officers; still others sold the notes and mortgages at disgraceful discounts on the Eastern market. They changed routes at will, leaving villages and farmers high and dry; they issued bogus stock; they continued to accept notes and mortgages after they knew that their roads were bankrupt. The panic of 1857 put on the finishing touches. Every railroad in the state defaulted on its bonds. The farmers now found themselves holders of worthless railroad stock and obligors on sizable mortgage notes they could not hope to pay. To demand interest payments from either the railroad company or the farmer was futile. The Eastern security holders therefore moved in with bills of foreclosure.

With foreclosure staring them in the face the farmers saw that the time had come for action. Individually they could do little; collectively they might hope to do much. They formed leagues throughout the state with a view to presenting a united front. For this they had precedent; a generation before, many of them had organized "claim clubs" to protect squatters from eviction. The Farm Mortgage Leagues multiplied and finally a Grand State League was formed to coordinate their activities. The mortgagors also established a newspaper, the *Hartford Home League,* which they kept going for four years, and in addition they controlled the policies of many rural weeklies. The primary object of the Leagues was to defend the mortgagors in the foreclosure actions, but they did more than this. They saw to it that the local enforcement officials—sheriffs and registers of deeds—were men friendly to their interests. And before long they jumped into state politics in order more effectively to protect their interests.

In this period of tension between North and South and close party battles on the national scene the farm-mortgagors' vote was crucial. In every election the farmers used their influence and their votes to return sympathetic lawmakers to Madison. Between 1858 and 1867 every session of the legislature except one passed some farm-mortgage legislation. But none of these laws went into effect, for the mortgagors had not reckoned with the Wisconsin Supreme Court. Resolutely the court stood its ground and declared the crucial farm-mortgage laws invalid or ineffective. When the mortgagors resorted to the time-tested remedy offered by the ballot box, they failed. Twice they ran friendly candidates for the Supreme Court and twice they were beaten.

So the foreclosures proceeded, and many of them were sad episodes indeed. There was some resistance: often the mortgagors packed the foreclosure sales and intimidated the prospective bidders; frequently railroad property was damaged. Inordinate delay, legalistic tricks, and lack of cooperation on the part of local officials prompted more than one Eastern security holder to settle his claim on the mortgagor's terms. One railroad made liberal provision for the settlement of claims in its reorganization plan, and eventually Congress turned over the

La Crosse and Milwaukee land grant to the state to help the mortgagors.[4]

* * *

HERE WAS the garden variety of economic colonialism in the United States: a well-organized, local debtor interest pitted against powerful out-of-state creditors. Both groups claimed to be the innocent victims of swindles and double-dealing. Both appealed to all agencies of law to intervene.

Of these agencies the legislature was especially sensitive to the plight of the mortgagor, since in general the climate of opinion was sympathetic to him. By organizing and using their political power effectively the farmers succeeded in electing representatives friendly to their cause.[5] The legislators attacked the problem from all sides. In the ten-year period 1858–68 they passed sixteen farm-mortgage laws. The most direct action would have been to get rid of the obligation altogether, to shift the loss from mortgagor to security holder. If the farmer had been free to plead fraud and false representation as a defense, this could usually have been accomplished, but he was forbidden by the common law to do so in the face of the holders' claims that they were innocent purchasers for value. The legislature soon set about to eliminate this obstacle.

An act passed in 1858 provided that the mortgagor could allege that the note and mortgage had been obtained from him by fraudulent representations and that if this were proved he was entitled to the court's decision or the jury's verdict. All documents, instruments, and representations were to be construed together and were binding on the assignee as well as on the original party. Finally, the law prohibited the assignee from alleging that he was an innocent purchaser of the note and mortgage without knowledge of the farmer's defense against the assignor.[6] The purpose of the statute was clear; any mortgagor could get enough testimony of fraud and double-dealing to convince local judges and juries that he had been swindled. As might have been expected, the Supreme Court declared the act invalid on the ground that it impaired the obligation of contract in violation of the federal constitution.[7]

Laws passed in 1860 and 1863 sanctioned the claim of fraud in a different way. They permitted the mortgagor to get a court order canceling his mortgage if he could prove that the original transaction had been fraudulent. To make the order effective against subsequent holders of the mortgage the statute authorized service by publication on unknown assignees and made the court's judgment binding on all parties so served. These laws seem to have been empty declarations; there is no evidence that the farmers made any use of them.[8] A fraud-defense section in a foreclosure stay law passed in 1861 fell with the rest of the act when it reached the Supreme Court, and another law providing for summary cancellation of mortgages, passed in 1863 over Governor Edward Salomon's veto, was apparently not used by the farm-mortgagors either.[9]

From the start the legislators attacked the problem in a still different way: They sought to make it difficult, if not impossible, for the security holders to enforce their rights. In 1858 they passed an act that delayed actual foreclosure for at least a year. The defendant was given six months to answer the complaint, and after entry of judgment all further proceedings were to be stayed for a similar period. The law, which was immediately challenged, was upheld by the Supreme Court, but for some reason the legislature at its next session saw fit to reduce both the six-month periods to ninety days, and a new law enacted in 1863 reduced them to twenty days and six weeks, respectively. Why the legislature should have retreated on this moratory legislation remains a mystery.[10]

Hard on the heels of the court's invalidation of the fraud-defense law of 1858 came the stay law of 1861. This measure provided that in foreclosure proceedings arising out of railroad farm mortgages the court must appoint on the demand of either party a "suitable and proper person" to take all the testimony and that all other proceedings be stayed while testimony was being taken. It permitted objections to testimony, motions on objections, with ten to twenty days to answer, and appeals to the Supreme Court from interlocutory orders. Finally, it required a jury trial on any issue of fact if either party applied for it. In short, it enabled the mortgagor to keep any plaintiff from ever reaching the point of final judgment in a foreclosure proceeding. The Supreme Court invalidated this law also, on the ground that it impaired the obligation of contract.[11]

The next step was taken in 1864, when the mortgagors succeeded in obtaining legislation providing for jury trial of all issues of fact in foreclosure proceedings. Obviously no local jury would render a verdict for a foreclosing Easterner, whatever the evidence might show. Twice the legislators tried this tack and twice they were rebuffed by the Supreme Court. The court construed the first law as discretionary only, and the second it characterized as an unconstitutional interference with the inherent powers of an equity court.[12]

After all attempts to shift the loss from mortgagor to security holder had failed the Grand State League played one more legislative card: it sought to shift the loss to the railroads. A law passed in 1862 permitted, but did not compel, railroad companies to contribute annually to a sinking fund for the payment of outstanding mortgages a sum equal to twelve per cent of their farm-mortgage indebtedness. No railroad volunteered to make the contribution, so two years later the legislature again took action. It passed two sinking-fund laws requiring certain railroad lines to make such contributions and authorizing the governor to appoint a receiver to force compliance if they failed to do so. The railroads did refuse to comply with the act, but the governor did nothing to enforce it, and again the farmers were without means of redress.[13]

Moses M. Strong

James H. Knowlton

Justice Luther S. Dixon

Justice Orsamus Cole

BYRON PAINE

GOVERNOR ALEXANDER W. RANDALL

Some mortgagors obtained relief when the Milwaukee and Prairie du Chien Railroad (successor to the Milwaukee and Mississippi) agreed to retire outstanding mortgages in exchange for a new stock issue that the legislature authorized in 1864.[14] What looked like substantial relief for others was available when Congress transferred the 1856 land grant to the Wisconsin Farm Mortgage Land Company. This agency was to sell the land and pay the proceeds over to mortgagors holding La Crosse and Milwaukee and Milwaukee and Horicon stock. But again the administration of the funds was enveloped in fraud and corruption. Of the half million dollars collected the mortgagors received only about twenty-seven per cent.[15]

The people of the state made a number of suggestions, but the legislature did not act on them: outright repudiation; assumption by the state of the whole debt; repeal of all railroad charters and appropriation by the state of the franchises and property; and imposition of a direct tax to raise the revenue needed to retire the mortgages. Some of these suggested solutions were scarcely possible, others would have entailed a kind of state intervention that would have been a generation ahead of its time.[16]

The executive agency of law likewise had reason to be preoccupied with the problem of the mortgagors' plight. It was a courageous sheriff who dared cry a foreclosure sale, and an unimaginative register of deeds who could not figure out some way to avoid entering transfers. On the state level, election returns were likely to be too close to permit a governor to ignore the farm-mortgagors' claims, as the election of 1861 proved. In that year the Democrats made the costly mistake of nominating Henry L. Palmer, an able lawyer but one forever tainted in the minds of voters by his former employment as an attorney for the La Crosse and Milwaukee Railroad, "the meanest corporation that ever disgraced any state."[17]

The issue made good political capital. Governor Alexander

Randall, as was his wont, identified himself at the start as the farmer's friend. "The railroad mortgages," he said, "were conceived in fraud, executed in fraud, and sold and transferred in fraud.... In the history of financial speculations of this country, ... so bold, open, unblushing frauds, taking in a large body of men, were never perpetrated. There was and is, no law to punish them; because such rascality could not have been anticipated." It was he who suggested as early as 1860 that the 1856 land grant be used to make settlements with the farmers.[18]

But aside from such rhetorical expressions of sympathy for the farmers and censure of the railroad corporations, Wisconsin governors took little positive action. True, they gave their official sanction, right down the line, to the farm-mortgage measures enacted; Edward Salomon was the only governor to veto such a bill, and he was not an elected official but an appointee serving out Governor Louis P. Harvey's unexpired term. Having approved the legislation, however, the governors were content to see it inoperative. Governor James T. Lewis, for instance, did not have the temerity to enforce the compulsory sinking-fund laws, which he had signed but which, presumably, he believed to be unconstitutional or unworkable. Had he been so disposed he could have made a tenable case for enforcement. In passing these measures the legislature was simply exercising the power over corporate charters reserved to it under the Wisconsin constitution. The mortgagors maintained that this section was implicitly a part of any charter or contract to which the state was a party. In addition, the company had failed to abide by its agreement to make the mortgagors' interest payments for them. The sinking-fund law could be regarded simply as a measure requiring the road to implement this agreement. At only one point did Lewis intervene positively, and then not to support the mortgagors but to warn them that they must not resort to violence in resisting foreclosure proceedings.[19]

The trial courts, like the legislature and executive, were

aligned with the mortgagors; the judges were too close to the farmers to defy them. In all but three of the major railroad farm-mortgage cases the mortgagors got judgment in the lower courts.[20] In the Supreme Court, however, they did not fare so well. The preliminary skirmish, which they won in 1859 when the court decided that the 1858 moratory law did not impair the obligation of contract but merely placed a reasonable restriction on the remedy, only delayed the crisis.[21]

The mortgagors needed a defense that went to the merits of their position. If they could find one they would need no remedial legislation at all. But this was difficult in the face of the Eastern mortgage-holders' claim that they were bona fide purchasers for value and that they were ignorant of any prior shady dealings between maker and payee. Many such statements were doubtless untrue, but the mortgagors found it hard to disprove them. That being so, the farmers had little chance of winning. The Wisconsin Supreme Court had approved the prevailing doctrine that a transferee of a negotiable note and mortgage, regular in form and transferred before maturity, took both note and mortgage free and clear of prior equities between the original parties.[22]

Only if the mortgagors could establish that the whole transaction had been illegal from the start, and that the holders knew or should have known of its illegality, might they have a chance of winning. This was the tack they took in the first foreclosure cases. Three such cases came up in the January, 1860, term of court—*Clark v. Farrington, Blunt v. Walker,* and *Cornell v. Hichens.* All of them were clearly test cases, but they were by no means collusive cases, and in each the court had to pass on the validity of the railroad farm mortgages.[23]

In all three cases the mortgagors relied on common-law defenses. Only in the Cornell case did they also urge the fraud-defense statute of 1858. They claimed that the railroad company had no power to accept notes and mortgages in consideration of subscriptions to stock, inasmuch as its charter did not grant such power expressly and it could not be regarded as an implied power reasonably necessary to carry out the company's objectives. The charter, while it specified with great particularity the procedure for opening books and receiving stock subscriptions, made no mention of accepting notes and mortgages as payment. The whole transaction was therefore an illegal one that bestowed no rights on anyone. No one could claim to be a bona fide purchaser of an instrument creating a nullity. The charters were public acts and stood as constructive notice to anyone dealing with the company. The note stated on its face that it was being given in payment of a stock subscription. Since this was not permitted by the charter, no purchaser could claim lack of notice. Hence the defendant was free to assert all his defenses.[24]

The Supreme Court rejected this whole line of argument. It pointed out that the railroad company could take notes and mortgages for some purposes, and that the purchaser was under no obligation to inquire into the specific purpose for which they were being taken.[25] In any event the court held that the company did have the right to take notes and mortgages as payment for stock; this was an implied power necessary to the fulfillment of the purposes of the charter. On this point the court felt no need to be cautious. To hold otherwise, it said, would unduly hamper railroad development in the state and it saw no good reason so to restrict the company. In *Clark v. Farrington* Justice Byron Paine said:

> The cash capital in this state was inadequate to the building of its railroads, or even to the payment of such proportion as is usually paid in cash for stock in the older and more wealthy communities. But the farmers along the routes, having confidence in the success of the enterprises, and the ultimate benefit to themselves, were willing to mortgage their farms for stock, placing the securities in the hands of the companies to negotiate and raise

the funds necessary for building the roads. This practice was extensively adopted along most of the roads in the state.[26]

In *Blunt v. Walker* Chief Justice Luther S. Dixon said:

We can discover no good reason for such a restriction; no good to be accomplished by it. On the contrary, it seems to us to conflict with the general purpose of the act, and to be purely evil in its consequences. It is difficult to perceive any reason why this company was to be so singularly and unjustly restrained.[27]

In the Cornell case the court ruled, as an antecedent step to deliberation on the fraud-defense law, that the plaintiff was a bona fide purchaser, whose status was not affected by any legislation passed after he had bought the note and mortgage. The act, said the court, therefore impaired the obligation of contract under the federal constitution.[28]

In the Clark case the mortgagors had presented a crude form of stock-watering argument. To permit such a transaction as this to stand, they contended, was to countenance a fraud on the subscribers who had put up cash for their stock. Whether this was true or not, the court pointed out, the mortgagors were not in a position to deny the validity of a transaction to which they had cheerfully assented. And the cash-paying subscriber had not complained.[29]

The farmers presented one other common-law defense. In *Crosby v. Roub,* decided three years later, they maintained that the series of documents involved in the transaction did not constitute a proper endorsement. Hence the negotiation was not in due form and the plaintiff was not free of prior equities existing between the immediate parties. Again the court held against the mortgagors. Even though the note and mortgage had not been endorsed by the railroad, it said, the bond the railroad had given the plaintiff operated as an endorsement constituting a negotiation that was regular in form. The plaintiff had therefore taken the note and mortgage free of prior defenses.[30]

The court heard many other cases in which the mortgagor sought to escape liability by asserting common-law defenses. In all of them its position was the same: rejection of the mortgagor's contentions.[31] Still other cases which had their origin in railroad farm-mortgage situations turned on procedural or ancillary issues.[32]

In 1862 the farm-mortgage stay law of the previous year came up on appeal. The court cut through the procedural veneer and saw the act for what it was: an impairment of the obligation of contract. "It is difficult to perceive," said the court, "how any candid person, capable of reading the law and comprehending its provisions, can fail to see upon its very face an intention to clog, hamper and embarrass the proceedings to enforce the remedy, so as to destroy it entirely, and thus impair the contract."[33] The court also held the statute invalid under two provisions of the Wisconsin constitution: the section guaranteeing all persons a remedy for any wrong done them and the clause relating to testimony in equity proceedings.[34]

A few years later, in 1866, the Supreme Court passed on another railroad farm-mortgage statute, the act of 1864 requiring that if either party so demanded, issues of fact in foreclosure cases be tried by jury. The case was argued mainly on two points: whether the documents involved in the transaction were so irregular as to put the plaintiff on notice—the ground taken in *Crosby v. Roub;* and whether there were conditions precedent the satisfaction of which the plaintiff must allege and prove before he could come against the mortgagor, such as the plaintiff's preliminary demand on the company for payment and other miscellaneous conditions that the company itself failed to meet. On both points the court ruled against the farmers. The trial judge had submitted some issues to the jury but had gone on to make additional findings himself. To this the defendant mortgagor took exception, asserting that under the 1864 law all issues of fact must go to the jury. The court pointed out that under the terms of the act the issues need not be submitted to the jury unless one of the parties to the action so demanded. The defendant had made no such demand, and he could not complain now.[35] The court could have stopped here, but it went on. "To avoid all misapprehension," said Justice Orsamus Cole, "my brethren think I had better add, that we do not suppose it to be incumbent upon the circuit court to submit in an equity cause the trial of issues of facts to a jury, unless it thinks proper to do so."[36] By this pronouncement the court took all the teeth out of the law. It made the statute merely declaratory of the well-established advisory verdict of equity procedure.

The second jury-trial statute, that of 1867, requiring all issues of fact to be tried by jury unless jury trial was waived, came before the court in 1868. Mindful of the fate of the 1864 law, the draftsmen had specifically abrogated the circuit court's power to pronounce judgment independently of a jury finding. Again the issue, which the trial court had submitted to the jury, was whether the plaintiff was a bona fide purchaser. The jury of course found that the plaintiff was not one and that the mortgagor's defense was good against him. The trial judge entered judgment on the verdict and the holders appealed.[37]

Speaking through Justice Paine, the Supreme Court declared the law invalid because it deprived the chancellor of his inherent power to decide issues of fact. This was strong doctrine. The Wisconsin constitution required jury trials in actions at law, but was silent about equity proceedings. By its decision the court attributed the procedural distinction between law and equity to the constitution. The language of the opinion barred the legislature from prescribing, for instance, that trial by jury should obtain in all actions, whether at law or in equity. The legislature could have abrogated the jurisdiction of the circuit court altogether, but it could not change the mode of trial. In support of its position all the court could do was to parade the horribles and pronounce a *non sequitur:* if the legislature could make the jury the judge of facts in equity cases, it could likewise make it the judge of the law.[38]

Thus the Supreme Court stood its ground throughout the whole affair. In only one case did it support the farmers: when it sustained the moratory legislation passed in 1858, but that act was later amended to reduce the moratoria time. In all the other cases the court shattered the mortgagors' hopes. It rejected their common-law defenses; declared the 1858 fraud-defense statute and the 1861 stay law unconstitutional because they impaired the obligation of contract; rendered the 1864 jury-trial statute ineffective by construing it to be discretionary only; and, finally, invalidated the 1867 jury-trial law on the ground that it deprived the chancellor of his inherent fact-finding power, which the court now enshrined in the Wisconsin constitution.

The farmers did not accept these decisions meekly. They went to the polls and there sought to apply the remedy that had been so successful with the executive and legislature. In 1861, when the unsympathetic Justice Orsamus Cole came up for re-election, they set out to defeat him. Wisconsin Republicans were in a dilemma: Cole had been their candidate, but they dared not risk the mortgagors' opposition. They therefore made no nomination, and Cole ran as an independent. The Democratic nominee withdrew after the race had begun. The mortgagors ran as their candidate James H. Knowlton, who had taken their side unequivocally by writing a scathing denunciation of the Supreme Court's decisions in the first farm-mortgage cases. The campaigning was spirited and bitter, but Cole won the election by about five thousand votes.[39]

The mortgagors made a second attempt to defeat a Supreme Court judge in 1863, when Chief Justice Dixon's term expired. The farmers regarded Dixon as a turncoat, believing that he had originally been on their side. In point of fact, however, he had not ony concurred with the majority in the first farm-mortgage cases but had written two of the opinions.[40] Again the Republicans refrained from making a nomination, and Dixon ran as an independent candidate as had Cole. This time the Democrats nominated the farm-mortgagors' candidate Montgomery M. Cothren. This too was a bitter campaign; Dixon was referred to as the "boy judge" and Cothren was branded a Copperhead. In the light of the first returns it looked as though Cothren had won, but then the soldier vote came in. The Copperhead epithet had done its work; Dixon won the election by some three thousand votes.[41]

Thus the mortgagors' attempts to control the judiciary from the ballot box failed. Their failure may, however, have been quite unrelated to the farm-mortgage issue. Certainly the charge of Copperheadism did much to defeat Cothren in 1863. And, as has been suggested, if the five thousand votes that constituted Cole's plurality in 1861 had not been cast for the Democratic candidate who withdrew, Knowlton might have won the election.[42] But the fact that the mortgagors failed had significant consequences. It greatly strengthened the tradition of an independent judiciary.

One other remedy might have been tried by the farmers. They might have pressed for relief through a constitutional amendment, but they did not do so.[43] At the outset they probably thought that so drastic a measure would not be necessary; they knew they had strength enough to work through other agencies of law and they had not foreseen the intractability of the court. By the time it had become clear that the court would not budge, the agitation was petering out. Easterners had compromised their claims, and the Milwaukee and Prairie du Chien had made its settlement. In any event, there was always more land.[44]

The Wisconsin constitution did figure in the affair, however, not only as the basis for the court's invalidation of legislation but as an underlying reason for the invention of the farm-mortgage scheme. The whole affair is partly attributable to the constitutional prohibition of state aid for internal improvements. The framers of the constitution had not been sufficiently aware of the tremendous pressure for capital that existed in Wisconsin; they had remembered only the sad experience of states burdened with huge debts born of their internal-improvement programs. But economic needs soon made an anachronism of the constitutional hostility to capital.

Many leading members of the state's legal profession played a part in the drama; the farm-mortgagors had come first for help to their lawyers. One of the farmers' chief purposes in organizing the Home Leagues was to pool funds for employment of good counsel. Attorneys' fees were not low. Lawyers in Monroe demanded a hundred-dollar retainer, a fee of four hundred dollars if they lost the case, and twenty-five hundred if they won it. The Grand State League assessed its members twenty-five cents each to raise a fund for retaining Matthew H. Carpenter to argue the constitutionality of the stay law. The mortgagors' cause did not suffer from default of counsel: in Monroe, Janesville, and Madison, for instance, they retained leading local attorneys.[45]

Like the local enforcement officials, the bar too was sensitive to pressure from the mortgagors. Life was made uncomfortable indeed for rural lawyers who took foreclosure suits for Eastern security holders. Ironically, the farm-mortgage scheme itself can be ascribed to the legal profession; its author was probably John H. Tweedy, an able lawyer who was a director of the Milwaukee and Mississippi Railroad.[46]

The mortgagors' candidates for the bench were also leading members of the bar. James H. Knowlton was a brilliant advocate and a prominent public figure. He had displayed great ingenuity and aggressiveness in his conduct of the legislative investigation of the land-grant scandal, and he had been a protagonist in a test case challenging the constitutionality of a local taxing statute. Montgomery M. Cothren had had almost ten years' experience on the circuit court bench.[47]

* * *

THE farm-mortgage cases had a perceptible effect on the growth of Wisconsin law. On common-law matters the law followed well-marked paths. The Wisconsin Supreme Court conformed to prevailing doctrine in characterizing the Eastern security holders as bona fide purchasers, thereby cutting off equities between prior parties. Indeed, the negotiation of these farmers' notes and mortgages seemed to be just the sort of situation the bona fide purchaser rule was designed to cover.

On the application of the contract clause Wisconsin followed the lead of the United States Supreme Court. In *Fletcher v. Peck* and *Dartmouth College v. Woodward* Marshall had refused to let the state itself rescind its grant; *a fortiori* the Wisconsin court could hardly countenance repudiation of a contract by a private person.[48] A majority of the Wisconsin judges also followed the Taney court's decision in *Bronson v. Kinzie*.[49] In *Von Baumbach v. Bade* they followed its rationale and in *Oatman v. Bond* they adopted its result. In the light of Chief Justice Dixon's language in the Von Baumbach case it is hard to see how mortgagors' counsel could have hoped that the 1861 stay law would stand.

But in another respect the Wisconsin court strayed from Taney. It did not share the mistrust of corporate power he had expressed as recently as 1853 when he remarked that grants of privileges and exemptions should always be strictly construed against the corporation and in favor of the public.[50] Knowlton, in his review of the 1860 farm-mortgage cases, took essentially the Taney position. He warned the court against "latitudinarian" construction of corporate charters and pointed out that incidental and convenient powers must not be unduly expanded. "The court has admitted a power to exist on a conceded-debatable hypothesis, without once adverting to results, or consequences. The doctrines laid down in the opinion apply to all corporations. If they are law, the rights of the people must soon lie buried beneath the crushing weight of irresponsible monopolies."[51]

The court might have considered the power of a corporation to take notes and mortgages in payment for stock subscriptions in this atmosphere of narrow construction and maintained that such power was beyond the scope of the charter. But the Wisconsin judges were not of Taney's mind. Greater than their fear of monopoly was their fear of the consequences of an overly narrow construction. They held that a private group such as a corporation to which a public function had been delegated should not be hamstrung by restrictive judicial interpretation. Justice Paine pointed out that to corporations was entrusted

> the accomplishment of "enterprises of great pith and moment," which, when properly executed, contribute greatly to the convenience and prosperity of mankind, and even to the advancement of civilization—enterprises impossible to private, unassociated capital, and which sometimes task even the enormous energies of corporations beyond their strength.... These considerations are sufficient to show that the rule that corporations can exercise no powers not delegated, should not, from an undiscriminating timidity or apprehension, be extended so as to unwisely and unnecessarily cripple and restrict them as to the means of executing the powers that are delegated. Powerful as they are, it must be assumed that the law is powerful enough not only to control and confine them within their proper limits, but also within a reasonable discretion in selecting among the various means that may be adapted to the execution of their power.[52]

Thus through judicial interpretation of the contract clause the law helped pave the way for corporate development in Wisconsin. The clause was a predecessor in economic regulation to the due-process clause of the latter part of the century. And against it the reserved-power clause in the Wisconsin constitution was an unsuccessful adversary. The mortgagors had maintained that this provision became an implicit part of all charters and legislation governing corporations, but the court was unwilling to permit it to infringe on the vested rights of third parties.

The court rightly assumed that capital was the crying need of a frontier community. But by permitting unbridled legislation of power to private groups in order to obtain that capital, it displayed a naïve faith in the good will and public spirit of nineteenth-century entrepreneurs.

The farm-mortgage struggle lent lasting prestige to the concept of a nonpartisan judiciary. The court had successfully defied prevailing attitudes on several points as, for example, when it invalidated the jury-trial statutes. It recognized, though it did not so state in its decision, that to uphold these laws would mean that no foreclosing creditor could ever collect. The fact remains, however, that in freezing this particular bit of equity procedure—i.e. forbidding jury trials in equity—in the constitution the court committed Wisconsin jurisprudence to an unfortunate rigidity. Counsel still feel the sting of *Callanan v. Judd.*[53]

The results of the judicial elections, whatever the determining factor, were interpreted as clear-cut victories for the independence of the courts. A Supreme Court justice, writing seventy years later could characterize the episode as "a chapter in the history of the Court of which every citizen may well feel proud. An elective bench in the midst of great popular clamor and threats of defeat preserved its judicial independence intact, refused to be coerced or dragooned and was finally sustained in its course by the people at large."[54]

Less can be said of the legislature. It was scarcely prepared, so early in its history, to grapple with the complex problems of railroad regulation and reorganization. In a very literal sense it was the people's agency of law, but it had a heart "too soon made glad." By bending so easily to the pressure of political winds, it engendered disrespect and even contempt for itself. Thinking people could not dissociate its behavior here from its collapse in 1856. Nor were party ties strong enough to stiffen the legislature's back. Neither party dared defy the farmers, and the farmers switched parties at will. In 1863, for instance, mortgagors who were normally Republican voted Democratic almost to a man.[55]

The farm-mortgage incident was also important in the history of private government—of *ad hoc* associations organized for political purposes. The Grand State League and the local Farm Mortgage Leagues were tightly knit units of power that permitted little deviation from their program and policy. The Monroe League, for example, resolved that no member should "make or accept any proposal to settle his mortgage without the consent of the League."[56] A generation later rebellious Grangers could hark back to the Farmer's Home Leagues for precedent just as farm-mortgagors had drawn upon the experience of the claim clubs.

The farm-mortgagors greatly strengthened anti-monopoly sentiment in Wisconsin. They had been badly burned, and it was to be a long time before they regarded railroad men as anything but scoundrels, and corporations as anything but agents of monopoly. They prepared the ground for the growth of the Grange and the Populist revolt. The episode confirmed farmers' suspicion that all Eastern investors were greedy speculators bent on illicit gains.[57]

The reverse of the medal was the public opinion engendered outside Wisconsin. In the Eastern states each new law passed in aid of the farmers provoked cries of protest, and at one point New York citizens threatened reprisals. The Easterners came to the conclusion that Wisconsin was a community "lost to honor, the abode of corrupt politicians and the home of a degraded people."[58] One wonders how they would have reacted if the farmers' schemes had been successful.

In the whole affair the law, balancing economic interests against each other, tipped the scales in favor of the Eastern creditors. Given the limitations of the times, however, perhaps the law did all it could. It tied things up for virtually a decade and forced creditors to compromise. Had it done more, the cost, in terms of the prestige of legal institutions, might well have been too great. True, it made no serious effort to give the farmer relief in the form of a public subsidy, but it was much too early for such a solution to recommend itself to the minds of men in the frontier state of Wisconsin.

III. The Formative Period of Wisconsin Railroad Law, 1858–1874

The railroads are the great public highways of the world, along which its gigantic currents of trade and travel continually pour.... They are the most marvelous invention of modern times.... There is scarcely a want, wish or aspiration of the human heart which they do not in some measure help to gratify.—JUSTICE BYRON PAINE in *Whiting v. Fond du Lac Railroad.*

RAILROADS made their first solid impact on Wisconsin society during the period between 1858 and 1874. If the farm-mortgage struggle was the only really dramatic episode in the relationship between the railroad and the law, this is not to say that other developments in that relationship were unimportant. As official agencies of law—mainly court and legislature—formulated and enforced rules of substantive policy from day to day in seemingly humdrum situations, they did more, perhaps, to fit the railroad into the life and times of the community than did dramatically contested elections, abortive regulatory statutes, and "great" cases.

But precisely because events were humdrum and the work was day-to-day, the law did not see broad implications in the questions presented to it. Nor did it develop new techniques to deal with new institutions. Instead it tried to make old doctrines fit new needs created by the railroads. In this process the courts did most of the work. This was necessary and natural, for only judge-made law was immediately available to take care of the many situations that inevitably arose. Sensing this need and mindful of their especial capacity to satisfy it, Wisconsin judges performed their lawmaking job boldly; they did not hesitate to enunciate broad governing principles of common law. The desirability of this course may be open to question, but conditions being what they were, there was no alternative. Legislative activity was inept and sporadic, and there was no administrative process. The court got its job by default.

The work of this generation of lawmakers covers five general areas in which the railroad impinged on the economic and legal order: 1) the railroad's relationships with strangers, including occupants of lands it took for rights-of-way and lands adjoining the tracks, as well as persons killed or injured by trains; 2) its relationships with users of its services, including both passengers and shippers; 3) its intracorporate and intercorporate affairs, covering relations with stockholders, officers, and directors, and problems of merger and consolidation, receivership and reorganization; 4) its relationships with government—state, local, and federal; and 5) its relationships with contracting parties auxiliary to its operations, such as building contractors, suppliers of goods and services, employees, purchasers of lands, and creditors other than holders of mortgage bonds. The table on page 68 shows, by five-year periods, the incidence of legal intervention, by way of general laws and Supreme Court decisions, in these various types of problems involving railroads.[1]

The Railroad's Relationships with Strangers

By far the greatest number of incidents that came before the law for official settlement involved strangers—that is, persons brought involuntarily into legal relationships with the railroads. Sometimes property rights were involved, sometimes invasions of personal rights.

INSTANCES OF LEGAL INTERVENTION

STATE LAWS AND SUPREME COURT DECISIONS

Pertaining to Problems Involving Railroads in Wisconsin *

FIELD COVERED	1858–63	1865–69	1870–74	TOTAL
RELATIONSHIPS WITH STRANGERS				
With landowners †	18	12	27	57
Injury to persons	2	11	7	20
Injury to livestock	5	11	2	18
Total	25	34	36	95
RELATIONSHIPS WITH USERS				
With passengers	2	5	3	10
With shippers	7	18	11	36
Total	9	23	14	46
INTRACORPORATE RELATIONSHIPS				
Charters and authority of officers	4	0	0	4
With stock- and bondholders	9	7	0	16
Farm-mortgage cases	15	13	5	33
Consolidation, merger, reorganizations, receiverships	3	12	2	17
Total	31	32	7	70
RELATIONSHIPS WITH GOVERNMENT				
With state government	11	11	6	28
With local governments	8	8	9	25
With federal government	3	1	1	5
Total	22	20	16	58
RELATIONSHIPS WITH OTHER CONTRACTING PARTIES				
With building contractors	2	8	5	15
With miscellaneous creditors	1	7	1	9
With employees	1	5	1	7
Total	4	20	7	31
Grand total	91	129	80	300

* Based on *Wisconsin General Laws* and on *Wisconsin Supreme Court Reports* for the years 1858–73. The private and local laws, which reached their greatest volume during this period, were not examined. The several categories into which the laws and court decisions have been divided overlap to some extent and do not, perhaps, always satisfy the requirements of logic.

† Comprising condemnation proceedings and damages to land and property from engine sparks.

Relationships with Landowners—Most numerous were problems involving relationships with landowners whose land the railroad took under the power of eminent domain. As a result of the nineteenth-century theory and methods of getting public jobs done, eminent domain proceedings represented relationships not with government but with private individuals. Lawmakers, while they realized that railroads were a public matter, delegated the task of building them to private concerns.[2] To enable these concerns to perform the task assigned to them the legislature had to give them authority to appropriate the land over which their roads were to pass. Any subsequent controversies involved primarily the landowner and the railroad.[3]

From the very first the special charters defined the railroads' power to condemn and take land. The details of the provisions varied, but the main outlines were the same: an express grant of power to condemn land upon payment of compensation to the owner, and a definition of procedures for arbitration and appraisal of the value of the land.[4] But on the question whether the railroads might enter on the lands before they made compensation, most of the charters were ambiguous. To resolve this ambiguity the legislature passed a general act in 1858 which stipulated that if the railroad did not make compensation within six months of appropriating the land the landowner might obtain an injunction halting all operations over his land until he received payment for it.[5]

Three other laws of a general nature were enacted during these early years. The first, passed in 1859, established a uniform procedure for condemnation, presumably obviating the need for detailed clauses in special charters. This law had a short life, however; the very next year the Supreme Court declared it unconstitutional. The act had apparently been sponsored by the railroads, for its central feature was a clause permitting the company to enter on the projected right-of-way before making compensation.[6] The railroad companies may have had in mind the advantageous position of the builders of mill dams under the Mill Dam Act of 1858. Under this law compensation to the owner whose lands were flooded was made only after the damage had been done, and then by a jury award. At an early day the Supreme Court had upheld this law, but, in its opinion invalidating the 1859 railroad condemnation act, the court expressed its regret for having sustained the provision of the Mill Dam Act.[7]

The section in the 1859 condemnation law that the court found objectionable provided that the only appraisal which must be made prior to the company's entrance on the property was an appraisal by an agent of the company and two disinterested freeholders of the country, who were, apparently, to be appointed by the company agent. After the agent had offered to pay the owner this appraised value, the railroad might enter on the lands. Speaking through Chief Justice Dixon, the court characterized this procedure as a mockery: it was an ex parte and secret appraisal in violation of the section in the state constitution requiring "just compensation." The fact that after the entry of the railroad the owner could, under the terms of the statute, petition the court for an appraisal by three impartial commissioners did not make the law valid. By this decision the Supreme Court established the proposition that before a railroad might enter on land it must compensate the owner —or give assurance that it would do so—on the basis of the value arrived at through an impartial and open appraisal.[8]

Another general law that also seems to have been railroad-sponsored was an 1861 act outlining a procedure for acquiring land which the railroad had already appropriated but for which it had not made compensation. The measure was more artfully drawn than its predecessor; it permitted the landowner to have appraisal commissioners appointed at the company's expense. But at the same time it expressly prohibited the court from granting an injunction preventing use and occupancy of the land until the amount of damages had been liquidated or until a final judgment had been rendered.[9] Six years later, in *Andrews v. Farmers' Loan & Trust Co.,* the Supreme Court sustained this statute, but on very narrow grounds. The court construed it as merely declaratory of the equitable doctrine of laches; when an owner, by acquiescence or otherwise, so postponed enforcing his rights, he forfeited his right to equitable relief by injunction. In the Andrews case the owner-plaintiff had waited four years after the defendant railroad had entered, constructed its tracks, and begun operations on its line.[10]

In the next case the court made the 1861 law impotent. It limited the prohibition against injunction to instances where the railroad had already constructed tracks, erected depots, and obstained the express or implied consent of the owner. "Had it been supposed," said the court, "that the statute was applicable to a case like the present, where by the facts alleged in the complaint it appears that the owner had never acquiesced at all in the actual operation or use of his land by the company, but has *in limine* and at the very first attempt of the company to take actual possession without an appraisement and tender of damages, resisted its so doing and commenced this action to stay and prevent such proceedings, it is very clear that this court could not, consistently with its previous decisions and with what it conceives to be the requirement of the constitution where private property is to be taken for public use, have held the act a valid and obligatory exercise of the legislative power."[11]

The third provision for condemnation proceedings enacted during this early period was incorporated in the general railroad law of 1872. Ten sections dealing with eminent domain included the requirement that an impartial and open appraisal be made before the company entered on the land.[12]

Thus condemnation procedures were defined partly by special act and partly by general law. And in both there were many blank spaces to be filled in by the courts. The courts shouldered, for instance, the task of defining what parties might take advantage of the injunctive provisions and under what circumstances—matters on which the legislature was usually silent; they determined whether the statute offered the landowner his only remedy; and, in the great bulk of litigation, they spelled out the procedures and terms under which the commissioners should make their appraisals and award. This was done under the hybrid general-special law pattern of condemnation statutes as well as under the provisions of the general law of 1872.[13]

Had the statutes been more adequate the courts need not have played so active a role in developing the law of eminent domain. But the legislature did not attempt to draw comprehensive condemnation procedures. When it defined such procedures at all, it failed to visualize their operation and ignored many points, with the result that much needless litigation was precipitated. Thus laws were thrust on the courts to administer through the cumbersome process of a lawsuit or through statutory appeals from commissioners' awards. The condemnation commissioners constituted a rudimentary form of the administrative process, but reviewing courts did not give their awards even presumptive effect. The courts were themselves performing the function of administration.

When the Supreme Court did intervene in matters of first-rank policy, it showed itself to be a creature of its time and place. In nullifying the 1857 law and emasculating the act of 1861 Wisconsin judges acted in accordance with the concept of "property" tied inextricably to land that was so typical of nineteenth-century agrarian society. As Chief Justice Dixon expressed it:

> It has been settled as one of the rights of private property secured to the owner by the constitution that it cannot, against his will, be taken from him, or entered upon and permanently occupied for public use, until its value has been ascertained by some legal and

proper proceeding, and has been paid to him. . . . It has also been settled that the attempt to enter upon and take permanent possession of land for public use without the assent of the owner, and without the damages having been first so ascertained, and paid or tendered to him, is, or would, if consummated, be in the nature of an irreparable injury for the prevention of which the writ of injunction constitutes the proper remedy and should, unless some peculiar reasons be shown for denying it, be issued when applied for in due form by the party whose constitutional rights are thus unlawfully invaded or threatened to be.[14]

The court shared the landowner's concern for a fair, open, and impartial hearing, but it showed no appreciation of the need for speed and expedition in getting land appropriated and tracks laid down. In any event one may wonder what purpose was served in vitiating the 1861 act by crabbed construction eleven years after its passage. During all this time, despite the court's doubts in the Andrews case, the railroads had presumably enjoyed the benefit of the statute and proceeded under its provisions.

Other actions between landowner and railroad included disputes over boundaries, over compensation for land that had depreciated in value since its acquisition under eminent domain, and over damage to a landowner's property resulting from the positive action of a railroad.[15] A new problem created by railroads was that of damage from fire started by sparks from locomotives. The Wisconsin court struggled manfully with issues of proof, negligence, and causation. On the issue of contributory negligence—i.e., whether the adjoining landowner must keep his property free from combustibles—the court made basic policy by adopting the reasoning of the English courts, which had first faced the problem, rather than that of the courts of the neighboring state of Illinois.[16]

Injury to Livestock.—Railroads also damaged chattels. Horses, cattle, and other farm animals were killed or injured. Before long the frequency of these casualties generated a response from the law. The legislature met the problem, not by imposing absolute liability on the roads for injury to livestock, but by making them fence their tracks. The act disposing of the northwestern part of the 1856 land grant, for instance, required the La Crosse and Milwaukee Railroad to fence its road in twenty-mile parcels as each stretch was built. In 1860 the legislature passed the first general act relating to fencing; it required the railroads to erect and maintain "good and sufficient fences" along their rights of way. Until they did so they were absolutely liable for death or injuries to animals. Afterward they were answerable only for negligence or wilful misconduct.[17]

It was soon apparent that this statute was not enough to force the companies to keep their fences in good repair. In 1867, therefore, the legislature passed an act permitting the landowner to make necessary repairs himself if, after due notice, the railroad failed to do so. The law authorized the landowner to recover his expenses plus interest in an action against the company. The general railroad law of 1872 incorporated essentially the terms of this act.[18]

Judicial construction put a heavy gloss on these statutes. Even before the legislature passed the fencing statute of 1867 the Supreme Court had spoken on the obligations of both the railroad and the livestock owner.[19] By the early seventies the courts had laid down a substantial body of law under both common law and statute on the subject of a railroad's liability for the death of animals straying on its tracks.[20] At one point the inevitable happened and a child was injured at a place where a fence was defective. The Wisconsin court permitted recovery by deciding, as a matter of self-conscious policy, that the purview of the animal-fencing statute included injury to children.[21]

Wrongful Death and Personal-Injury Actions.—The size and speed of railroad trains inevitably took a heavy toll in life and limb. This problem had plagued society from the very first, and mid-nineteenth-century law met it with the only tool it had—the law of torts. Significantly, it chose a principle that imposed liability only for fault or substandard conduct—in other words, the doctrine of negligence. It need not have made this choice; it could have used the principle of strict liability, by terming the railroad a "dangerous instrumentality" or an "inherently dangerous" activity. The fact that the law did not do so reflects the attitude of the times. Strict liability, according to the current concept, was too high a price to exact from an infant economic institution upon which material progress depended; the railroad ought to bear the loss only if it had been negligent.

Legislation in the interest of greater safety began as early as 1856. In that year an act was passed requiring a train to come to a full stop before crossing the tracks of another line, and in 1870 a measure required similar stops before drawbridges.[22] But legislation dealt with only a small part of the problem; it was the court that normally administered redress for personal injuries inflicted by railroads, and, to judge from the number of cases reaching the Supreme Court, the injuries were numerous. "This is one of those actions, now so frequent," said Chief Justice Dixon in *Butler v. Milwaukee & St. P. R.*, "for injuries caused by negligence in which the principal questions are whether there was any evidence of negligence on the part of the defendant to go to the jury and whether the evidence also showed that the party injured was free from fault or did not contribute by his own want of care to the injury complained of."[23]

In England the advent of the railroad and the accidents it caused created pressures that ultimately brought about the passage of Lord Campbell's Act, the first wrongful-death statute.[24] In Wisconsin the legislature included a wrongful-death section in its railroad-crossing law of 1856 and the next year passed a wrongful-death statute modeled after the British act.[25] The courts passed on these statutes many times. In giving them effect they were likely to limit recovery by employing a mechanically narrow and rigid construction, but they laid down procedures and practices which held for many years and which helped prepare them for the flood of litigation that was to follow in the next generation.[26]

Railroads and Their Users

In controversies between the railroads and the persons who used them it was again the courts that did most of the detailed work. The legislature participated by enacting some general regulatory principles which were important but which covered only a part of the field and were inadequately implemented.[27]

Relationships with Shippers.—In disputes between shippers and railroads the courts had as precedents judicial decisions setting forth the general principles of the law of bailments, but over the years the sheer volume of cases resulted in the promulgation of virtually a new body of law.[28] Most of the disputes concerned damage to goods in transit and posed the question whether carrier, shipper, or consignee should bear the loss. The carriers soon tried to limit their liability by contract, and these contracts, too, came in for judicial review. Many controversies involved that no-man's land between the time goods reached their destination and the time the consignee picked them up. Others involved wrongful or mistaken delivery. As goods came to be shipped over successive carriers, the question became still more complicated; which carrier was then to be held responsible?[29]

The very number of such cases ought to have made the Supreme Court an expert on the commercial handling of goods. But the court did not often refer to business and commercial practice; it rested most of its decisions on legal doctrine. Even so, it was probably better that the bewildering variety of problems came before the courts rather than the legislature.

Relationships with Passengers.—The increasing volume of travel and the speed and size of trains brought before the courts new problems pertaining to injuries to passengers. The attitude that governed the court's refusal to impose absolute liability for injuries inflicted on strangers also governed its assessment of liability for injuries suffered by passengers. In accordance with common-law precedent, however, the court did hold the railroad to a higher degree of care in protecting passengers.[30] Questions of negligence—of both railroad and passenger—constituted the main issues in the cases. Again the legislature took no part; this was entirely judge-made law. The cases involved persons who had been riding on cars at the time they were injured as well as those who had been in the act of boarding or alighting from the train.[31] The question whether the plaintiff was in fact a passenger was necessarily involved in, and often determinative of, the decision.[32] The main task of the courts was to untangle the facts and apply an appropriate legal rule; very little new policy was made by these decisions. The common-law principles of carrier liability to passengers had been fairly well settled by this time.

Intracorporate and Intercorporate Relationships

This new transportation agency employed the corporate device as a means of doing business. As working institutions corporations are people, and it was therefore natural that the relations between them would find their way to the law for definition and delineation.

The formal grant of power was contained in the railroad's charter. Since a charter was the prerequisite of corporateness, the legislature perforce played an active role. The consideration of special railroad charters probably consumed more of the lawmakers' time and occupied more space in the statute books than any other single subject, especially during the years 1866–71, despite the fact that there existed both a constitutional provision designed to discourage special grants and a body of general railroad legislation adequate to cover most articles of incorporation. But the words of the constitution were not heeded and the facilities of the general statutes were not used. Railroad companies continued to come into existence by special act. Governors and newspapers inveighed against the proliferation of special charters, but not until 1871 was the pressure great enough to effect the passage of a constitutional amendment outlawing them. The next year the legislature passed the general railroad act controlling all railroad corporations.[33]

The special charters came frequently before the courts, and by their interpretation of various clauses in them judges helped determine the scope of corporate power. From the first the Supreme Court took a latitudinarian position in defining the railroad's authority under its charter from the state. It saw too many disadvantages in restrictive construction:

> The charters of these companies impose such restrictions and requirements upon them as, in opinion of the legislature, the public interest and public policy demand. And it having done so it must be assumed that within these limits the company is left to accomplish the enterprise as best it may. And the mere fact that in some agreement it may appear that motives of private interest may, to some extent, operate in influencing its action, ought not to be held to make such agreement void as against public policy. It is vain to suppose that such enterprises can be accomplished without the operation of such motives. They constitute the mainspring of human action and must inevitably operate to a greater or less extent, in the execution of all great enterprises of this character, and we think it may be assumed that so long as the company complies with the requirements of the charter, the struggle between conflicting private and local interests will, from the necessity of the case, be so adjusted as best to advance the enterprise and accommodate the public generally.[34]

The most important litigation between stockholder and railroad involving the authorized power of corporations was of course the series of farm-mortgage controversies that plagued court and legislature for twenty years, but there were many people other than farm-mortgagors who, having optimistically subscribed for stock, wanted to escape their obligations when insolvency overtook the railroads. They too used a variety of methods to get out of paying for the stock they had contracted for, and in so doing presented to the Supreme Court many times the question of the validity and interpretation of subscriptions to stock. In all these cases the court laid down broad principles of corporation law and set its face against a narrow construction of the powers granted by the charters.[35]

Twice the legislature came to the aid of the stockholders. In 1858, after exposing the land-grant scandal, it passed an act requiring the railroads to make stated reports and disclosures to the secretary of state for the information of all stockholders. The next year it enacted a measure permitting stockholders to petition the court for a stockholders' meeting and authorizing the court to compel the calling of such a meeting if the directors failed to respond. In 1866 the legislature enacted a law making it unnecessary for a judge to disqualify himself from sitting on a case, as Judge Jason Downer had recently done, simply because he was a stockholder in a railroad that was a party to the action. As the act was worded it apparently became mandatory for such a judge to sit, but it is doubtful whether the legislature intended to interfere with the court's discretion in an extreme case.[36]

At this early date the authority of directors and officers was still governed largely by the principles of the common law of agency. On the few occasions that the law intervened to determine the legal effect of an officer's actions, it construed the authority of presidents and vice-presidents narrowly. None of the cases reported indicates what position the court took on the authority of directors. Presumably their authority was as broad as the scope of the railroad's charter.[37]

During the sixties the law faced for the first time a number of problems arising out of railroad mortgage foreclosures, receiverships, reorganizations, consolidations, and mergers. This was Wisconsin's first big era of railroad consolidations; of the many roads chartered in the fifties, only two—the Chicago, Milwaukee and St. Paul and the Chicago and North Western—survived until the seventies. By 1874 these two lines controlled the entire network of Wisconsin railways.[38]

Consolidations were effected in different ways. Sometimes the charter itself expressly granted the necessary authority, sometimes it was implied in language less precise. As early as 1857 the railroad interests succeeded in pushing through a general consolidation law broad enough to cover all situations. Under the aegis of this statute the two dominant roads embarked on their programs of amalgamation. By the mid-sixties they had carried the process so far that a strong anti-consolidation sentiment developed, with the result that in 1864 the legislature repealed the general consolidation act. But this action did not really hamper the consolidationists, for no act was passed prohibiting consolidation, and the railroads continued to get authorization by special act. In 1867 the legislature passed a law expressly prohibiting the two major roads from consolidating. But even this did not prevent a merger in fact: in 1869–70 the two roads were run by interlocking directorates and Alexander Mitchell was president of both![39]

Thus at the very time that sentiment against monopoly and consolidation was strong, railroad consolidation went on at a breakneck pace. It is hard to explain this inconsistency. In part it lay in a failure to understand the railroad problem. The contemporary assumption was that all monopoly was a bad thing and therefore to be condemned. But this view ran counter to stubborn fact. By its very nature the railroad was in part a monopoly; unbridled competition never had a place in railroad transportation. The trend toward consolidation was not only more or less inevitable but to a great extent desirable for efficiency of operation.[40]

The inconsistency stemmed also from a lack of realism about the efficacy of law. Merely to condemn the evil of monopoly was not to put a stop to it. Yet in these early statutes the legislature made no provision for even the most rudimentary enforcement of its declared policy. At the same time, putting the policy into words served to salve an uneasy collective conscience.[41]

The two companies that ultimately dominated Wisconsin's railroads emerged from the panic of 1857 by picking up the ruins of the many lesser roads that had fallen by the wayside. The decades of the sixties and seventies saw a spate of foreclosure sales and receiverships, during the course of which railroad-reorganization lawyers learned their skills.[42] The foreclosure of the many La Crosse and Milwaukee mortgages, the gallant but futile resistance of the directors of the Milwaukee and Prairie du Chien to engulfment by Stimson and Company, an Eastern investment firm, and the final arrangement of interlocking directorates between the Milwaukee and North Western roads are among the more dramatic incidents of the period.[43] The foreclosures also gave birth to less dramatic conflicts over the priority of mortgage bondholders and the effect of after-acquired property clauses.[44]

Influential mortgage holders also went to the legislature for relief. One of the trustees of the La Crosse and Milwaukee, W. Barnes, was allegedly the proponent of an 1859 act that permitted trustees under a mortgage or deed of trust to bid in at the foreclosure sale. Barnes held a junior mortgage on the road and after passage of the act he proceeded, as trustee, to foreclose on his mortgage first.[45] In the same year the legislature enacted a law permitting trustees and mortgage holders to redeem from the foreclosure-sale purchaser within a year by depositing with the court the purchase price plus interest.[46]

Out of these reorganizations came procedures and details of judicial administration in which the Wisconsin Supreme Court laid the foundation of Wisconsin railroad-reorganization law.[47] The bigger cases, involving out-of-state bondholders, found their way into the federal courts, including the United States Supreme Court, which spoke several times on railroad foreclosures and reorganizations in Wisconsin.[48]

Railroads and Government

In delegating the building of the state's railroads to private entrepreneurs Wisconsin lawmakers were not denying that the job was a public responsibility nor suggesting that it was to be entirely exempt from state control. The very life of a railroad corporation was derived from a charter granted by the state, which, under the constitution, reserved the power to repeal or modify it.[49] Recurrent relations between the state and the chartered corporation were therefore to be expected.

Relationships with State Government.—The malodorous events surrounding the disposition of the 1856 land grant did not prevent Congress, eight years later, from donating a second tract of land in aid of Wisconsin railroads. These lands the state legislature gave to the corporation that eventually became the Wisconsin Central Railroad Company. Presumably the legislators had learned something from the experience of their notorious predecessors who had disposed of the first grant for their own purposes. At all events there was not the incidence and atmosphere of political jobbery here that had characterized the earlier transactions. In 1868 the legislature passed an act requiring recipient roads to select their land-grant tracts within a year's time or suffer forfeit.[50]

Every special charter and every amendment to it involved

a relationship between railroad and government. The mine run of these charters give little evidence that the promoters sought any special favors; on the contrary, they seem to have been content with acquiring routine powers to do business as a corporate organization. Only in the special laws authorizing consolidations did the railroads seek special favors from legislators. But the pressure for special charters and amendments (in which applications for railroad charters bulked large) became so great that the legislators were forced to devote a disproportionate time to them. Only then did the demand for a flat constitutional prohibition of special charters bear fruit. With the passage of a general railroad law in 1872 the grant of a charter to a company meeting the requirements became a mere ministerial function of government. By shifting the machinery from the legislative to the executive branch the legislature freed itself for other duties.[51]

In the field of taxation the relations between state and railroads were likewise fraught with problems. Early in their history the railroads pressed for favorable tax treatment and by 1854 had achieved a special position under a law imposing an annual tax of one per cent of their gross receipts in lieu of taxes based on the assessed valuation of their real and personal property. This law, which placed upon the railroads a far lighter burden than ordinary tax assessments would have done, had many ups and downs in the Supreme Court before it was finally affirmed. In the initial challenge the court affirmed its validity but wrote no opinion. In a test case brought by James H. Knowlton the court overruled the first decision by implication and invalidated the tax, and in a third case it expressly overruled the unreported case. Then, in a subsequent case, which was argued twice, the court again reversed its position and once more sustained the tax.[52] In the meantime the legislature had passed new taxing statutes, couched in terms of "license fees" for the privilege of doing business, that were designed to overcome the lack of "uniformity" the court had criticized in its opinions invalidating the 1854 law.[53]

Here were two agencies of law working at cross purposes; the ultimate effect of the court's vacillations was to make the legislature's action superfluous. In employing a mechanically rigid interpretation of the uniformity clause in the state constitution the court ignored the possibility that railroad taxation presented a unique problem. It acted in a purely negative way, suggesting no workable alternative, and it accomplished very little by its venture into tax policy except to create embarrassment for itself.[54] The license-fee technique of railroad taxation lasted, in one form or another, until the turn of the century, when Governor Robert M. La Follette made revision of railroad taxation a major part of his program. The other cases that came up under these laws dealt mainly with the question of what constituted "railroad property" meeting the qualification for exemption from regular taxes.[55]

The state government made some sporadic attempts at general regulation during these early years, but they were neither effective nor lasting. The laws were either completely riddled by railroad-lobby amendments, or they regulated unimportant areas, or they proved difficult if not impossible to enforce.[56] They either included no enforcement clauses at all or they made the district attorney or the aggrieved party responsible for initiating a lawsuit to get relief.[57] The railroad companies abused their powers and discriminated shamelessly in freight and passenger rates.[58] The result was an ever-growing sentiment against them, which finally culminated in the passage of the Potter Law in 1874.

In the early seventies the executive agency of law, functioning through the attorney general, stepped into the regulatory process. By an information in the nature of quo warranto the state successfully invoked the original jurisdiction of the Supreme Court and asked for the dissolution of the West

Wisconsin Railroad. The court accepted jurisdiction but declared it was not constitutionally empowered to grant the equitable relief of dissolution. This was only a precursor to actions initiated under the Potter Law by the attorney general shortly before the institution of the injunction proceedings in *Attorney-General v. Railroad Companies,* which elicited the now-famous opinion of Judge Edward G. Ryan.[59]

Relationships with Local Government.—Because of the important part they played in early railroad financing, local units of government became inextricably entangled in the companies' affairs. In lieu of the direct state aid forbidden by the constitution the railroads received from towns and villages subscriptions for stock, which were paid for with bond issues, as well as outright gifts of securities. This required much enabling legislation; scores of local laws were passed authorizing cities, towns, and counties to give financial aid to railroads.[60] In 1870 these were supplemented by a general act prescribing the procedures for giving municipal aid to railroads.[61] Thus for a time local aid, like condemnation procedures, was governed partly by special law and partly by general law. After all local and private legislation was outlawed by the constitutional amendment of 1871 the legislature enacted general provisions that controlled all municipal aid to railroads thereafter.[62]

When the railroad bubble burst, many local governments sought to repudiate their obligations. The easiest tack they could take was to claim that aid to railroads was not an expenditure for a "public purpose" and that the tax levied to pay for municipal bonds was therefore invalid.[63]

Here the Wisconsin Supreme Court drew a fine distinction. It upheld the legislature's power to authorize a city to levy taxes for the payment of bond issues exchanged for railroad stock, but denied the legislature power to enact a law permitting a municipality to make an outright donation to the railroad.[64] This denial, voiced by Chief Justice Dixon in *Whiting v.*

Sheboygan & Fond du Lac Railroad, ran counter to decisions of other state and federal courts.[65] The court conceded that railroads were quasi-public bodies for the purpose of exercising the power of eminent domain; but this did not necessarily mean that taxation levied to aid them was for a public purpose. The court laid special stress on their private nature and their organization for private profit. When a city or county subscribed for railroad stock in exchange for a bond issue, the unit of local government was acting as part owner and within its authorized powers; when it gave securities to the railroad, it was not.[66]

Justice Byron Paine dissented on all grounds; public purpose for taxation, he said, was the same as public purpose for eminent domain, and he saw no difference between subscribing for stock and making an outright subsidy. Logic may have been with the majority, but the facts were with Paine. His real grounds were probably those that appeared later in his dissent:

> But if the question were reexamined anew, no different conclusion could be arrived at. Railroads are the great public highways of the world, along which its gigantic currents of trade and travel continually pour—highways compared with which the most magnificent highways of antiquity dwindle into insignificance. They are the most marvellous invention of modern times. They have done more to develop the wealth and resources, to stimulate the industry, reward the labor, and promote the general comfort and prosperity of the country, than any other and perhaps than all other mere physical causes combined. There is probably not a man, woman or child, whose interest or comfort has not been in some degree subserved by them. They bring us to anticipate and protract the seasons. They enable the inhabitants of each clime to enjoy the pleasures and luxuries of all. They scatter the productions of the press and of literature broadcast through the country with amazing rapidity. There is scarcely a want, wish, or aspiration of the human heart, which they do not in some measure help to gratify. They promote the pleasures of social life and of friendship; they bring the skilled physician swiftly from a distance to attend the sick and the wounded, and enable the absent friend to be

present at the bedside of the dying. They have more than realized the fabulous conception of the eastern imagination which picture the genii as transporting inhabited palaces through the air. They take a train of inhabited palaces from the Atlantic coast, and with marvellous swiftness deposit it on the shores that are washed by the Pacific seas. In war they transport the armies and supplies of the government with the greatest celerity, and carry forward, as it were, on the wings of the wind, relief and comfort to those who are stretched bleeding and wounded on the field of battle.

And yet, notwithstanding all these tremendous results, ... we are now told that the public has not sufficient interest in the construction of a railroad to sustain an exercise of the taxing power, because, forsooth, in executing the great public work, the state has made use of the agency of a private corporation, and left it to the comparatively petty and unimportant profits to be derived from the actual operation of the road! I confess that such a conclusion is so utterly in conflict with what I had supposed to be the settled law, so inadequate to what seem to me the real merits of the great question involved, that it is a matter of astonishment that it could have been adopted by any mind.[67]

In a subsequent decision the court found occasion to narrow the holding of the Whiting case, and two years later the United States Supreme Court repudiated the Whiting rationale in *Olcott v. the Supervisors*.[68] In this case, which arose out of the very same facts, the federal court held that the Wisconsin act authorizing the municipal bond issue was valid, inasmuch as the question of "public use" as related to taxation was a matter of "general law" rather than of construction of the Wisconsin constitution. The United States courts, accordingly, might determine the matter for themselves; they were not bound by the decisions of the Wisconsin judges.

Further consideration of the problem of local financial aid to railroads was limited to technical, jurisdictional, and procedural issues; other relationships of railroads to local governments that came before the law were few and relatively unimportant.[69]

Relationships with the Federal Government.—Aside from

granting lands in 1856 and 1864 in aid of railroads, the federal government intervened only indirectly in the events growing out of railroad construction. Of great importance to the fortunes of Wisconsin's roads was the disposition the United States Supreme Court made of the mortgage-foreclosure cases brought before it. The Eastern men of capital who were involved appealed the cases to the highest court because the stakes were high. On their outcome depended what interests would be in control of the roads. Most of the suits involved the hapless La Crosse and Milwaukee Railroad.[70]

In two other cases problems of federalism touched state court jurisdiction. In 1861 the Wisconsin Supreme Court declared unconstitutional that part of the Judiciary Act of 1789 which provided for removal from state to federal court of a suit between citizens of different states.[71] In 1865 it refused to assume jurisdiction if a cause was already in the federal courts.[72]

Finally, in deciding the Olcott case contrary to the decision of the Wisconsin Supreme Court on identical facts, the United States Supreme Court pointed a way out of the Whiting rule for those parties who could get into the federal courts.

Railroads and Other Contracting Parties

Cases involving disagreements between the railroad promotor and the railroad contractor—who more often than not might be classed as an enterpreneur—were not uncommon. The Newcomb Cleveland contract, which came before the Wisconsin court twice during the sixties, gave rise to this sort of litigation.[73] Subcontractors, too, petitioned the law for relief, mainly with respect to the enforcement of materialmen's liens.[74]

Still other creditors, such as suppliers of building materials and vendors of land, had occasion to seek help in collecting from recalcitrant or insolvent roads. Most commonly the issue involved was that of priority of liens.[75] Some cases posed the question whether a debt against a defunct road was good against its newly organized successor, and there were many other examples of the creditor's quest for financially responsible defendants.[76] Disputes over sales of railroad timber stumpage frequently reached the courts.[77] The legislature intervened once in favor of subsequent creditors and purchasers when it required mortgages on locomotives and other equipment to be recorded in the same manner as land mortgages.[78]

Employees of the railroad called upon the law to settle wage claims and award damages for personal injuries suffered in the performance of their duties. The several wage-claim statutes passed by the legislature in the years 1855–60 all came before the courts.[79] Personal-injury and wrongful-death actions initiated by employees against the railroads were surprisingly few in view of the fact that this new mode of transportation was fraught with great hazards, and many employees must have been injured. The Wisconsin Supreme Court, overruling its first opinion on the subject within a year after it was handed down, self-consciously brought Wisconsin jurisprudence into line with the prevailing view that recovery should be denied if a worker's injury was due to the negligence of a fellow servant.[80] It was not until the next generation that lawmakers made inroads on that doctrine.

* * *

It is obvious that the chief work of the law during the early decades of railroad transportation in Wisconsin consisted mainly in fashioning instrumental and administrative legal tools rather than in laying down broad substantive policy. Such tools were vitally necessary in the day-to-day adjustment to the host of problems created by the railroad, and the law, sharing the prevalent attitude, did what needed to be done immediately. This is reflected, as the table on page 68 shows, in the number of controversies between the railroads and shippers, and in the many adjustments that were made in the administration of condemnation proceedings. Even within the general category of cases involving relations with government—which seemingly might call for first-level policy decisions—such matters of instrumentation as the administration of the terms of the land grant and the fashioning of special charters were most numerous.

The law's failure to meet problems of substantive policy as squarely as it did the need for administrative tools is better attributed to lack of sophistication and inertia than to hostility. The law simply failed to realize how radical an innovation the railroad was. When the railway companies went bankrupt after the panic of 1857, they unleashed a myriad of problems that put a great strain on agencies of law. These insolvencies created interests—notably the farmer-mortgagors and numerous local government bodies—bent on getting out of the obligations they had so blindly incurred. True, some of the earlier canal, plank-road, and banking companies had also become insolvent, but never before had the law had such great financial difficulties thrust upon it wholesale. Apparently that fact was not recognized; the law dealt with these problems just as though it were dealing with controversies between two individuals, affecting their rights alone.

After its complete collapse in the fifties the legislature remained at its nadir for more than a decade. It was dominated by the railroad interests, and they got just about what they wanted. Their success is not attributable to corruption and bribery alone; the legislators, like Wisconsin's citizenry in general, were confident that the railroad would usher in the millennium. True, Wisconsin lawmakers made anti-railroad noises from time to time, but these smacked of empty ritual; seldom did a legislator oppose legislation favorable to roads operating in his own district.[81]

When legislators did take the floor in opposition, they were completely outmaneuvered, as they were when they tried to prevent Stimson and Company from gobbling up the Milwaukee and Prairie du Chien and when, at W. Barnes's behest, they passed an act permitting him to foreclose a junior mortgage in advance of a prior one. What little the legislature did was largely ex post facto. It showed no imagination in anticipating problems and contributed nothing to preventive law.

It was not the legislature but the court that fashioned the bulk of railroad law. The court was not ideally suited to do much of this. It had to shape its policy within the formal framework of a lawsuit—a ponderous, wasteful, and often irrelevant procedure.

Like the legislature, the court did its major work in the field of instrumentation. It deliberated repeatedly over details of condemnation procedure; reviewed the awards of condemnation commissioners; set out procedures for the execution of the wrongful-death statutes; considered the availability of garnishment in personal-injury suits; decided many procedural points implicit in the struggle of municipalities to avoid payments on their stock subscriptions; hammered out administrative details in mortgage-foreclosure and receivership suits; decided whether wage-earning employees of contractors could garnish the railroad; established the priority of mortgages of competing creditors; construed the fencing and wrongful-death statutes; deliberated on the rights and duties of shippers and carriers; spent time untangling facts in personal-injury suits; construed the language of special charters; and interpreted contracts to which the railroads were parties. All these were procedural, instrumental, administrative, and second-level policy tasks. This is not to say that such work was not proper; it is what courts are for. But the fact remains that much of the court's work would have been minimized if not eliminated altogether had legislation been drafted more carefully. Many other situations could have been better handled under rules and regulations issued by administrative agencies, but such agencies were yet to be created.

Even in those fields where the case-by-case method of building up law is said to be most valuable, the record of the Wisconsin court is not a notable one. In controversies between shippers and railroads the case-by-case method was probably preferable to lawmaking by a mid-nineteenth-century legislature, but this does not alter the fact that the court evinced in its opinions very little awareness of the relevance of commercial dealings and business practices.

Even when the court did occasionally intervene in matters of first-level substantive policy it did not function as a really effective creative force. In the Whiting case it took a stand against the donation of municipal bonds to railroads, but in the light of prevalent municipal practices, the United States Supreme Court decision in the Olcott case, and even its own later opinions, one may question whether its decision had any lasting effect. Its position in the Whiting case is in marked contrast to its stand in the farm-mortgage cases, where it upheld the obligation and refused to relieve the farmer-mortgagor of his debt. In both cases two tough common-law doctrines overrode consideration of the facts: the concept of "public purpose" in taxation and the doctrine of the favored position of a bona fide purchaser without notice.

Only Justice Byron Paine pushed to its logical conclusion the rationale of delegation of public power to private companies. The question was simply stated: how much public aid should the state give the railroads? Justices Luther S. Dixon and Orsamus Cole sanctioned aid derived from self-help under the power of eminent domain, aid from cities and towns in the form of purchases of stock, and, presumably, aid in the form of land grants. Paine would have permitted the outright donation of municipal bonds. He had facts on his side; there was very little difference between buying worthless securities and making outright gifts. And the restrictions in the Whiting case could not be allowed to stand; the United States Supreme Court repudiated them expressly, and the Wisconsin court carved them away almost to the vanishing point. It is hard to see how the majority in the Whiting case were motivated by anything other than a desire to see Fond du Lac County get out of a bad deal.

The Whiting case and others point to the conclusion that the court was no more aware than the legislature that a new economic institution was creating new problems calling for new solutions. The majority of the bench saw nothing unique about the railroads to justify public subsidies; they stated that there was no difference between railroads and private educational corporations.[82] Similarly, in the tax-uniformity cases the court apparently recognized no reason why railroads should be regarded as different from other taxpayers.[83] Nor did the court's treatment of the early general condemnation laws reveal any appreciation of the distinctive aspects of railroad construction. Similarly, nothing in the cases involving construction contracts points to an awareness of the railroad's financing problem, and nothing in the personal-injury cases indicates any realization that the injured plaintiff and the railroad defendant did not have equal bargaining power.

When judges worked at cross-purposes with the legislature they had little to show for their efforts except frustration of legislative policy and judicial embarrassment. And by its broad assertion of judicial review the court nullified the weak beginnings of the administrative process that were implicit in the procedure of condemnation commissioners' awards.

The Development of Sanctions

In any substantial sense, public policy is not alone what the law says; it is also what the law does. The care, skill, vigor, and courage with which men contrive means to implement policy will generally have at least as much importance as the formal declarations of policy in determining the real impact of law on community life. This is especially true where stakes are large, contending interests sharply divided, and issues varied, technical, and complicated. On all these counts the growth of the railroad posed problems testing to the utmost the law's capacity to make itself effective.

The period from 1858 to 1874 offered the law an opportunity to design sanctions appropriate to railroad problems—not only sanctions as conventionally defined but likewise many rules of law, evidence, and procedure that may properly be called sanctions also. Not much was made of that opportunity. The law's record in developing new enforcement techniques was a barren one.

The Courts.—The courts made not only the largest body of substantive policy but they also showed the most creativeness in developing sanctions. In doing so they relied heavily on the traditional flexibility of equity jurisprudence. The power to reform instruments and to grant or deny injunctions, for instance, can be regarded as judicial fashioning of sanctions. The same may be said of specific relief at law: mandamus, quo warranto, and ejectment.[84]

The courts could also create effective sanctions by modifying rules of law, procedure, and evidence. For instance, by controlling the limits on damages, submitting issues to, or taking them from, the jury, reversing findings of lower courts on the ground of errors in instructions, and implying conditions precedent in stock certificates they attached penalty or reward to conduct of which they approved or disapproved.[85]

Judicial construction of statutes also enlarged or contracted the area of workable sanctions. *A fortiori* the power to declare statutes unconstitutional was a formidable enforcement club. Matters of jurisdiction and procedure likewise worked to promote or hinder the effectiveness of sanctions. By using rules of evidence, presumptions, and the burden of proof, courts could vary the ease or difficulty of recovery.[86]

The Legislature.—Legislative contributions to new sanctions were even less imaginative than those of the courts. Many acts, for example, called the judicial process into play only by implication, containing no enforcement clauses of any kind. Presumably the legislators relied on the common-law doctrine that violation of a statute was a misdemeanor.[87]

By and large the legislature responded to the new problems by creating new causes of action, changing the rules of liability, and providing new forms of injunctive relief rather than by developing new techniques of enforcement.[88] Such penal sanctions as were laid down followed the well-worn path of fine and imprisonment. The technique extended to matters as diverse as prohibitions against track-walking and fence-removing and the requirement that railroads accept all grain for shipment at the usual charges.[89] A statute prohibiting shipment of gunpowder provided for fines against both the company and the officers.[90] Another act required trains to come to a full stop before crossing a drawbridge, on penalty of a five-hundred-dollar fine for each violation, "to be recovered in an action of debt" by the district attorney of the county where the violation had occurred. In addition, fine and imprisonment could be imposed on any conductor or engineer who "wilfully and knowingly" violated the act.[91]

The legislature also clung to such old techniques as informers' statutes. The penal section of the first general railroad act imposed a penalty of fifty dollars for each violation of any section of the act, half of which was to be paid to the person in whose name the action had been brought and half to the county treasury for the benefit of the school fund.[92]

For the enforcement of other legislation more drastic sanctions were imposed. If a railroad failed to pay its annual license fee, the attorney general, upon receiving notification from the state treasurer, could effect a forfeiture of the railroad's franchise and charter.[93] The state also imposed forfeiture of all unselected land-grant lands upon a railroad that failed to make its selection within a year's time. The act did not state how the lands returned to the state, but it seemed to imply that the revision was to be self-executing.[94] The very severity of these sanctions practically guaranteed that they would seldom, if ever, be used.

Licensing as an enforcement technique was little used. The legislature employed it in regulating river ferries, but apparently did not recognize that the same policies could be applied to the state's network of railroads.[95] The "license" fee imposed on the railroads was simply a form of tax, having no regulatory significance whatever.

The legislature passed no appropriation act for the express purpose of furthering enforcement of any law pertaining to railroads. It frequently made special appropriations for its own committees but apparently saw no need to extend similar aid to the enforcement agencies of the executive branch.

Wisconsin legislators also failed to take account of inertia in their development of new types of sanctions. The courts, in devising presumptions, in shifting the burden of proof, and in employing other procedural and evidentiary devices, helped to put the force of inertia behind enforcement instead of against it. But the legislature always placed the burden of initiating proceedings on the aggrieved party, sometimes by creating private causes of action, more often by assigning the responsibility for enforcement to the prosecuting attorneys, who seldom acted without a complaint from the aggrieved party. And when it left enforcement to the district attorneys, it merely increased the likelihood that little would happen. Legislators failed to see that one of their primary tasks was to overcome the inertia that defeated the purposes of their legislation. It was much too early for effective use of licensing as a regulatory technique or for the development of non-coercive sanctions by means of publicity and education.

The Executive.—The enforcement of sanctions, upon which their effectiveness depends, is the job of the executive branch of government. How much the attorneys general and district attorneys made of existing statutes is hard to say, for the reported cases are few. District attorneys had wide discretion in deciding which laws to enforce and how rigorously to press enforcement. In all probability they enforced very few of them, and these few only half-heartedly, either because of enforcement difficulties inherent in the laws themselves or recalcitrance on the part of enforcement officials.

Occasionally the governor invoked the ultimate sanction, as Governor Randall did when he forestalled transfer of lands to a railroad that had not completed the requisite amount of track.[96] For the most part, however, the governors confined themselves to hortatory activity; almost without exception their annual messages included suggestions for railroad legislation, and in 1874 Governor William R. Taylor offered a ten-point program.[97] But they vetoed very little railroad legislation, however inadequate or railroad-inspired it may have been, and when they did it was usually for reasons of technicality or detail.[98] Nor, apparently, did any governor use his power to institute, through the attorney general, proceedings for the forfeiture of lands against a railroad that had not paid its license fee.[99]

* * *

THE railroads, therefore, had little to worry about so far as enforcement of existing laws was concerned. It is not surprising that they had things pretty much their own way. Not until the very end of the period, in the mid-seventies, was there any real attempt—in the Potter Act—to tailor the law to the railroad.

IV. Railroads Versus the State: The Impact of a Judge

The question will arise in your day, though perhaps not fully in mine, which shall rule—wealth or man; which shall lead—money or intellect; who shall fill public stations—educated and patriotic freemen, or the feudal serfs of corporate capital. Gentlemen, when money wages that war on intellect, the country will demand: Videant jurisconsulti ne quid republica detrimenti capiat.—EDWARD G. RYAN in an *Address Delivered before the Law Class of the University of Wisconsin,* June 16, 1873.

FOR A DECADE and a half after 1858 the railroads reached out to new areas, serving an increasing number of people and becoming ever more indispensable to Wisconsin's economy. At the same time they grew more powerful, more indifferent to the public good, and more arrogant and intractable. Through consolidations, mergers, and interlocking directorates, control of the roads became more and more concentrated, competition less important, and rates increasingly arbitrary and exorbitant.[1]

All these excesses flourished without much hindrance from the law. Such regulatory measures as were enacted were haphazard and devoid of effective implementation. Governors proclaimed sonorously the necessity of dealing with the problems created by the railroads, but the legislators did almost nothing. Throughout most of the Civil War decade railway lobbyists dominated the legislature, and the interests of the public at large were all but ignored.

The people of the state became increasingly dissatisfied; they knew they were not getting a fair deal. They lamented the railroads' pervasive influence on men in public life, of which the "free pass" was the symbol; they deeply resented the domination of the legislature by the lobbyists; and, above all, they protested the excessive carriage charges, which channeled far too large a portion of the farmer's proceeds into the coffers of the railroad companies.

This sentiment contributed to the growth of the granger movement in Wisconsin and other states of the Northwest. Farmers organized themselves into so-called granges, the number of which in Wisconsin increased during 1873 and 1874 from thirty-three to more than four hundred. Ignoring a clause in their constitution forbidding political activity, the grangers entered state politics and helped effect a "Reform" coalition. In 1873 this coalition succeeded in electing its gubernatorial candidate, William R. Taylor, and in winning control of the Assembly and close to control of the Senate. True, they had the help of Alexander Mitchell and other railroad men, but only because the railroad interests disliked Cadwallader C. Washburn, the incumbent governor, even more than they did his opponent.[2]

The advocates of reform and regulation seemed to dominate at Madison in 1874; even the Republicans were advocating reform of some sort. At the outset the problem of railroad regulation was referred to a joint select committee on tariffs and taxation, which a few weeks later submitted a carefully phrased report that seemed to represent an impartial, forthright approach to the whole problem of regulation. The committee conceded that it had become necessary to regulate the railroads and asserted that the state had the power to do so by virtue of its constitutional right to amend or repeal any legislative act, including charters and corporate franchises. The people of Wisconsin were "therefore not at the mercy of the railroads" and there was no cause for alarm. The power of the state extended even to financial matters, such as rates and tolls. At this point the committeemen were not prepared to make concrete recommendations, for, they said, the matter was a most intricate one, and it seemed to them almost impossible to legislate on some aspects of it with perfect justice to both sides. Granted that rates had sometimes been oppressive, it was not yet clear how the evil could be remedied by a "legally fixed, inflexible rule"; other states had endeavored to do so, but without much success. In any event the criterion of exorbitance was not the rate per se but its relation to the amount of "*bona fide* capital employed by the carrier in carrying on his business."[3]

The committee therefore recommended that, in lieu of immediate legislation, a board of three commissioners be created to collect data and draft a bill for consideration of the next session of the legislature.[4] In so doing the committee failed utterly to gauge the temper of the times. Much as it might have pleased the railroad interests, there was not the slightest chance of such postponement. Some sort of legislation was bound to be enacted, and all the railroads could do was to work for as palatable a measure as possible.

Three bills were introduced early in the session, including the one ultimately passed—that introduced by R. L. D. Potter, senator from Waushara County. After much parliamentary maneuvering, substitution of bills, and sundry amendments, both houses, by a bipartisan vote, finally enacted the Potter bill into law, and Governor Taylor signed it at once. The measure was the most radical of the several bills that had been introduced, and it is just possible that the railroad companies supported it for precisely that reason—in the hope, that is, that even the fanatical Grangers would reject it as too extreme. However that may be, by the end of the session the situation had resolved itself into a choice between the Potter bill and no legislation at all.[5]

The Potter Law divided all railroads or parts of railroads operating in Wisconsin into three classes: Class A, comprising the Milwaukee and St. Paul, the Chicago and North Western, and the Western Union Railway systems; Class B, the Wisconsin Central, the Green Bay and Minnesota, and the West Wisconsin systems; and Class C, all others. For each of these classes the maximum passenger rate per mile was stipulated. The provisions governing freight rates were most complicated. Articles of freight were divided into four general and seven special classes, but the railroad commission created by the act was empowered to make a reclassification within prescribed limits. For the seven special classes of freight specific maximum charges were set, and for the general classes the maximum was defined as the rate that the particular railroad had charged on June 1, 1873. Higher charges than those authorized by the act were expressly prohibited.[6]

The Potter Law also embodied the beginnings of an administrative process. It directed the governor to appoint, with the consent of the Senate, three railroad commissioners for staggered terms of three years. To forestall domination of the commission by the railroad interests it was stipulated that no person should be eligible for appointment who owned any railroad bonds, stock, or property, who was in the employ of any railroad company, or who was "in any way or manner interested" in railroads.[7]

The statute was a pioneer step toward obtaining an official collection of data pertinent to the economics of the railroad industry. The commissioners were authorized to administer oaths, to send for persons or papers in accordance with their own regulations, and to examine the books and records of any railroad operating in the state. In making an examination pursuant to their duties they had power to issue subpoenas and, in the event of wilful disobedience on the part of a person summoned, to compel his appearance by suing out a writ of attachment in the circuit court. Anyone convicted of such disobedience was guilty of a misdemeanor and subject to fine and imprisonment. The law directed the commissioners to make detailed reports on the cost of operation of each railroad, gross receipts and net earnings, interest-bearing indebtedness, and amount of interest paid. These reports and records were to be available to the governor, the secretary of state, and the legislature.[8]

Of the direct regulatory powers vested in the railroad commissioners the most important was the power to reclassify all articles of freight except those included in four of the special classes. These exceptions made the power more nominal than real, inasmuch as they comprised (1) grain; (2) flour and lime; (3) lumber, laths, and shingles; and (4) livestock. The commissioners were further empowered to reduce the rates on any class of freight when in their judgment it would in no way injure the railroad; but they had no authority to raise rates. The salary of the commissioners was set at twenty-five hundred dollars a year, a thousand dollars less than Supreme Court justices were receiving.[9]

In the matter of sanctions the law was decidedly less than adequate. It did give the shipper a complete defense against a railroad corporation that sought to collect an excessive charge and permitted the aggrieved party to sue the corporation for three times the amount of an overcharge. It authorized the state to sue agents of the corporation for violating rates set either by statute or by the railroad commissioners, and to bring a criminal action against the company itself for imposing charges in excess of those set by the commissioners. What it did not provide for was suit of the state against the corporation itself for violation of rates set by the act. In other words, the state was authorized to take remedial action against either the company or its agents for violation of administrative rate orders but not against the company for violation of rates set by statute.[10]

This deficiency may have represented merely an oversight on the part of the framers of the law, or it may be that they considered violation of a statute a misdemeanor at common law for the punishment of which the state needed no specific authorization. That the omission may have been deliberate, however, is suggested, first, by the fact that justices of the peace were given concurrent jurisdiction in actions under the statute. Secondly, the form the commissioners used for complaints of violations of statutory rates looked only to actions against agents or actions by aggrieved parties for triple damages. Whatever the reason, the only avenue open to the state for violation of statutory rates was to bring suit against the agents.[11]

The act did not expressly prohibit discrimination in charges and rates. True, obedience to its provisions would in itself have eliminated discriminiation, but in view of the clamor the shippers had raised against the practice, explicit prohibition of it might have been expected, especially since it had been included in both the other bills introduced in the 1874 legislature.[12]

The first appointees to the Railroad Commission were Joseph H. Osborn of Oshkosh, a leader of the Grange, John W. Hoyt, a newspaperman of Milwaukee, and the influential Democratic politician George H. Paul, also of Milwaukee. The commissioners proceeded at once to draw up classification tables and to announce the rates that were to be effective. But it soon became apparent that enforcement was to be more difficult than enactment.[13]

* * *

WHATEVER may have been the railroads' role in the enactment of the Potter Law, there was no ambivalence in their attitude toward enforcement. Both Alexander Mitchell and Albert Keep, respective presidents of the Chicago, Milwaukee and St. Paul and the Chicago and North Western, wrote Governor Taylor that they refused to be bound by the law and would not abide by the rates. They had obtained opinions from such eminent counsel as William G. Evarts, Rockwood Hoar, and Judge Benjamin R. Curtis, all of whom agreed that the statute was patently unconstitutional and that the courts would so declare. The issue was sharply drawn.[14]

Governor Taylor made the first response. If, as was reputed, he had had the support of the railroads in the campaign of 1873, he must certainly have lost it by this time. On May 1, 1874, he countered Mitchell's and Keep's challenge with a proclamation outlining what he conceived to be his constitutional duty as executive to "expedite all such measures as shall be resolved by the legislature, and to take care that the laws be faithfully executed." The law of the land, he stated, must be respected and obeyed. If the Potter Law was oppressive or defective in some details, it was still the law of the land, enacted by the legislature in the exercise of the powers granted to it and in accordance with "the clearly expressed sentiment of the people of the state." Everyone had the right to test its validity through the proper channels, but this right was coupled with the duty of obeying the statute until such time as it should be declared invalid by competent authority. If the railroads persisted in the course they had announced they would suffer the penalties of the law and the condemnation of the people. He enjoined the roads to submit peaceably to the Potter Law, and he pledged exercise of all the functions of his office to secure its faithful execution. Toward that end he invoked the "aid and cooperation of all good citizens."[15]

To counteract the influence of the prominent persons whom the railroads had enlisted to denounce the Potter Law, the advocates of regulation called upon another eminent representative of the legal profession, Matthew H. Carpenter, United States senator from Wisconsin and one of the ablest lawyers in the midwest. Carpenter wrote an opinion sustaining the constitutionality of the Potter Law in which he undertook to refute the arguments of Evarts and Curtis.[16]

At the same time the governor took further steps in pursuance of his executive duties. Having obtained from the attorney general an opinion affirming the constitutionality of the act, he issued to the people of Wisconsin an "Address" in which he spelled out in detail the responsibilities of citizens and law-enforcement officers. The origins of the law, said Taylor, lay deep in the popular conviction that the tolls being exacted by the railroads were excessive. The railroads had sought to prevent remedial legislation by the systematic exercise of the "very powers conferred upon them for the public good, as well as for their corporate advantage." Their charge that the law was unreasonable was not sufficient ground for suspending it until its validity should be determined by the "tedious processes of courts delayed by appeals and every possible legal artifice." Such submission would only open the way for a continuation, perhaps at even greater expense to the people, of the extortionate charges by which the railroads swelled their profits. Moreover, what guarantee was there that they would comply with the law more readily if it were upheld by the courts? If they were permitted to regard a law as inoperative until it was approved by the courts, what assurance was there that even the courts could effect a peaceable compliance? It was not to be tolerated that any law enacted by the legislature and approved by the executive should be "put in abeyance and treated with open disobedience and flagrant contempt by any person, corporation or combination of corporations, on the plea of unreasonableness, or upon any plea whatever. Such a sufferance would tend to a subversion of all legal authority."[17]

Taylor did not stop with denunciation. He showed the people how they could help to make the law work. In so doing he pointed out a grave defect in the enforcement sections of the Potter Law: while defining the conventional procedures for the prosecution and punishment of violators, the act made no provision for expeditious handling of any such extraordinary and flagrant violation of the state's statutes as the railroads were here proposing. It gave justices of the peace concurrent jurisdiction with the circuit courts in order that ample facilities might be available for the trial of offenders, but, as in other criminal actions, the governor explained, *"no prosecution can originate otherwise than in complaint made by the injured party or some other person having knowledge of the offense."* That being the case, the executive must depend, in the face of an organized and general defiance of the law on the part of wealthy corporations, on all good citizens of the state to make use of the only means provided for redress and on subordinate officials to give him their hearty cooperation. With faith that they would "bring promptly and manfully all the aid and cooperation" owing the state "in any time of peril to her institutions, her authority or her laws" he appealed for their support. "I call upon and enjoin every citizen of this state," he said,

> to observe with scrupulous care the requirements of the law herein referred to, in every instance and particular of business dealings with any railroad company of this state, especially the companies herein named; to pay as a traveler no higher fare than the law prescribes; to pay as a shipper or receiver of freights no higher rates than the law prescribes, all of which rates the Railroad Commissioners have fixed and published; and that in any exigency or necessity he should suffer any sum in excess of legal rates to be extorted from him by any agent of such company, he notify, with all convenient dispatch, the district attorney of his county of such violation of law.
>
> I further enjoin all constables and police officers within the state to inquire of all such offenses, and to complain against the offenders before some justice of the peace, and diligently to take care that this law be not violated in their own precincts with impunity....
>
> In the possible contingency of a sufficient resistance to the local authorities to require the interference of the executive, the guarantees contained in my proclamation of May 1st can be relied on with the utmost confidence.[18]

But the state needed more than Taylor's exhortations and the opinion of Attorney General A. Scott Sloan to implement its position. The railroads gave no sign of yielding; on the contrary, they instructed their agents and conductors to exact the "full fare"; they conducted a vigorous publicity campaign against the act, inveighing against it in their annual reports and enlisting the support of influential newspapers.[19] Early in June the companies brought suit in the federal circuit court for the District of Wisconsin to test the constitutionality of the Potter Act. The plaintiffs—out-of-state bondholders and stockholders—asked for a preliminary injunction restraining the railroad commissioners from executing the provisions of the statute. Here the state won an initial skirmish: the plaintiffs' motion was denied and the state's position sustained on the merits of the controversy. Such regulation of rates was proper, said the court, under the reserved-power clause of the Wisconsin constitution. The case came up again before a three-judge circuit court, and the state's position was again upheld on demurrer. This decision was later affirmed by the United States Supreme Court as one of the "Granger cases."[20]

Meanwhile, activated by Governor Taylor's exhortations and the proddings of the attorney general, the state instituted suits against company agents who, acting under orders, were exacting the "full fare" for carriage. The railroads decided upon a strategy of delaying prosecutions as long as possible by posting bail in all cases and appealing every decision in order that the issue of constitutionality might be passed upon by the appellate court. Instructions for the execution of this policy were issued to George B. Smith, Madison counsel for the North Western, who served as coordinator for all suits instituted against agents in Wisconsin and made arrangements for the employment of counsel to defend them in the various Wisconsin communities.[21]

Prosecution of individual agents proved to be insufficient. There was local dissatisfaction with these suits, and general confusion among the people as to how the act should work. Many expected the railroad commissioners to play a prosecutor's role and were disappointed when they did not do so. At any rate, the railroads seemed to be holding the winning hand in this delaying game. The state had to take more positive action, but it was handicapped by the limitations the Potter Act placed upon it.[22]

On June 2, the attorney general filed informations in the nature of quo warranto in the Supreme Court against the two railroads, in the hope, possibly, that it would prove as successful as had a similar action which the state had brought against the West Wisconsin Railroad earlier in the year for noncompliance with its charter and for abandonment of the route prescribed by statute.[23] The informations prayed that the two railroads be deprived of their charters for imposing rates in excess of those set by statute.[24] Actually, of course, the state did not want, nor did it dare, to put its two leading railroads out of business; it merely wanted to compel them to obey the law. To do this it must obviously find some other remedy, one which would both establish its own supremacy and keep the railroads running. Presumably the state might appropriately have applied for issuance of a writ of mandamus to compel the railroads to comply with the terms of the Potter Act. This writ the Supreme Court also had original jurisdiction to entertain. For some reason the attorney general did not choose to do so, but instead brought a suit to enjoin the railroads from imposing unlawful rates.[25]

Shortly after the institution of the quo warranto informations there was a significant change in the personnel of the Supreme Court. Chief Justice Luther S. Dixon, who was thought to be sympathetic to the state's cause, resigned from the bench and Governor Taylor had to appoint a new justice.[26] He wrote George H. Paul, one of the railroad comissioners, to inquire about the qualifications of several men who had been suggested to him: Edward G. Ryan, Henry L. Palmer, William

Pitt Lynde, George B. Smith, Silas Pinney, and Ithamar C. Sloan. What he was looking for, said Taylor, was a man who was "honest, [of] good cool judgment and learned in the law, popular now and available next spring too and who is instinctively in sympathy with the people as against aggregated capital and oppressive monopolies"; the present situation, with an "apparently irrepressible conflict on hand," was different, Taylor wrote, from what it would have been a few months earlier.[27]

In his own mind Taylor seems to have narrowed the possibilities he had mentioned to one or two men, for only two days later he wrote Paul again to ask, "Can you ascertain definitely the position of E. G. Ryan on the R. R. question and Lynde too—but Ryan sure—*I won't* appoint a man in three months unless I know his position on the R. R. question. I think Ryan and Lynde all right but I must know it or no appointment. Don't know as will appoint either of them."[28] And, as a matter of fact, he did tender the post to another man, the brilliant young Madison attorney William F. Vilas. For personal reasons Vilas declined the offer, and on June 17, 1874, the governor appointed Ryan to the post.[29] The stage was set for the now-famous injunction suits.

On July 8, four days after the federal circuit court handed down its decision in the bondholders' suit, the attorney general filed two informations in the Supreme Court praying for writs of injunction to restrain the Chicago and North Western and the Chicago, Milwaukee and St. Paul from exacting passenger or freight tolls in excess of the maximum rates established by the Potter Law. Apparently the railroad companies sensed that this was to be an all-out struggle. They obtained leave to delay filing their answer and spent the rest of the month deliberating on the strategy to follow. They seem even to have considered abandoning their policy of disobedience and complying with the rates while the Potter Law prosecutions and the federal court suits were pending.[30] The Supreme Court heard the motion for injunction during the first week in August and on September 15, after the completion of arguments and submission of supporting affidavits, handed down its opinion sustaining the state on every point and granting the injunction.[31]

Both sides were represented by distinguished counsel. The state had Attorney General A. Scott Sloan and his brother Ithamar C. Sloan, Harlow S. Orton, and Luther S. Dixon, all leading members of the early Wisconsin bar. Both the Sloans were able lawyers, and A. Scott Sloan had spent several years on the trial bench and earlier in the term had successfully argued a railroad quo warranto proceeding in the Supreme Court.[32] Dixon, who apparently played an important part in the prosecution, had argued the merits of the bondholders' suits in the federal court. Orton was a distinguished jurist, who was later to serve as dean of the University's Law School and, from 1878 to 1895, as a justice of the Wisconsin Supreme Court.[33]

The railroads had equally eminent counsel. Representing the Chicago and North Western were Burton C. Cook, general solicitor of the road, Charles B. Lawrence, and George B. Smith of Madison. Cook was a leading member of the Chicago bar; Lawrence had been chief justice of the Illinois Supreme Court and had written the opinion declaring the Illinois railroad-regulation law unconstitutional. Smith, Madison counsel for the road, was a prominent railroad attorney and a masterful tactician in the trial of cases. The Chicago, Milwaukee and St. Paul employed John W. Cary of Milwaukee and Philip L. Spooner of Madison. Cary had been instrumental in launching the mortgage-foreclosure and reorganization proceedings of the old La Crosse and Milwaukee and had made the arrangements for the consolidation of the several small roads that became the Chicago, Milwaukee and St. Paul. Philip Spooner, father of John C. Spooner, was a member of the University's recently organized law faculty.[34]

The new chief justice, Edward G. Ryan, wrote the opinion of

the court. Whether or not his presumed views on the impending litigation were decisive in Governor Taylor's appointment of him, they were almost certainly one of the significant factors. And the governor had no reason to regret his choice; he got the decision he wanted and he certainly found someone "learned in the law." Ryan had had a distinguished and tempestuous career at the bar, and he had long been ambitious for the robes. Indeed, as he once remarked, he had waited so long for the opportunity that he had ceased to hope for it. He had been a delegate to the first constitutional convention and he had played a part in such famous Wisconsin cases as the Radcliff murder trial, the trial of the fugitive slave Sherman M. Booth, the impeachment of circuit judge Levi Hubbell, and the Bashford-Barstow gubernatorial contest. In his partisanship there was much ambiguity, for he was that rather paradoxical combination of technician and man of policy one finds in many leaders of the bar. He often lent his technical skill to causes completely alien to his personal philosophy and deepest convictions. He could be injudiciously frank; anecdotes about Ryan's candor abound in Wisconsin lawyers' lore.[35]

The Railroad Companies case was the first that Ryan heard and among the most important, involving as it did important questions of high policy and having wide political implications. His opinion, a long one, was the greatest he ever wrote. Had it been his only one he would merit a prominent place in the history of Wisconsin jurisprudence. It reveals, as do his other opinions and his nonjudicial writings, a classical training his colleagues lacked—a training acquired as part of the liberal education he had received in Ireland. This is not to say that Ryan was a cold intellectual. He had an unusually irascible nature and an uncontrollable temper; as one of his contemporaries put it, Ryan was engaged all his life in a struggle with himself.[36]

Perhaps the outcome of the Railroad Companies case would have been the same had William F. Vilas accepted Taylor's offer. But it is hard to see how anyone could have presented a more forceful, eloquent, and irrefutable vindication of the state's position than Edward G. Ryan did in *Attorney General v. the Railroad Companies.*

* * *

In many ways, Ryan stated, the most vexing problem in the case was the first question the court had to decide—whether the Supreme Court had power to entertain the cause under the grant of original jurisdiction in the Wisconsin constitution:

> The supreme court, except in cases otherwise provided in this constitution, shall have appellate jurisdiction only, which shall be co-extensive with the state; but in no case removed to the supreme court shall a trial by jury be allowed. The supreme court shall have a general superintending control over all inferior courts; it shall have power to issue writs of habeas corpus, mandamus, injunction, quo warranto, certiorari, and other original and remedial writs, and to hear and determine the same.[37]

At first blush, said Ryan, it would seem that the powers here defined clearly included suits for injunction, and it had been so assumed twenty years before by Judge Abram D. Smith in *Attorney General v. Blossom.*[38] But in the Railroad Companies case counsel had pointed to a significant difference between the equitable writ of injunction and the prerogative common-law writs included in the constitutional provision. The common-law writs were traditionally "jurisdictional" writs; the mere exercise of them established jurisdiction; they were truly prerogative in scope and they represented the command of a superior authority to a person or agency whose affairs that authority was empowered to oversee. But historically injunction was merely a "judicial" writ. It operated only in an ancillary or auxiliary fashion—in aid of a judgment, for instance—in cases where equity jurisdiction had already been established. Whence, then, did the Supreme Court derive the original jurisdiction over the railway companies that empowered it to hear a motion for an injunction?[39] It was, said Ryan, implicit in the policy underlying the general grant of jurisdiction to the Supreme Court: "to make this court indeed a supreme judicial tribunal over the whole state; a court of first resort on all judicial questions affecting the sovereignty of the state, its franchises or prerogatives, or the liberties of the people."[40] He found his conclusion reinforced when he examined the policy behind the other prerogative and original writs named in the section; under the aegis of the maxim *noscitur a sociis,* therefore, he determined that the writ of injunction was expressive of the same policy. Specifically, he compared the writs of injunction and mandamus and found their purposes to be the same: "The latter commands. The former forbids. . . . And so near are the objects of the two writs, that there is sometimes doubt which is the proper one; injunction is frequently mandatory, and mandamus sometimes operates restraint."[41] This was perhaps a bootstrap doctrine. But it was a doctrine that squared with the facts of the case; at issue here was the very sovereignty of which he wrote.

Ryan placed limitations on his doctrine. Certainly the attorney general could not invoke the original jurisdiction of the Supreme Court merely by asserting that the cause affected the sovereignty of the state. "Hereafter the court will require all classes of cases, as it has hitherto done some, in which it is sought to put its original jurisdiction in motion, to proceed upon leave first obtained, upon a *prima facie showing that the case is one of which it is proper for the court to take cognizance.*"[42]

Secondary arguments concerning original jurisdiction Ryan disposed of without difficulty. Counsel for the state had alternatively based their case on a statute which, had it been applicable, would have defeated the state's claim at the outset. Ryan pointed out that it was obvious on the face of the statute that it had no application to the Supreme Court's original jurisdiction but referred only to the powers of the circuit court.[43] Finally, the objections that neither information had been verified and that the information against the Chicago, Milwaukee & St. Paul described the road as the "Milwaukee & St. Paul" Ryan disregarded as technicalities that could not be taken seriously.[44]

But even if the original jurisdiction of the Supreme Court were established, it still remained necessary for the state to show that the controversy was one calling for a proceeding in equity. Here Ryan dealt with the so-called visitatorial power of a court of equity over corporations. Ryan himself did not use that term, but Harlow S. Orton had used it in his brief for the state.[45]

On this point Ryan had an imposing array of authority against him, including an opinion of Chancellor Kent and the preponderance of contemporary American decisions. Equitable jurisdiction had usually been denied in suits of the attorney general for injunctions against private corporations. It was otherwise with the English courts, as Ryan pointed out at great length. But, he went on to say, the list of American authorities denying equitable jurisdiction was less impressive than was generally supposed. He cited United States cases in which the authority had been recognized, and he examined cases in which it was thought to have been denied. He then sought to show that at best the denials represented mere dicta.[46]

Ryan was most troubled by Chancellor Kent's opinion in *Attorney General v. Utica Insurance Co.*, which denied an application for an injunction against a corporation for usurping banking powers contrary to law.[47] Ryan saw in it two significant differences from the case before him. In the first place, no public injury was shown. Therefore no injunction could properly issue, and Kent's remarks about the general impropriety of injunctions at the suit of the attorney general were entirely gratuitous. Secondly, the case antedated the rise of great corporations, and the use of equitable jurisdiction to restrain cor-

Chief Justice Edward G. Ryan

William Taylor　Alexander Mitchell　Albert Keep

porate abuses had not yet been fully established, a fact to which he attached great importance. Earlier in his opinion Ryan had said:

In our day the common law has encountered in England, as in this country, a new power, unknown to its founders, practically too strong for its ordinary private remedies. The growth of great corporations, centers of vast wealth and power, new and potent elements of social influence, overrunning the country with their works and their traffic throughout all England, has been marvelous during the last half century. It is very certain that the country had gained largely by them in commerce and development. But such aggregations of capital and power, outside of public control, are dangerous to public and private right; and are practically above many public restraints of the common law, and all ordinary remedies of the common law for private wrongs. Their influence is so large, their capacity of resistance so formidable, their powers of oppression so various, that few private persons could litigate with them; still fewer private persons would litigate with them, for the little rights or the little wrong which go so far to make up the measure of average prosperity of life. It would have been a mockery of justice to have left corporations, counting their capital by millions—their lines of railroads by hundreds, and even, sometimes, by thousands of miles—their servants by multitudes—their customers by the active members of society—subject only to the common law liabilities and remedies which were adequate protection against turnpike and bridge and ferry companies, in one view, of their relations to the public; and, in another view, to the same liabilities and remedies which were found sufficient for common carriers who carried passengers by a daily line of stages, and goods by a weekly wagon, or both by a few coasting or inland craft; with capital and influence often less than those of a prosperous village shopkeeper. The common law remedies, sufficient against these, were in a great degree, impotent against the great railway companies—always too powerful for private right, often too powerful for their own good.[48]

Ryan also disposed of the defendants' arguments that there were, in this instance, adequate remedies at law by the suits under the Potter Law itself and the pending quo warranto actions. The Potter Law, he pointed out, provided for action by the attorney general only on rates set by the railroad commissioners. The act gave the attorney general no authority to proceed against violators of legislatively prescribed rates. As to the quo warranto proceedings, Ryan said that here, as in England, the attorney general was free to choose between an action in equity and one at law. If in his judgment the public interest was better protected by the preventive remedy of injunction than by the drastic remedy of forfeiture, the court would not intervene.[49]

Counsel for the roads also objected that their clients were in effect being denied a jury trial on matters relating to their franchises. Ryan's reply was that such matters as this had been strictly of equitable cognizance at the time the Wisconsin constitution was adopted. Furthermore, there was here no dispute with regard to the facts; the controversy involved only matters of law.[50] Finally, to the technical objection that the bill contained no formal averment of the public injury Ryan replied that it was enough that the law had been violated.[51]

* * *

HAVING decided that the Supreme Court had original jurisdiction and that the state had made out a case for equitable cognizance, Ryan was ready to pass upon the validity of the Potter Law itself. Defense counsel had leveled their heaviest fire against the principle that the legislature could constitutionally prescribe maximum charges for transportation services. The railroads contended that their charters bestowed rights—the right to own property, to exercise the power of eminent domain, to fix charges—which were inviolate contracts with the state. Granted that these rights might legitimately be curtailed in the future, the state could not constitutionally regulate and modify interests already in existence by virtue of these rights. Thus *Dartmouth College v. Woodward*[52] stood in Ryan's way at every juncture. He met it head on, and he also skirted around it. He questioned it from start to finish, he stated that it had served its purpose, and he pointed out that many able commentators and jurists had cast doubt on the wisdom of it. "It deprives the states," he said, "of a large measure of their sovereign prerogative, and establishes great corporations as independent powers within the states, a sort of *imperia in imperiis,* baffling state order, state economy, state policy." Well might a distinguished judge of the United States Supreme Court "start back, shocked at the claims of corporate immunity from law."[53]

Nevertheless Ryan finally yielded, though unwillingly, to the Dartmouth College decision. But he then went on to show that it was not applicable to railroad corporations like the defendants in the Railroad Companies case. Marshall himself had said that the contract clause, as defined in the Dartmouth College case, did not extend to municipal corporations and instrumentalities of the state. And that was exactly what railroads were. Ryan repudiated the dichotomy of public and private corporations that the railroads had urged to immunize them from state control. It was difficult at this day, he said, to accept as sound the distinction between municipal and quasi-private corporations which underlay the presumption that it was essential to have legislative control over all municipal corporations "of every grade and nature," but not over other corporations. Each of the defendants exercised more power over the public interests, the public welfare, and the prosperity of Wisconsin than did the largest municipality in the state with its ninety or one hundred thousand souls. To the railroad the state had entrusted the exercise of the sovereign right of eminent domain; the construction and operation of hundreds of miles of thoroughfare jeopardizing public safety; a virtual monopoly of transportation in its district, amounting almost to the control of all commerce within its reach; and a power over its people approaching the power of life and death. And yet it was a private corporation and as such had a charter exempt from legislative control, whereas the most insignificant town in the state, having no influence outside its own area, was "invested with the dignity of a public corporation," over which it was "unsafe to deny legislative control."[54]

The situation had changed since the days of *Dartmouth College v. Woodward,* said Ryan. That decision had been made "long before what were then private corporations had become of more public significance than municipal corporations were then, long before our present civilization hinged almost as much on *quasi* private corporations, as Hallam says early modern civilization did on municipal corporations; before Judge Story had lived to see a bank, which he defined to be a private corporation, notwithstanding its public relations, wage war, unequal at last, but long doubtful war, against the federal government itself."[55]

"The difficulty," Ryan said, "arises probably from applying old names to new things; applying the ancient definition of private corporations to corporations of a character unknown when the definition arose, corporations of such great and various public relation and public significance; a definition which, as applied to them, is wearing out, so that courts are beginning to call them *quasi* private corporations and *quasi* public corporations, as in truth they are."[56]

Ryan's analysis was realistic, but it was one that was dying and that a later generation of judges was to repudiate completely. He saw with keen insight the "sovereignty" involved in delegating major economic power to corporations. But as the economy developed, the mere fact of corporateness seemed less and less to be the essence of this sovereignty.

In any event Ryan saw a better escape from the Dartmouth College decision. The Wisconsin constitution authorized the legislature to amend or repeal any general or special law it had passed under the provisions dealing with non-banking corporations.[57] This reserved power over corporations, he asserted, had been included in the constitution for the precise purpose of overcoming the restrictions imposed by the Dartmouth College case. With copious citation and discussion he demonstrated that this had been the unanimous construction placed upon the section by previous decisions of the Wisconsin Supreme Court.[58] By force of this constitutional provision and the judicial construction placed upon it, he concluded, "the rule in the Dartmouth College case, as applied to corporations, never had place in this state, never was the law here. The state emancipated itself from the thralldom of that decision, in the act of becoming a state; and corporations since created here have never been above the law of the land."[59]

The defendants' lawyers conceded that the legislature could alter or repeal the franchise it had granted, but insisted it could do no more than that. It could not withdraw what it had not granted, and hence could not affect property acquired under the franchise, although it might affect the franchise itself. When the state modified the ownership of property by limiting the realizable income from it, it was appropriating property without just compensation and was exceeding its legislative powers. The railroad lawyers also contended that "due process" had been violated, generally on the ground that property had been taken without compensation. Judge Lawrence, however, went even further in his brief and grounded his "due process" argument on the Fourteenth Amendment. This was an early instance in United States legal history of the use of the "due process" argument which later was to have great vogue.[60]

Ryan did not yield to these arguments. Again he resorted to economic facts: the reserved power was meaningless if, by the merest act under its charter, the company could put itself outside regulation. This would be merely a denial of the reserved power in another form. The reserved power, he went on to say, was applicable to all property acquired under the franchise; it was a condition under which the companies agreed to hold their property when they accepted a charter from the state.[61] The rest of his opinion on this point has a modern ring:

We listened to a good deal of denunciation of [the Potter Law] which we think was misapplied. We do not mean to say that the act is not open to criticism. We only say that such criticism is unfounded. It was said that its provisions, which have been noticed, were not within the scope of the legislative function; as if every compilation of statutes, everywhere, in all time did not contain provisions limiting and regulating tolls; as if the very franchise altered were not a rebuke to such clamor. It was repeated, with a singular confusion of ideas and a singular perversion of terms, that the provisions of the chapter amounted to an act of confiscation; a well-defined term in the law, signifying the appropriation by the state, to itself, for its own use, as upon forfeiture, of the whole thing confiscated. It was denounced as an act of communism. We thank God that communism is a foreign abomination, without recognition or sympathy here. The people of Wisconsin are too intelligent, too staid, too busy, too prosperous for any such horror of doctrine; for any leaning towards confiscation or communism. And these wild terms are as applicable to a statute limiting the rates of tolls on railroads, as the term murder is to the surgeon's wholesome use of the knife, to save life, not to take it. Such objections do not rise to the dignity of argument. They belong to that order of grumbling against legal duty and legal liability, which would rail the seal from off the bond. They were not worthy of the able and learned counsel who repeated them, and are hardly worthy even of this notice in a judicial opinion.[62]

Defendants' counsel also put forward the argument of vested rights: even if the reserved-power clause did apply to a contract between the railroad and the state—that is, the charter—it could not affect the contractual rights of third parties, such as bondholders and other creditors, who had in the meantime dealt with the road. Ryan called this contention an absurdity resting on the proposition that a mortgagor could vest in his mortgage a greater estate than he had himself. Regulation might lessen the means for payment of a contract, but that was not to impair the obligation of the contract. The defendants had accepted their franchise, and their creditors had invested their money, subject to the reserved power, the exercise of which inflicted no legal wrong on them.[63]

The defendants argued finally that the constitutional amendment prohibiting local and special legislation represented a repeal of the reserved-power clause in the constitution, hence any modification of charters must be accomplished by general law. The Potter Law, they said, was special legislation. At best, Ryan replied, this would amount to repeal by implication, and in a matter of such importance as this the court would not pronounce a repeal by mere implication.[64]

One concession Ryan made, for a time, to the defendants. Faced with the question whether the Potter Law was applicable to that portion of the Milwaukee Road which, as a part of the Milwaukee and Waukesha, had been organized before Wisconsin became a state and therefore before the reserved power over corporate charters had been provided for, Ryan bowed to the authority of the Dartmouth College decision and excepted that portion of the Milwaukee from the terms of his decree.[65] But this was a short-lived victory for the defendants. When the attorney general later showed that the Milwaukee and Waukesha had not accepted its charter before the acquisition of statehood, Ryan modified his decree to cover all parts of the Milwaukee Road.[66] A similar argument, that since defendants had not indicated acceptance of the Potter Act it could not properly be regarded as an amendment to their charters, Ryan dismissed as irrelevant.[67]

One other contention—that two laws also passed in 1874 had constructively repealed the regulatory sections of the Potter Law—Ryan disposed of authoritatively after examining the legislative journals and finding no intent to work a constructive repeal. He went on to point out that, furthermore, the two laws could stand side by side with the Potter Law without inconsistency.[68] Matters not properly put in issue—questions of interstate commerce and the scope of the railroad commissioners' powers—Ryan dismissed summarily.[69]

* * *

As a product of judicial creativeness Ryan's opinion ranks high in every respect. As a whole it went beyond the presentation of counsel's briefs, and on at least two issues it deviated from the dominant line of American authority. Ryan conceived of himself as doing a creative job, for he stated that he had received no help from the bar in solving the difficulty he faced.[70]

His opinion was the first exhaustive discussion of the nature of the Supreme Court's original jurisdiction to issue writs of injunction. Twenty years earlier, in *Attorney General v. Blossom,* Judge Abram D. Smith had, without discussion, lumped injunction with common-law prerogative writs. Ryan came to the same conclusion and said that Judge Smith was "more apparently than really inaccurate."[71] In the Railroad Companies case Smith and Lamb had argued and briefed the jurisdictional point for the Chicago and North Western, but their presentation, creditable though it was, was much less thorough than Ryan's. So also was Cary's argument for the Milwaukee Road.[72]

In the course of his discussion of original jurisdiction Ryan expressed a view of the Supreme Court's discretionary control over its docket that was unusual among his generation of judges. In blocking out the area within which the court would exercise original jurisdiction—requiring a prima facie showing that a case was one of which the court could properly take cognizance —Ryan was in effect suggesting that the time, energy, and dignity of the Supreme Court be kept free for cases involving major policy.

In dealing with the impressive authority arrayed against him on the visitatorial power of a court of equity Ryan produced a decision and an opinion that has become a truly leading case.[73] Here he got almost no help from the briefs. Nor did American treatises on railroad law present the problem in its significant setting of the modern large-scale business corporation; they talked more about narrower issues, such as injunctions against wrongful encroachments on public ways. The research and analysis underlying Ryan's decision were almost entirely his own.[74]

On the general problem of the power of the state over railroad companies he had more help. Briefs of counsel labored the point, and all the extra-judicial polemic was concerned with this issue. The subject had been dealt with by the United States Supreme Court, and it was a favorite topic in the legal periodicals.[75] Ryan probably reflected the prevalent pattern of ideas. Yet even on this point he was willing to go farther. He would have rejected completely the distinction between "private" and municipal corporations as it applied to railroads. But this was a view destined to disappear; it could not withstand the rush of events and the onslaught of due process that came during the next few decades.

Ryan showed a basic understanding of the realities of the case in shaping his decree. When the defendants urged him to exercise judicial discretion and withhold the writ because it would work great hardship, he refused. He was moved by their appeals, he said, but in a case like this, seriously involving the public interest, issuance of the writ was not a matter of judicial discretion. For discretion could be exercised only in injunctions in aid of private remedies; it was not applicable to writs involving "things *publici juris*." "We have held that here is positive violation of positive public law to positive public injury, and that we have jurisdiction of this writ, as a prerogative writ, to restrain it. There is no room for discretion. The duty is positive, *ex debito justiciae*. The discretion which we were urged to exercise would be discretion to permit the violation of the laws which we sit here to enforce. It was said to us by counsel, in a professional and not offensive sense, that we dare not issue these injunctions. We reply that, holding what we have held we dare not face the judgment of the profession for withholding them."[76] Here again Ryan broke new ground. The general view was that the issuance of an injunction was a matter not of right but of the court's "sound discretion."[77]

Ryan did attach one condition to his issuance of the writ, namely that the attorney general dismiss the pending quo warranto proceedings. He also took cognizance of the fact that the roads needed time to adjust their rates and gave them until October 1 to comply with the law.[78]

* * *

RYAN'S opinion was in the best tradition of common-law craftsmanship. He showed, as have all great judges, an awareness of the real issues underlying the controversy—that it was a "political" suit in the broader sense to determine whether the government was more powerful than the railroads. He recognized the growth of corporations as the great economic development of his time, and the one that would pose the greatest problems for the law. For while they were "private" agencies in organization and structure, they were actually, in their effect upon society, as "public" as any agency could be. They were, for our times, the center of power in the community, holding a part of its sovereignty.[79]

Ryan dealt with these issues in the light of his philosophy of the judge's job, a philosophy that was ahead of his time. On the one hand, he did not shirk the responsibility of choice: he asserted, as a matter of conscious policy, that the state must be stronger than any private concentration of power within it. At the same time, recognizing the distinctive character of judge-made law, he preached judicial self-restraint to a degree unusual for his generation of judges; it was the legislature, not the judiciary, he said, that should determine what were reasonable rates and formulate the means of dealing with pressing public problems.[80] He also advised the court to be cautious in interfering with the right of coordinate branches of government to make a choice between alternative modes of procedure; the attorney general, for instance, should be free to choose between injunction and the drastic remedy of forfeiture in seeking preventive relief. Finally, he refused to pass on issues not presented by the pleadings and he contemptuously dismissed pettifogging and hypertechnical arguments as unworthy of consideration.[81]

The technical craftsmanship he displayed in his opinion was a model for the nineteenth-century judge. On each important issue he reviewed the facts in their historical setting and made a meticulous examination of all the leading cases.[82] He did not hesitate to criticize precedent with which he disagreed, notably *Dartmouth College v. Woodward.*[83] He was skillful in defining the issues and in mobilizing and distinguishing prior decisions to support the exercise of his own responsibility; he did not delude himself as to the extent of the constraint actually imposed by precedents, and it was not his temperament to pretend to a constraint he did not feel. On the other hand, he was a man of the law, steeped in its professional tradition, and he was prepared to pay obedience to *stare decisis* when rigorous analysis showed that governing precedent existed. He knew and used the techniques of common-law judging: he was a master not only at distinguishing cases but in drawing the lawyers' distinction between holding and dictum; he did not hesitate to use dissenting and concurring opinions to support his contentions; and, like many great common-law judges before him, he was not averse to passing out advice to the legislature.[84]

* * *

THUS it was a court-order that forced the two railroads to abide by the provisions of the Potter Act; from now on, presumably, the rates specified in the law would prevail throughout the state. The railroads took no appeal to the United States Supreme Court and stated that they would abide by the statutory rates and abandon their policy of disobedience and defiance.[85]

This did not mean that they acquiesced in the principle of rate regulation. They simply turned their efforts in another direction and campaigned hard for the repeal of the Potter Law. They covered the state with polemics on the bad effects it would have on Wisconsin: they memoraliezd the legislature, issued denunciatory reports to their stockholders, and enlisted the support of many of the newspapers. They attributed to the Potter Law almost every existing ill and they warned the people that investments in railroads would cease unless the law was repealed. But the Grange carried the day in the elections of 1874, with the result that in its next session the legislature made only a slight upward revision of the seven special rates and a reclassification of the class B railroads.[86]

The popular victory was short-lived, however. In 1875 the railroad interests succeeded in electing a governor—Harrison Ludington of Milwaukee—and a legislature sympathetic with their position. The Vance bill of 1876, repealing the Potter Act, marked the end of the brief period of Granger legislation in Wisconsin. In reducing the Railroad Commission to a single member and stripping it of all but advisory powers, it represented a complete surrender to the railroads.[87] The experiment in regulation had not accomplished what had been hoped for, partly because of defects in the Potter Law itself, partly because of other factors affecting the health of the railroad industry: economic depression, competition, and general railroad development.

On the other hand, there can be no question that Judge Ryan's decision had a strong impact both on the minds of Wisconsin's citizens and on the judiciary. It was truly a crucial decision, forcing the capitulation of the arrogant and irresponsible companies and investing the law with new prestige in the popular mind. It also established important precedents in Wisconsin jurisprudence; Ryan's discussion of the original jurisdiction of the Supreme Court gave the state a potent weapon, and the decision was followed by a spate of cases invoking the court's original jurisdiction, though many of these were not of a crucial character.[88] In a very real sense the sovereignty of the state was at stake in the Railroad Companies case. It was a drastic situation demanding a drastic remedy and Ryan saw this as the true criterion for resort to extraordinary jurisdiction. Judges in later cases did not.

The decision was likewise a landmark among state court decisions for its treatment of the state's power to regulate railroad rates. Here—on the issue of the state's reserve power over corporations—Ryan had the better of the argument; but logic could not stem the rush of events. The next generation, by the use of "due process," again placed the railroads outside the realm of regulation. Judge Lawrence's brief was a harbinger, and the kind of doctrine spun by defendants' counsel in the Railroad Companies case contributed to the pattern of substantive due process.

If, in establishing the power of the state to regulate the railroads, the court made an important contribution to Wisconsin jurisprudence, it is equally clear that the Potter Law failed as an instrument of regulation. As a technique it was altogether inadequate, and it was probably a good thing that it was so soon repealed. It became evident that the problem was one which could not be solved by legislative rate-making and that the Potter Law was unduly weak in that it made most inflexible the freight rates on the very items which were most vital to the Wisconsin economy: grain and flour, certain lumber products, and livestock. In setting these maximum rates the legislature may have been responding to a popular demand that it assume a positive role in preserving the balance of power, but other provisions of the law greatly confused the issue. On the one hand the Railroad Commission was presumed to be an utterly detached body; it was denied even the power to initiate proceedings to enforce the policy laid down in the act. On the other hand, in stipulating that no one connected with any railroad should be eligible for appointment, the law insured the selection of men sympathetic with regulation.[89] Taylor adhered to this condition, with the result that the state had three pro-grange and pro-regulation commissioners who had no power to do anything.

Closely related was the other major deficiency of the Potter Law—the lack of adequate sanctions. The framers either failed to appreciate what effect human inertia would have on the operation of the law or they did not know what to do about it. People simply did not bring the actions contemplated by the statute, and the district attorneys soon tired of carrying on alone. In any event they could not normally take action until the aggrieved party brought the violation to their attention. Finally, enforcement was seriously crippled by the fact that the state could not take action against the company itself for violation of statutory rates.

Other aspects of the act lent themselves to propagandizing activities of the railroad companies. The state's citizenry was told that the stringency of the terms was bound to affect the operations of the carriers, if not put them out of business altogether. The result was a disposition on the part of the people to ascribe any curtailment of service to the Potter Law. The many enforcement suits against agents and conductors were unpopular, too, with the people in the local communities, who felt that instead of prosecuting their neighbors the state should go after the corporations.[90]

The question remains whether judicial regulation, through the visitatorial power of an equity court, might have offered greater promise than the statutory rate-making which was so obviously ineffectual. Certainly it promised greater flexibility, and if the level of judicial sophistication possessed by Ryan could have been assured, it would probably have been superior to regulation by statute. But it is not safe to rely upon regulatory measures that work only in the hands of unusual men; most governing responsibilities must be adjusted to average talent. And as a whole the judicial process was no better equipped—in knowledge, available time and energy, and aggressive motivation—to administer rate-making machinery than was the legislature. What was needed, apparently, was a special agency to perform the task,[91] an agency clothed with both legislative and judicial powers and functions.

One question implicit in judicial regulation touched the very basis of American government: who had the final voice with respect to the reasonableness of rates, the legislature or the court? At first this issue was not the most prominent aspect of the case, but it loomed larger as the contest shaped up. The railroads took their ultimate constitutional ground on the claim that the question was one for the courts to decide, whereas Ryan asserted that it was the legislature which must decide whether rates were reasonable and that the remedy for inequitable rates must be sought at the polls. Ryan's view had the support of a few contemporary commentators and it resembled the view taken in Waite's majority opinion for the United States Supreme Court in *Munn v. Illinois*.[92] But it was soon to be discarded; the next generation of judges, by defining in their own terms what constitttued a "reasonable" rate, in effect performed the job of regulation. Many years were to elapse before the courts returned to Ryan's view.

The federal cases that grew out of the Potter Law specifically and the granger laws generally, made the same points that Ryan made in the Railroad Companies case. But their pronouncements were more significant from the standpoint of the subsequent development of the railroads and of railroad regulation.

When the Supreme Court, too, repudiated its position fifteen years later it also undid much of Ryan's work.[93]

Nothing in Ryan's position indicated that he foresaw what direction railroad regulation was to take. He did not realize that federal regulation was to be the eventual solution. For this he cannot be criticized; few others of his time saw it either. It was the power of the state rather than that of the federal government which was the great battle ground during his time.[94]

One positive contribution to the techniques of regulation the Potter Law did make. It set up a special administrative agency to deal with a unique situation. Granted that the functions were not adequately defined, the Railroad Commission was nevertheless a significant beginning. The growing realization that it was futile to set rates by statute and the popular discontent over the commissioners' lack of authority to initiate proceedings engendered at least the beginnings of some sophistication about the kind of administrative structure needed. Another advance, also, may be ascribed to the commissioners. They began the process of collecting statistics on railroad operation and rate-making, which were indispensable to any solution of the problem.

* * *

THE struggle between public and private power fought out in the Railroad Companies case is a bench mark for two recurring themes in United States legal history. First, it mirrored the varying degrees of prestige enjoyed by the several agencies of law. This was revealed most clearly in the conduct of the railroad companies. Without qualm or embarrassment two powerful companies announced that they simply would not obey the legislative rates. Yet at no time, probably, did they have any thought of defying the courts, as Governor Taylor feared they might. Their general solicitor wrote privately that they certainly did not intend to disregard an injunction.[95]

Why should they have felt less compunction in disregarding

a statute than a judicial order? At the very least their attitude reflected the notion that law made by the legislature was of a different order than that emanating from the courts. It probably represented also the great depreciation of prestige the legislature had suffered over the preceding fifty years.

The respect accorded the courts by even the most rugged individualist was denied not only the legislature but also the executive. Taylor's proclamation frightened no one, and the attorney general's opinion convinced only the attorney general and the governor. And as yet no one knew how to regard the work of the railroad commissioners. Thus it fell to the judicial agency to establish the supremacy of law over private power.[96]

The incident is significant also in that it represented one of the last official expressions in Wisconsin of the view that the nature of the railroad-building job was, in essence, a public one, even though it might be accomplished by private corporations. Earlier both legislature and court had stated that the state had delegated a public task to private concerns better prepared to undertake it. Now the railroads had been built. In the meantime the companies had grown so strong that when the time came to reassert public control over them it proved almost impossible to do so. Ryan's opinion saved the day.

The outcome owed much to two of the state officials involved in the battle. Governor Taylor realized how crucial for the public welfare the proceedings against the companies were, involving as they did the prestige and even the sovereignty of the state; and he showed enough sophistication to spot the basic defects in the Potter Law sanctions.[97] Finally, it was indeed fortunate that Ryan was on the bench to write the opinion. There was probably not another man in Wisconsin who could have done so professional a job. More important, no one could have met the issue more frankly and asserted the power of the state so unequivocally.

V. Wisconsin Railroad Law from 1875 to 1890

One precedent creates another. They soon accumulate, and constitute law. What yesterday was fact, today is doctrine.—*The Letters of Junius.*

AFTER the dramatic conflict staged in the injunction suits Wisconsin railroad law again went through a period of relatively unspectacular growth and development. Railroads continued to build their lines, routinize their operations, and perfect their intracorporate procedures without much interference from formal agencies of law. New roads came into existence as areas like northern Wisconsin with its rich pinelands set up a cry for railroads, sought land grants, and offered local aid.

The table on the next page shows the extent of the law's intervention in various types of relationships between the railroad and the Wisconsin community. One striking fact emerges from these data: that only in a few instances did the law intervene in the railroad's intercorporate and intracorporate affairs. And this was during a period when the railroad was expanding greatly and in face of the fact that it was the first major industrial institution to be drawn into the swirl of the post–Civil War financial revolution. The significant economic and industrial advances, in other words, took place outside rather than inside the law.

INSTANCES OF LEGAL INTERVENTION, 1875–1890
STATE LAWS AND SUPREME COURT DECISIONS
PERTAINING TO PROBLEMS INVOLVING RAILROADS IN WISCONSIN *

	1875–80	1881–85	1886–90	TOTAL
RELATIONSHIPS WITH STRANGERS	58	58	78	194
With landowners	30	28	35	93
Death and personal injury	15	9	11	35
Injury to livestock	13	21	32	66
RELATIONSHIPS WITH USERS	25	19	25	69
With passengers	12	12	8	32
With shippers	13	7	17	37
INTRACORPORATE RELATIONSHIPS	22	8	2	32
Charters and authority of officers	9	4	2	15
With stockholders and bondholders	4	2	0	6
Farm-mortgage cases	1	0	0	1
Consolidation, merger, reorganization, receivership	8	2	0	10
RELATIONSHIPS WITH GOVERNMENT	81	64	28	173
With state government	54	44	16	114
With local government	23	20	10	53
With federal government	4	0	2	6
RELATIONSHIPS WITH OTHER CONTRACTING PARTIES	40	27	22	89
With building contractors	17	6	10	33
With miscellaneous creditors	0	0	0	0
With employees	23	21	12	56
Total	226	176	155	557

* Based on *Wisconsin Session Laws*, 1875–1890, and *Wisconsin Supreme Court Reports*, Vols. 35–78 (1875–1890).

THE RAILROADS' RELATIONSHIPS WITH STRANGERS

Relationships with Landowners.—During these years, as in the preceding period, many relationships between railroad and landowner were brought to the law for settlement. Most numerous were cases involving problems arising out of condemnation and eminent domain proceedings and claims for damages to property resulting from fires set by railroad engines. Despite the fact that the general railroad law of 1872 set out with great particularity the procedure for taking land by eminent domain, the legislature found it necessary to pass five additional laws on the subject. Two of these merely extended existing condemnation proceedings to new activities—the building of spur tracks and the construction of underpasses. The others set a limit on the period of delay and continuance granted the condemnation commissioners under the general act; authorized Wisconsin railroad companies to condemn land in an adjacent state if the laws of that state so permitted; and defined more specifically the rights of owners of abutting land by excepting land taken under eminent domain from the provisions of a statute governing damages recoverable by landowners.[1]

But again it was court rather than legislature that dealt with most of the problems born of the condemnation power. On two questions the court made substantive policy: it laid down fundamental principles of the law of excess condemnation when it placed on the railroad the burden of proving why more than the usual hundred-foot right of way was needed, and it wrestled with the difficult question of whether depreciation in the value of land not physically invaded constituted a "taking" for which compensation was paid.[2] The rest of the court's work was mainly instrumental: it construed the condemnation provisions of the general railroad act of 1872—consistently with its contruction of earlier condemnation laws—as requiring compensation prior to entry;[3] it deliberated many times on the measure of damages;[4] it determined the propriety of appraising the value of lands held by different landowners;[5] and it passed on a host of jurisdictional, procedural, and miscellaneous questions in the course of rendering its opinions in condemnation cases.[6]

Damages from fires caused by locomotives sparks continued to occupy the court during this period as they had in preceding decades. The court's main job was to untangle the facts, after which it simply applied, with or without modification, the tenets it had laid down earlier. In so doing it added also to the body of the Wisconsin law of evidence and it constantly tried to draw the wavy boundary line between judge's and jury's responsibility.[7] In 1882 the Wisconsin legislature, taking its cue from Eastern states, passed an act giving railroad companies an insurable interest in property along their rights-of-way which might be damaged by fires caused by locomotives.[8]

Remaining instances of the law's intervention between railroad and landowner included three legislative acts imposing liability on the roads—one for interference with navigable streams and the other two for failing to keep land along the right-of-way free of debris—and a spate of judicial decisions dealing with liability for interfering with use and enjoyment of property.[9]

Injury to Livestock.—During this period the legislators continued to tinker—partly because of the advent of barbed wire—with the fencing laws their predecessors had passed.[10] But the Wisconsin Supreme Court, viewing these acts as in derogation of the common law, tended to construe them crabbedly. It insisted that plaintiffs bring themselves within the literal language of the statute; it imposed on them a heavy burden of proof to sustain the charge of negligence; and at times it demanded that they lead blameless lives themselves, free from contributing or imputed fault.[11] In administering the fencing laws the court found, in case after case, that its main task was to unravel the facts and assess damage.[12]

A broad assertion of policy broke through when the court refused to let the legislature abolish the defense of contributory negligence. The fencing statute, passed in 1872, imposed absolute liability on the roads for damages to livestock "occasioned by the failure to erect such fences and cattle-guards as herein required."[13] Early courts had assumed that the act meant what it said: absolute liability meant absolute liability, and contributory negligence was no defense.[14] But this was too much for Chief Justice Ryan; he was too deeply rooted in the common law to accept any such interpretation. To him "occasioned" meant "caused" and hence if the plaintiff's own negligence contributed to the injury, the mishap could not have been caused by the defendant's failure to erect the fence:

> The rule [abolishing contributory negligence as a defense] can no longer be upheld. The rule of this court must be taken as sustaining the defense of contributory negligence to actions against railroad companies, for injuries occasioned by failure either to erect or to maintain fences on the line of their roads, as in other actions for negligence. . . . The essential danger of railroads requires diligence on both sides; a high degree of diligence in the management of the road, and at least ordinary diligence on the part of adjoining owners. The rule of absolute liability appears to be as unwise in policy as unsound in legal construction.[15]

Ryan's decision did not last long. The very same year it came down, in 1878, the legislature amended the section by imposing on the railroad absolute liability for all damages "occasioned in any manner, in whole or in part, by the want of such fences or cattle guards."[16] This change in language, slight though it seems, was enough to enable Chief Judge Orsamus Cole, seven years later, to hold that the statute ruled out contributory negligence as a defense.[17]

Death and Personal Injury Actions.—In dealing with death and personal injury caused by railroads the legislature merely tinkered with existing legislation. The laws it passed, mainly amendatory to earlier ones, were directed primarily toward the prevention of accidents by requiring protective devices or conduct by the roads: guards and blocks on every frog in the track, and attendants at unlocked turntables.[18]

Again it was through the judicial agency that the law did most of its work. An avalanche of death and personal-injury claims reached the Wisconsin Supreme Court during this period. Most of them arose out of accidents occurring at intersections of tracks and highways or accidents caused by runaway horses, by pedestrians walking on the right-of-way, or by the existence of holes, turntables, or other obstructions on railroad property.[19] Many cases involving strangers came up under the wrongful-death statute. In these the court traveled along the paths it had marked out during earlier years.[20]

The sheer volume of cases gave the Wisconsin Supreme Court opportunity to explore almost every aspect of the law of negligence, causation, and damages. By 1890 the court had blocked out the Wisconsin law of negligence, and, partly as a result of the widespread use of the statutory special verdict, it had also laid down a controlling body of precedent regarding the role of judge and jury and other principles of adjective law.[21]

Railroads and Their Users

Relationships with Shippers.—The whole controversy over governmental regulation, exemplified in the Potter Law and the Railroad Companies case, of course represented intervention of the law in the relationships between railroads and the people who used them. But apart from this major effort of the agencies of law, their activity during this period was either sporadic or routine. The legislature did very little: it passed laws dealing with construction and maintenance of warehouses and sidings, requiring shippers to provide partitions in cars, and permitting railroads to regulate the time and manner of transportation of passengers and property, providing that no "unjust preference, advantage, or monopoly" was given to any person doing business in more than one station.[22]

The court, again, played a more active part, but even its role was less prominent than in other fields or than it had been in the formative period. For the relationship between railroad and shipper was in the domain of contract, the basic principles of which had already been established. During this period, great as railroad expansion and the consequent increase of shipping were, relatively few disputes reached the courts. In its administration of those contractual relations that did reach it for settlement, the Wisconsin court added little that was new to the body of doctrine it had previously laid down; controversies concerning shipments of goods, inter-carrier relationships, and the efficacy of exculpatory clauses were disposed of in more or less routine fashion.[23]

Relationships with Passengers.—Neither court or legislature added significantly to the body of existing law governing the railroads' relationships with passengers. In the regulatory statute of 1876 that had eviscerated the Potter Law and in the law permitting the roads to prescribe the time and manner of transporting goods and passengers, the legislature necessarily addressed itself to the questions of fares, rules, and regulations.[24]

In addition, two laws were enacted in the interest of passenger safety—one requiring the companies to place an axe and saw in each car and the other prohibiting the conductor from locking doors leading from one coach to another while the train was in motion—and two more in the interest of the public morality —one empowering conductors to arrest persons using indecent or profane language, and the other outlawing gambling, particularly three-card monte, on railroad cars.[25]

Again the main job of the court in suits involving injuries to passengers was to establish the facts. When it decided the cases that came before it in monotonous profusion, it merely reasserted principles of law laid down during the formative period.[26]

Intracorporate and Intercorporate Relationships

The general railroad law of 1872 established the pattern of railroad incorporation and drew the formal lines of corporate power in more or less permanent form. The law's activity during the next two decades did little to modify or alter those forms.[27] The legislature addressed itself almost entirely to changing specific details, as when it authorized railroads to change their names, routes, and location of stations, to build bridges across navigable streams, and to guarantee payments of bonds.[28] It also dealt with the authority given to boards of directors and, in general, expanded that authority: it prescribed details as to the manner and time of board elections, authorized staggered boards, vested in the board of the Milwaukee Road the power to execute mortgages without a stockholders' vote, and, in the 1876 replacement of the Potter Law, prohibited directors from having any financial interest in competing roads or in firms supplying their roads with material.[29] Only once did it come to the aid of stockholders, when it passed a law requiring a two-thirds affirmative vote for the transfer of land-grant holdings from one road to another.[30]

On the one occasion when the Supreme Court had opportunity to intervene in an intracorporate conflict between stockholders and management, it dismissed the plaintiff-stockholders' suit on the technical ground that they had not made a formal request of the corporation to sue nor, alternatively, alleged in the complaint that it would have been futile to make the request.[31]

Anti-consolidation sentiment found some expression in the 1876 substitute for the Potter Law. The new act prohibited consolidation of parallel lines and forbade interlocking directorates of competing roads. But it assigned to the jury rather than to the Railroad Commission the task of determining whether the roads were "parallel" or "competing."[32] Aside from this limitation, railroad consolidationists generally had their own way. In 1875 the legislature unobtrusively re-enacted sections of an earlier law dealing with consolidation which it had repealed in 1864. A law passed in 1880 and refined by certain amendments in 1882 and 1883 granted broad consolidation powers to roads "where it can be lawfully done"—i.e., where their roads were not competing—and when the surviving road constituted one continuous line.[33] By 1890, therefore, anti-consolidation statutes became largely empty declarations of policy having little effect on the tide of merger and consolidation.

Relationships with mortgage bondholders—other than holders of farm-mortgage bonds—were dealt with three times by the legislature. In 1876 it legalized a consolidated sinking-fund mortgage executed by the Milwaukee Road and two years later gave holders of these sinking-fund bonds certain voting rights; in 1877 it passed a law prescribing the procedure under which purchasers at foreclosure sales might continue the business.[34]

Problems of intracorporate and intercorporate affairs occupied the Wisconsin Supreme Court far less in this period than other relationships between the law and the railroads. When the law did anything at all in this area it acted through the legislature.

Railroads and Government

The Twilight of State Regulation.—The Potter Law and Judge Ryan's opinion marked the apogee of state regulation of railroads in Wisconsin. All that followed was anticlimactic, and by the 1890's direct state regulation of rates had practically ceased. But by this time state regulation was no longer important, for in 1887 Congress had passed the Interstate Commerce Act.

No sooner had Ryan's opinion come down than agitation appeared on all sides for modification of the Potter Act. The law hung on in principle for two years. Amendments enacted in 1875 made certain reclassifications of lines and minor modifications in procedure, but in 1876 the Potter Law came to an end.[35] Repeal became inevitable with the election of Governor

Harrison Ludington and a legislature friendly to the railroads. Ludington laid the blame for lagging railroad construction and impairment of the state's credit squarely on the Potter Law and recommended its repeal. What he wanted in its place is none too clear. He urged substitution of legislation that would abolish "unjust discrimination" and prevent extortionate rates by establishing maximum rates not greater than those fixed by the companies when they made their own tariffs. Such tariffs, he observed, "may be presumed to be sufficient to enable them to earn a fair return upon capital actually and in good faith invested." With this limitation, Ludington stated, the railroads should be free to establish their own rates.[36]

This was all the 1876 legislature needed. It amended the Potter Law and took out all its teeth. It is one of the ironies of history that the 1876 law—in intent and operation a repudiation of the Potter Act—was, from a regulatory point of view, a better drafted statute than its predecessor. It included, as the Potter Law did not, an outright prohibition of discrimination and substituted for the elaborate rate schedules that would have made the Potter Law impossible to administer, two simple and general sections. Section 5 provided that "No railroad corporation shall charge, demand, or receive from any person, company, or corporation an unreasonable price for the transportation of persons or property, or for the handling or storing of any freight or for the use of its cars, or for any privilege or service afforded by it in the transaction of its business as a railroad corporation." Section 11 rolled back rates for the Milwaukee and North Western railroads to those set forth in their own schedules of June 15, 1872, and prohibited those roads from charging more. Establishing rates by roll-back is not good industrial economics, but even this was an improvement over the cumbersome schedules of the Potter Law.[37]

The 1876 law was doomed to impotence because it failed to set up administrative machinery adequate to enforce its provisions. It reduced the Railroad Commission from three men to one and failed to arm the commissioner with any enforcement powers whatsoever. After receiving a complaint the commissioner could investigate alleged unreasonable charges or discrimination, but he could go no farther. He had to turn his report over to the attorney general, who, short of an action of quo warranto, perhaps, could not be compelled to act.[38] As has been mentioned two other substantive provisions of the act—Sections 8 and 9—prohibited consolidation of parallel lines and interlocking directorates of competing companies, but withheld from the railroad commissioner the power to make the necessary factual determinations and placed it instead in the hands of the jury.

Recognizing the difference in remedies, the 1876 act included a saving clause for the disposition of pending Potter Law prosecutions.[39] But the legislature had not anticipated the reaction of the Wisconsin Supreme Court. In the first case to come before it the court, through Ryan, declared the saving clause ineffectual on the ground that the legislature could not save the remedy without saving the right and that it was for the court, not the legislaure, to declare the effect of a repeal. "*Lis pendens,* under a statute repealed, becomes *lis nuda;* a fruitless pursuit of extinct rights and liabilities."[40] The zeal Ryan had shown for the Potter Law in the Railroad Companies case could not survive a clash with his predisposition for the supremacy of court over legislature. And so the Supreme Court closed the door on prosecutions under the Potter Law. But it left a window slightly open; it permitted Potter Law plaintiffs to amend their complaints and base their actions on the common-law remedy for excessive charges.[41]

Wisconsin governors seemed unconcerned about the turn of events regarding direct regulation of rates. Governor William E. Smith asserted that "the total absence of all serious complaint against railroads, shows most conclusively, that our present law is well suited to the purposes for which it was enacted, and, under the watchful supervision of the Commissioner, is being faithfully obeyed."[42] Governor Jeremiah M. Rusk stated that "the Railroad Commissioner system in Wisconsin has been a success," and that over the years "not a single case of litigation has grown out of a complaint lodged with the commissioner, but in every instance amicable adjustment has been made, satisfactory to all parties concerned."[43]

Of the railroad commissioners only Nils Haugen saw defects in the 1876 law. He regarded discrimination in favor of one locality over another, rather than increased rates, as the greatest cause for dissatisfaction. He was keen enough to observe that "the fixing of rates can not at present be said to rest on any fixed principle, unless it be to charge that rate which will produce the most revenue for the time being."[44] But his was a voice crying in the wilderness. His predecessor, Andrew J. Turner, had ruled that the provision of the act outlawing discrimination prohibited only "unjust discrimination" and discrimination between shippers "for like services." Turner conceded that almost every service rendered was in some way different from every other, and he could find nothing anti-competitive in the prevalent railroad practice of pooling rates.[45]

Thus ended attempts by the state government to regulate railroad rates directly. But during this period came also the only feasible solution—the intervention of the federal government in 1887 through passage of the Interstate Commerce Act.

Taxation and License Fees.—During the fifties the basis of railroad taxation had been established: the roads paid a tax (technically a license fee) at a specified percentage of their gross earnings per mile of line in Wisconsin. This principle served the railroads well, for it enabled them to allocate their earnings to Wisconsin as they chose. This basis of taxation remained unchanged for approximately fifty years: the legislature merely passed one law in 1876 changing the specified percentage, and another in 1883, amended in 1885, including sleeping and parlor car companies within the purview of the taxing statute.[46]

Both these laws came before the Wisconsin Supreme Court. The first was passed upon in a case involving the question whether the earnings of leased roads should be added to the earnings of the lessor and the percentage applied to the aggregate amount. The court delivered a setback to the roads when it sustained the state treasurer's ruling that the earnings should be combined.[47] The other statute—taxing sleeping- and parlor-car companies—reached the court when the companies contested the basis of the tax: the gross earnings from the use of the cars as reported to the railroad commissioner and by him certified to the state treasurer. The companies contended that the act might include only the gross earnings from passengers who got on or off in Wisconsin. In this case the Supreme Court agreed with the companies: it held that the interstate commerce clause of the federal constitution prohibited the interpretation urged by the state.[48] As so limited the act proved almost impossible to administer; a troublesome task for the railroad commissioner.[49]

This was the period of railroad construction in northern Wisconsin and the northern roads did not wait long to obtain from the legislature exemptions (usually for a ten-year period) from the real property tax on their land-grant holdings. The Supreme Court sustained the validity of the exemption statutes, making it clear that exemptions were matters of legislative grace that might be withdrawn at any time without running afoul of the contract clause of the federal constitution.[50] One exemption act directed the state treasurer to apportion the receipts from the license fees paid by the road to the counties in which the exempted lands lay. When the counties sought to compel the treasurer to make the apportionment, the Supreme Court quashed their writ of mandamus because the ten-year exemption period had expired and with it the treasurer's statutory power to make the apportionment.[51]

Land-Grant Problems.—With the building of the northern railroads the Wisconsin legislature began to dole out the remaining portions of the two federal land grants. By an act of 1879 it gave some of the northwest lands of the original 1856 grant to the Northern Wisconsin Railway Company. It appended conditions regarding the number of miles of construction to be completed annually, exempted the lands from taxation for ten years, gave the company the privilege of reserving the stand of timber on any land it sold, and stipulated $2.50 an acre as the maximum price at which it could sell to settlers. The act paid its respects to *Dartmouth College v. Woodward* by declaring that "this act shall not be taken or deemed to be a part of the charter of the said North Wisconsin railway company or an amendment thereto."[52] Three times the legislature had to waive forfeiture of the lands when the road failed to complete the required miles of construction.[53] And when the Chicago, St. Paul, Minneapolis & Omaha Railway absorbed the North Wisconsin, the legislature authorized the Omaha to succeed to the interest in the land grant.[54]

In 1874 the legislature gave a portion of the 1864 grant to the Chicago and Northern Pacific Air Line Railway Company and in 1878 extended for another three years the period allowed for fulfillment of the terms. This line also came under the sway of the Chicago, St. Paul, Minneapolis & Omaha, and in 1882 the 1874 grant was revoked and conferred on the Omaha.[55] By the early eighties, therefore, the Omaha had received the major portion of the railroad land-grant tracts in northern Wisconsin. In connection with the 1882 act revoking the grant the legislature passed a law directing the Omaha to deposit with the governor a specified sum of money to pay laborers' claims incurred by the Northern Pacific Air Line Railway. When the governor later refused to pay certain of these claims and the claimants brought a mandamus proceeding against him, the Supreme Court declined to intercede, declaring that the governor's action was well within the discretion given him by the statute.[56]

The 1879 grant to the Northern Wisconsin stated that the lands should be deemed "agricultural lands," but this was a fiction: they were timberlands and their economic value consisted of a magnificent stand of virgin pine. From the outset timber stealing had plagued the area and the problem was not alleviated by the transfer of the lands to the railroads.[57] In a separate act the legislature had decreed that transfer of title should include assignment of any causes of action the state held against timber thieves. Other statutes provided for the appointment of timber agents and modified traditional common-law remedies against trespassers.[58] The only case under these statutes that reached the Supreme Court was one involving a claim for attorneys' fees earned by defending suits brought against timber agents who had seized logs cut by trespassers.[59]

The final claims of the hapless farm-mortgagors and the ultimate fate of the 1856 land grant were settled before the mid-eighties. The Wisconsin Supreme Court disposed of the last of the railroad farm-mortgage cases,[60] and before long the Railroad Farm Mortgage Land Company, created in 1868 to administer the remainder of the 1856 land grant, got into difficulty. Its first brushes with the law were over matters of mere administrative detail, but in 1883 the scandals accompanying its operations finally engendered a full-scale legislative investigation.[61] Thus the story of the 1856 land grant ended as it had begun—with a legislative investigation of wholesale fraud.

Miscellaneous Relationships with the State Government.—In one additional instance involving direct relationships between railroads and the state government, the legislature touched on a point of basic policy. In 1887, the same year that Congress passed the Interstate Commerce Act, the Wisconsin legislature enacted a comprehensive statute prescribing the terms under which foreign railroad corporations might extend their lines

Atley Peterson

Nils P. Haugen

into the state.[62] Other legislative acts were more special and less important: acts regulating narrow-gauge railroads, establishing terminals, amending franchises to impose conditions with respect to rate of construction, and establishing filing fees and the manner of service of process.[63]

In a few instances the court, too, dealt with matters of basic policy. The Railroad Companies case had demonstrated what a powerful weapon was the original jurisdiction of the Supreme Court. Consequently, in two cases the parties sought direct relief from the Supreme Court. In the first the attorney general filed a quo warranto information praying that a foreign railroad be deprived of its charter for failing to maintain a principal business office in Wisconsin.[64] In the second a railroad sought injunctive relief against the state in a case involving state debts; the Supreme Court refused to entertain the suit on the ground that there was no express statutory authorization for it.[65]

In one case, decided in 1890, the court denied specific performance of a lobbying contract on the ground that to enforce the contract would be contrary to public policy. Judge Cassoday's opinion was grounded in common-law precedent; only by way of a note at the end of the opinion did he point out that the case fell within the four corners of the 1858 anti-lobby law, which both court and counsel had overlooked completely![66]

Relationships with Local Government.—Financial aid to railroads by city, village, county, and other local units continued to occupy Wisconsin agencies of law during the seventies and eighties. The general law of 1872 had set the pattern for local aid, but the legislature found occasion to amend it several times. In 1875, for instance, it prescribed the maximum tax that might be imposed and limited the municipality's liability to the amount collected, whether by tax or by sale of lands for uncollected taxes.[67] Other amendments simply made the 1872 act applicable to particular situations, such as narrow-gauge railroads.[68] Yet in many instances the general law itself was, apparently, inadequate. Conseqently the statute books are sprinkled with local-aid legislation tailored to special circumstance that seemingly could have been handled under the general law with minor amendments, at most.[69]

Northern Wisconsin towns soon found themselves, as their neighbors to the south once had, embarrassed by their local-aid obligations and they too came to court and legislature for relief.[70] But the Wisconsin Supreme Court was plagued by the dichotomy of the Whiting case—sustaining aid by bond issue and taxation but invalidating outright donations—which it reaffirmed in cases it decided during these years.[71] Once the Wisconsin court strayed, only to invite a stinging rebuke from Chief Justice Ryan. The court declined to void a municipal stock subscription because it felt it could not upset a valid contract between town and railroad. Ryan, who concurred with the majority on a technical point alone, deplored his brethren's treatment of the Whiting rule and lectured them on their misconception of the nature of the judicial process:

> The distinguished gentlemen who represented the bondholders on the argument warned the court, with great emphasis, against repudiation. That is the keyword of the cant of speculators in questionable public securities.... That word of reproach, any such words of reproach, can have no influence on the mind of any judge fit to hold his office. It is as much the duty of courts to avoid illegal, as enforce legal contracts. Courts having nothing to do with the consequences of judgments rendered on settled principles of law. Far better that these bondholders should lose their money invested in these bonds, than that principles of judicial decision should lose their control of the judgments of the court. It is the strict duty of this court to pass upon the validity of the statute under which the bonds in this case were issued upon fixed rules of judicial decision, in disregard of all outcry from counsel, clients or other. And it would be far better and more honorable to this court to encounter the slang of repudiation, than to earn the reputation, as may have happened to other courts, of being a court of claims for speculators in abortive evidences of public debts in Wall

street or elsewhere. Such a threat—it sounded like one—can have no influence on me to swerve a line from what I believe to be the law or my duty to declare it at all hazards. Unfortunate the court wanting in courage to declare unpalatable right against pretentious, palatable wrong.[72]

The court found avenues of escape for the cities in addition to the distinction made in the Whiting case. It granted relief when the railroad materially changed its route from that authorized by charter, when the parties failed to follow the statutory procedure, and when the municipality acted in excess of its authority.[73] On some occasions, however, the court declined to rescue defaulting localities and refused to listen to technical and formalistic defenses they presented.[74]

Miscellaneous relationships between railroads and local government were dealt with by the legislature in enabling acts delegating to local bodies a measure of police power: authorizing the county board of supervisors to enter into "amicable arrangements" for constructing viaduct crossings and giving city officials power to direct the erection of gates at critical crossings.[75] Other relationships with local government came before the courts in actions by railroads against local taxation and suits by municipalities to recover expenses from the roads, to enjoin construction, and to adjudicate disputed ownership of stock.[76]

Relationships with the Federal Government.—Wisconsin railroads had to deal with the federal as well as the state government during this period. Land grants of course came originally from Congress, and the northern roads, like their southern predecessors a generation earlier, prevailed upon the Wisconsin legislature to memorialize the national legislators for grants.[77] Before a road could build a bridge over a navigable stream it had to get federal as well as state approval.[78] Federal circuit courts—that is, trial courts—were also busy with railroad problems. Cases involving local aid and foreclosures and receiverships outnumbered all the rest combined. In their adjudications on local aid federal judges proved to be less tractable than their state brethren in helping defaulting municipalities escape their obligations, and in the financial mopping up after wholesale railroad insolvencies Wisconsin federal judges gained rich experience in the important administrative job of supervising railroad reorganizations and receiverships.[79] Other issues before the federal courts were basically the same as those the state courts dealt with: condemnation, liability to shippers and passengers, title to land-grant property, and controversies with suppliers.[80]

But the problem of federalism impinged on railroad law in much more subtle ways. Wisconsin lawmakers, like those of other states, struggled with the difficult problem of confining a national business to state boundary lines. In 1887 it passed a detailed qualification act subjecting foreign roads to at least minimal regulation under Wisconsin law, but by this time the need for federal rather than state regulation was painfully apparent.[81] In 1882 the Supreme Courts of Iowa and Illinois had come to diametrically opposite conclusions as to the validity of state regulation of interstate railroads.[82] Nils Haugen, the Wisconsin railroad commissioner, set out the two court opinions side by side as though to point out the inevitability of federal regulation.[83] Governor Rusk also saw the need for uniform regulation and discussed it in his annual message of 1882. He voiced the hope that interestate commerce would soon be regulated by a "national statute."[84] In 1887 Congress responded to this need by passing the Interstate Commerce Act.

Railroads and Other Contracting Parties

Relationships with Vendors and Purchasers of Land and with Suppliers.—Railroad land grants enabled the roads to finance construction by selling the lands to settlers. Good and merchantable title, accordingly, was of prime importance. Twice—both times in 1876—the Wisconsin legislature intervened: it passed a law "to protect purchasers of railroad land grants" which spelled out with great particularity the mode of conveyance from state to railroad and from railroad to settler; and it extended the time that settlers were allowed to acquire title to land-grant tracts of the North Wisconsin and the Chicago and Northern Pacific Air Line railroads.[85] And as owners, vendors, and purchasers of land the roads of necessity brought many of their transactions to the courts for settlement in suits for rent, ejectment, foreclosure, and acquisition of rights-of-way.[86]

In the relationship between the railroads and their suppliers the legislature again intervened twice, and again both times in the same year. It prescribed a technique that was remarkably farsighted for the time, namely, a central filing system (with the secretary of state) for protection of equipment companies' security interests, and it also authorized equipment companies to issue equipment trust certificates—a technique that had been developed in the East—and to classify their property into as many divisions as the board of directors deemed necessary.[87] Other problems involving railroad and contracting parties came before the courts in routine disputes arising out of the contractual relationship: enforcement of suppliers' and mechanics' liens and garnishment suits.[88]

Relationships with Employees.—The employer-employee relationship thrust a problem of first magnitude on Wisconsin railroad law, a problem that it failed to solve and probably did not fully recognize. This was the problem of industrial accidents, which by now had become acute; the injustice of harsh common-law doctrine haunted Wisconsin lawmakers—court, legislature, and executive—throughout these years.

In the formative period the Wisconsin Supreme Court had first rejected the fellow-servant rule, but within a year it had reversed itself and brought Wisconsin law into line with contemporary jurisprudence.[89] The legislature dealt with this issue in 1875 when it passed a law abrogating the fellow-servant rule and rendered ineffective any contract or regulation that purported to exempt the railroad from the liability imposed by the act.[90] This law—excoriated by the railroads and others as "class legislation"—lasted only five years; in 1880 it was repealed.[91]

But industrial accidents were too numerous and the harshness of the fellow-servant rule too apparent to permit the legislature to remain permanently silent. In 1889 it passed another act, extremely circumscribed in scope, which abolished the fellow-servant rule only where damage had been caused by the negligent conduct of "any train dispatcher, telegraph operator, superintendent, yard master, conductor or engineer, or of any other employee, who has charge or control of any stationary signal, target point, block or switch."[92] This was a response, though a feeble one, to the "felt necessities of the times," but if the response was feeble its net effect was even more so. For it was the Wisconsin Supreme Court that directed the course of the law of railroads' liability for injuries to employees. An avalanche of employee-accident cases descended upon it and generalization as to its handling of them is virtually impossible.

An employee injured on the job had a formidable task indeed in charging the railroad with liability and recovering compensation for his injuries. First of all, the vagaries of doctrine and the technicalities of an ordinary tort action for negligence stood in his way: he must establish a duty—that is, a standard of care—owed to him by the defendant, show the breach of that duty, link up the breach with his injury (in other words, the problem of causation), and prove his damages with reasonable certainty. More than that, he was confronted with the unholy trinity of common-law defenses that his employer could present to bar recovery: contributory negligence, assumption of risk, and the fellow-servant rule.[93]

With this array of legal doctrine able railroad attorneys rendered recovery a herculean task. They found in Wisconsin's special-verdict statute, moreover, a valuable tool for limiting plaintiff-mindedness of juries. Yet the Supreme Court could not blind itself to compelling equities; on occasion it modified and bent doctrine to permit recovery. In the mid-seventies for instance, it followed the lead of other state courts in softening the rigor of the fellow-servant rule by adopting the so-called "vice-principal" doctrine, which rejected the defense if the negligence causing the accident was that of a supervisory employee.[94] But as often as not ultimate recovery, put through the wringer of a suit at law, rested on fortuitous circumstances quite unrelated to the merits of the controversy. So the court wended its way, granting recovery here and denying recovery there, through the maze of cases arising out of railroad accidents incident to such activities as switching and coupling operations, employees' conduct on trains in motion, work in and around the yards, shops, and bridges, and other functions of railroading.[95]

The increasing incidence of industrial accidents did not go unnoticed by Governor Taylor. In his annual message of 1875 he asked for a statute to abrogate the fellow-servant rule. "Such a statute," he said, "would tend to secure the employment of more cautious and reliable men, and thus afford greater security to the traveling public." He went on to recommend, presumably lest the companies object too much, that "for the liabilities thus increased, the companies should receive increased compensation."[96] The legislature responded and passed the first statute abolishing the fellow-servant rule. With Taylor's administration, however, leadership from the governor's mansion seemed to end. Although the legislature repealed the 1875 law abrogating the rule and industrial accidents were increasing yearly, subsequent governors were seemingly little concerned. None of them called for re-examination of the question or for amendatory legislation.

The railroad commissioners, who were closest to the problem of industrial accidents, expressed alarm over the increasing toll of life and limb. Even Commissioner Andrew J. Turner, who was in most respects not unfriendly to the roads, said that although the statutory abolition of the fellow-servant rule had been called "class legislation," he could not help but feel that the hazardous nature of the work entitled railroad employees to special consideration.[97] Commissioner Nils Haugen was more specific. In 1882 he noted that the increasing number of injuries sustained by persons in the employ of the roads "cannot be viewed but with alarm." He believed that the source of most injuries was the coupling of cars, and that the state could hope for no reduction in accidents until the roads adopted an automatic coupler.

> Eighty-five employees killed or crippled in coupling cars should impress on their humane employers the necessity of a change from the present link and pin and it is to be hoped that the national convention of the master carbuilders, who considered the subject at their last meeting, will, at their next, be able to agree upon the adoption of some one or more of the more numerous contrivances invented to obviate the going between cars.[98]

He was also forced to infer, from the frequency of collisions, that someone must be at fault, since the two trains often had no knowledge of each other's proximity. Appropriate legislation of a criminal nature, he concluded, would lessen the danger.[99]

Haugen's successor, Atley Peterson, also decried the number of accidents attending the coupling of cars. He printed eight pages of letters he had received from railroad officials concerning the progress being made in automatic couplers. Nevertheless he was not prepared to make their installation compulsory forthwith; the existing state of the art, he felt, made legislative requirement of automatic couplers unnecessary; the roads were installing them as rapidly as possible. He suggested the interesting technique of placing control of the matter in the railroad commissioner and authorizing him to determine when and how automatic devices should be put into operation.[100]

RAILROAD ACCIDENTS IN WISCONSIN, 1874–1890*

	1874	1875	1876	1877	1878	1879	1880	1881	1882	1883	1884	1885	1886	1887	1888	1889	1890	Total
Passengers																		
Killed	18	18	0	2	2	1	0	0	3	3	3	1	4	22	8	4	3	92
Injured	37	30	10	6	2	6	2	30	74	25	18	11	10	23	42	59	51	436
Total	55	48	10	8	4	7	2	30	77	28	21	12	14	45	50	63	54	528
Employees																		
Killed	28	13	15	12	18	12	21	39	51	43	36	61	34	48	63	52	69	615
Injured	80	108	147	56	110	67	148	263	252	103	112	166	168	320	537	844	748	4229
Total	108	121	162	68	128	79	169	302	303	146	148	227	202	368	600	896	817	4844
Others																		
Killed	†	†	27	20	26	21	29	0	59	42	53	51	53	73	62	72	111	699
Injured	†	†	40	21	41	26	27	34	50	26	21	47	43	52	74	82	112	696
Total	†	†	67	41	67	47	56	34	109	68	74	98	96	125	136	154	223	1395
Totals																		
Killed	46	31	42	34	46	34	50	39	113	88	92	113	91	143	133	128	183	1406
Injured	117	138	197	83	153	99	177	327	376	154	151	224	221	395	653	985	911	5361
Total	163	169	239	117	199	133	227	366	489	242	243	337	312	538	786	1113	1094	6767

* Although not so stated in the tables, it is assumed that only accidents which occurred within the state were here included.
† "Others" were included with "Passengers" in the 1874 and 1875 tables.

What the railroad commissioners did, however, was perhaps more significant than what they said: they kept yearly statistics on the number of deaths and injuries resulting from railroad accidents. The table on page 155 is a summary of these tabulations. After the railroad commissioners' reports began to be published the companies took care to distinguish between accidents "owing to the employees' own want of caution" and others. Commissioner Haugen saw through this strategem. "The companies' reports in that respect must be taken with some allowance, as juries not unfrequently differ with the officials as to the cause of accident and it is but natural that in doubtful cases the company in its reports should take the benefit of the doubt."[101] Beginning in 1890 the statistical tables divided accidents befalling persons other than passengers and employees into "trespassers" and "nontrespassers," classifications presumably authored by the railroads.

Other employer-employee relationships involved wage claims and obligations of employers to furnish board for their employees. The Wisconsin Supreme Court passed on both these matters.[102] Legislative intervention dealt only with liability for wages of successor roads.[103]

The beginnings of organized activity by labor in the United States elicited no public response by court or legislature in Wisconsin and inspired only alarm in Wisconsin governors. Governor Jeremiah M. Rusk probably typified the prevailing attitude toward the role of law in adjusting relationships between employer and employee when he remarked that

> . . . where one person engages to work for another, on another's premises and material, and with another's tools or machinery, it is equally clear that the product belongs to the employer; the workman's claim ends with the receipt of his stipulated wages. The State's duty and province in such cases is simply to maintain individual rights and enforce the fulfillment of contracts. Everyone's rights to work for himself, or for anyone else, on such terms as he

may choose to make, must be maintained at all hazards. He who interferes with this principle, tramples upon the most sacred of human rights and upon a consecrated principle of American liberty.[104]

* * *

DURING the years 1875–90 the role of law in adjusting the relationships between railroad and community was for the most part dull and dreary. It met most problems in a humdrum fashion and only occasionally came to grips with first-level substantive policy. In general the only noticeable difference between these years and the formative period was an increase in the volume of controversies.

Thus the Wisconsin Supreme Court disposed of some three hundred cases, of which no more than a third, by even a generous test of importance, could be said to deal with general policies. Most of the work consisted in routine development of the details of policy, such as construing condemnation and fencing statutes and establishing facts in accident cases. When the court dealt with a problem of first magnitude, such as the problem of industrial accidents, it contributed very little to an effective and permanent solution. To be sure, it supplemented the work it had done in the formative period by creating a tough body of common-law doctrine and a storehouse of techniques in judicial administration. In so doing it performed part of its task as a court and enhanced its position as the foremost agency of law in the minds of nineteenth-century Wisconsin citizens. But its prestige did not derive from effective handling of railroad problem; the court took little cognizance of the economic realities underlying the growth of the railroads.

So, too, on the legislative side. During this period the legislature enacted some hundred and seventy distinct laws dealing with railroad affairs, the great majority of which dealt either with local aid to railroads or with the parcelling out of the remainder of Wisconsin's land grants. In neither field did the legislature manifest the wisdom that it might be presumed to have gained from its experience during the formative period. It showed, as it had earlier, extreme sensitivity to the railroads' entreaties for land, tax exemption, and special privileges. When it did recognize a need for lending its power to the public interest, its efforts were weak, naïve, and ineffectual: it suffered direct regulation of rates to die of inactivity; it could not withstand the pressures that induced it to restore the fellow-servant rule to Wisconsin law in 1880; and its attempt to abrogate the rule again in 1889 was half-hearted and inadequate.

The governor's role was even smaller. The chief executives who followed William R. Taylor saw no issues that demanded a positive and supervisory role for law in the growth and development of railroads. Nor is there any evidence of significant activity on the part of the other executive officials. When the legislature abolished incorporation by special act in 1872, it transferred to the secretary of state the duty of passing on railroad charters and amendments. The effect of this was to give the railroads *carte blanche:* a document filed—if it complied with the technical requirements of the statute—was a document approved; no inquiry was made into the desirability, purpose, or effect of granting the charter. The railroad commissioners, stripped of authority by the 1876 act, did no more than collect data and make recommendations. Their chief value was that they kept the office alive and compiled basic data, so that when effective regulation did come under Robert M. La Follette, it had an institutional framework upon which to build.

In the meanwhile railroad building, development, and financing went on undisturbed. Unhampered by the weak "parallel line" limitation, consolidation and merger continued unabated, and companies staked out railroad systems with standards, ends, and means all of their own choosing. The financial revolution of the times went unrecognized in Wisconsin law, and the supervision of equity courts over foreclosure and receivership proceedings was meager and inadequate at best. Railroads built up, developed, parcelled out, and exploited the economy, and the law remained aloof. Perhaps the law was too weak to intervene; probably it saw no need to do so.

For Wisconsin lawmakers, particularly governors and railroad commissioners, like most nineteenth-century opinion-makers, saw no significant conflict of interests between the railroads and other groups of society. "Agrarian" was a term of opprobrium, not of description; "[Farmers] are not agrarians," said Governor Taylor.[105] Governor William D. Hoard's pronouncement was probably not atypical of his time and genre:

> . . . demagogues have sought to commend themselves to this element by advocating legislation of a most radical and destructive character. That they have hitherto failed in Wisconsin is due to the well informed conservatism of the farmer . . . and so, at the best, a large proportion of the difficulties which confront us, whether real or imaginary must find their solution in the great unwritten law of common sense and mutual interest. . . .
>
> Fortunately for the best interests of all concerned there has existed for years a friendly spirit of cooperation between the people and the roads, evolved from economic consideration of their mutual and correlative dependence.[106]

The Growth of Sanctions

From 1875 to 1890 Wisconsin law was no more creative in fashioning sanctions to implement policy dealing with problems foisted on it by the railroad than it was in designing the basic policy itself. Its record during the formative period, therefore, may well be incorporated by reference; there was little here that was new.

The Courts.—Wisconsin courts continued to create and fashion what were in effect sanctions out of rules of evidence, jurisdiction, procedure, and judicial administration. When it became necessary, for instance, to dull the edge of the fellow-servant rule, the Supreme Court adroitly used legal fictions, presumptions, constructive knowledge, and the burden of proof to carry deserving plaintiffs over doctrinal obstacles.[107] By directing trial courts to submit crucial issues to the jury, it expanded the possibilities for recovery. The court refused to entertain pending Potter Law prosecutions—in spite of a saving clause in the 1876 statute—yet it went on to fashion its own remedy: a common-law action for damages based on excessive charges.[108]

The power and prestige that contemporary opinion attached to judicial, as distinct from legislative, sanctions did not go unnoticed by the railroads. When they wanted relief they often resorted to one of the extraordinary remedies—frequently invoking the original jurisdiction of the Supreme Court—just as the state had done in the Railroad Companies case.[109] The court was careful not to expand the use of these extraordinary writs: in the second hearing of the original suit against the Milwaukee, for instance, Judge Ryan criticized the attorney general for overzealous use of the remedy of injunction.[110]

The Legislature.—Legislators showed little ingenuity in departing from conventional techniques for enforcing declared policy. Fines, imprisonment, and informers' statutes comprised the major part of the enforcement provisions of acts dealing with policies ranging from land-use programs to disorderly behavior on railroad cars and theft of railroad equipment.[111] Minor alterations in familiar techniques reveal little advance in sophistication: for violation of the fencing laws, for instance, the legislature merely prescribed a fixed fine rather than an action against the road for the value of the repairs.[112]

Even when a problem was *sui generis,* legislators showed little originality in designing sanctions. To implement its policy requiring foreign railroad corporations to appoint a statutory agent to accept service of process, the legislature levied a fine on the company for each violation. A far more effective remedy —as state legislatures were later to learn—was to deny access to the state courts to corporations failing to qualify.[113] In administering the land-grant property the legislature showed some sophistication when it put inertia on the side of action rather than inaction: it provided that where the railroad broke a statutory condition of the land grant, the attorney general might proceed in the Supreme Court to obtain a decree of forfeiture if the legislature had not already repealed the grant.[114]

In dealing with complicated intercorporate issues—the problem of interlocking directorates, for instance—the legislature displayed complete faith in the common-law fact-finding body: it placed determination of "parallel" or "competing" lines in the hands of the jury.[115] In its regulatory efforts it inadvertently replaced the Potter Law with a measure that was administratively more feasible, but at the same time prevented effectiveness by failing to provide adequate sanctions for its enforcement. Minor defects in the sanctions provided in the Potter Law the legislature noticed and attempted to remedy. By the amendments of 1875 it gave an aggrieved party an action against the corporation as well as against the agent; but in 1876 it substituted for this remedy an action for treble damages to be instituted by the attorney general on complaint of a private party submitted first to the railroad commissioner. Chief Justice Ryan, in sustaining the act, pointed out the difference in the two remedies and also showed an appreciation of the basic defectiveness of the change:

> Obviously the actions of 1874 and 1875 were given as a private, personal right. The action of 1876 appears to be given as a matter of state control over *quasi* public corporations, though the penalty goes to the injured party. That disposition of the penalty was probably intended to encourage injured parties to complaint to the proper officer of the state. But the change of the action was manifestly designed to relieve servants of the corporations from liability, and to protect the corporations themselves from being harassed by action at the personal discretion of parties claiming to be injured. The private actions of the two former statutes appear to have gone for private wrong alone. The *quasi* public of the latter statute

appear to go upon the public right also; redressing the private wrong indeed, but redressing it only by the state, when it shall be deemed material to public policy to redress it. The wisdom and justice of this provision may be questionable. But with that the court has nothing to do. It can only administer statutes as the legislature sees fit to pass them.[116]

When legislative prestige was at a low point, the power of investigation proved to be a powerful sanction. By exposing the scandals accompanying administration of the Railroad Farm Mortgage Land Company, as it had done with the disposition of the 1856 land grants twenty-five years before, the legislature probably regained some of the prestige it had lost and demonstrated once more its latent power to operate in the public interest by airing the dirty linen of Wisconsin officials who had perpetrated wholesale fraud.

Governor and Attorney General.—Wisconsin chief executives provided very little leadership in developing or even recommending effective sanctions. They displayed complacent satisfaction with the situation as it was; they saw no need to change existing methods of lodging complaints with the railroad commissioner, to improve administration of the tax laws, to supplement judicial handling of the problem of industrial accidents; they did not invoke the negative sanction they had at their command by refusing to certify transfer of land-grant tracts. Despite the fact that certain parts of the line of the Wisconsin Central Railroad had not been completed as required, Governor Taylor went ahead—reluctantly, to be sure—and certified the lands for transfer because the Secretary of the Interior had already done so. His duty, Taylor stated, was exclusively and simply ministerial.[117]

There is very little evidence that the attorney general and district attorneys were active in instituting enforcement suits under railroad statutes. After the Railroad Companies case they did invoke, sometimes too eagerly, the original jurisdiction of the Supreme Court and apply for the extraordinary remedies of injunction and quo warranto.[118] There is no way of knowing how many complaints lodged with the railroad commissioners found their way to the attorney general's desk nor how many of these he decided to act on. The number of reported cases instituted under the fine and imprisonment sections of the various railroad statutes indicates that district attorneys were also not particularly zealous in carrying out declared legislative policy.

The Railroad Commissioners.—The regulatory act of 1876 not only reduced the number of railroad commissioners from three to one but also limited the functions of the office to the compilation of statistics and the investigation of complaints and submission of findings to the attorney general. The law did not even make it the railroad commissioner's duty to include recommendations as to prosecutions in his report, and he had no power to institute compaints on his own initiative. To Wisconsin lawmakers of the day, however, this was as it should be. "The Commission in Wisconsin," said Governor Rusk, "is . . . one of suggestive and advisory powers, rather than arbitrary; and in no State has the commission system been productive of better results or more good than in our own, and I commend you to a careful study of the commissioner's report for the details of railroad work and railroad operation."[119] Weak though the office was, it now and then showed some vitality; by refusing to certify the sleeping-car companies for a license, for instance, the commissioner at least brought forth the issue for determination. But it was the state treasurer alone who had power to issue the license, and it was the court that, by holding with the railroads, refused to impose the sanction.[120]

Statutory changes in the commissioners' powers and duties enacted after 1876 were of little consequence. An act passed in 1885 required him to investigate any complaint within thirty days and report his findings to the attorney general within ten days thereafter.[121] At the very end of the period, in 1889, two changes of some significance were made. One act, insignificant on its face, permitted railroads to pass over drawbridges without stopping if they had interlocking devices *that had been approved by the railroad commissioner.*[122] Here at least was some legislative recognition of a function beyond the mere power to recommend. The other act also had significant implications for the growth of the administrative process. It permitted incorporated and unincorporated associations, as well as citizens, to lodge complaints, and it stated that if the commissioner "shall find . . . that the charges are well founded, he shall so decide, and the decision of the commissioner respecting such charges so investigated shall be final and conclusive, unless appealed from within twenty days from the service of such decision on the offending corporation to some court of competent jurisdiction in the county where complaint resides."[123] Thus the hole in the 1876 act was partly plugged; the commissioner's finding was at least entitled to some weight. The statute did not say how much and we do not know what weight the courts actually gave it in litigated cases. Presumably an appeal from a commissioner's award was subject to de novo review. Other statutory tinkerings with the office of railroad commissioner involved appropriations, appointments, and miscellaneous ministerial duties.[124]

One must not write off the whole railroad commissioner experiment as a failure. The mere fact of continuity was important, and the railroad commissioners' reports made two significant contributions: they included a body of reasonably accurate statistics on which future regulation could be based; and they mirrored, as possibly no other public documents did, the pattern of ideas about railroads and the law that pervaded the Wisconsin atmosphere in the 1880's. The 1876 act required railroads to submit certain data that the commissioner might request, but it went no further. It said nothing about the subpoena power to get data from reluctant roads. The legislature apparently did not want too much information: twice it passed laws limiting the length of the commissioner's report. Nevertheless the body of statistics compiled during these years is impressive.[125]

The contrast between the reports submitted by the three-member Potter Law commission—pro-Granger in outlook—and the subsequent officials is striking. From 1874 to 1876 the commissioners, though armed with no real enforcement power, evinced a willingness to enforce the policy of the statute. Subsequent commissioners regarded themselves as arbitrators, impartial in any conflict between the railroads and the law.[126] They failed to see the potentialities even of the weak position they occupied. The 1874 document ran to more than five hundred printed pages, of which about one-fourth constituted the report proper, as distinct from the accompanying documents, tables, statistics, etc. The first compilation under the 1876 act—Dana C. Lamb was railroad commissioner—contained only an eighteen-page report and reports of succeeding years were approximately the same length.

Of all the post-Granger commissioners, Nils Haugen was most aware of the basic defects of his position. He saw how unsatisfactory was the arrangement under which the facts pertaining to a license tax were determined by the commissioner whereas the state treasurer issued the license, sometimes without waiting for the commissioner's recommendation; he saw the economic reality that ran counter to the public cry for competition among roads, noting that parallel competing lines often led to needless duplication and suggesting that the railroad commissioner be empowered to determine the need for a parallel line as the Massachusetts commissioner was; and he saw through railroad practices of padding their mileage and writing down their earnings in order to reduce their license taxes.[127] To a lesser extent his successor, Atley Peterson, also saw basic defects in the act.[128] But it is doubtful whether even these two commissioners saw the fundamental fallacy in the theory underlying the act they were trying to administer, namely that it failed to define the commissioner either as arbitrator or as enforcement official but made him a little of each. Haugen and Peterson also probably shared the view of their contemporaries that there were really no basic conflicts between railroads, farmers, and the public for the law to administer, and that, by tightening up procedures here and there, all would be well in the Wisconsin community.

VI. Who Made the Decisions?

The inn that shelters for the night is not the journey's end. The law, like the traveler, must be ready for the morrow.
—BENJAMIN N. CARDOZO in *The Growth of the Law.*

THE morrow broke over Wisconsin when the railroads came and Wisconsin law was not quite ready. That it was unready is not surprising; never before had so formidable an economic institution, one creating so many complex problems, thrust itself on the attention of Wisconsin lawmakers. Between 1850 and 1890 railroads took a permanent place in the Wisconsin community as they had in the states to the east. By 1890 they had almost completed their network of lines, built their financial structures, routinized their operations, and refined their ways of dealing with public and private bodies. All this they did with considerable help and very little supervision from the law.

Law and the Delegation of Power.—During those four decades events moved fast and the pattern of ideas took a new form. The notion that railroad-building was a public function, widely accepted at the beginning, was faint indeed at the end. True, even at the time the first railroads were being built in Wisconsin, men of law no longer thought that the state itself was the proper agency to build the lines. But they did pay passing deference to the concept that construction by private associations was essentially a delegation of authority from the state. This explains in part the provision in the Wisconsin constitution giving the state a reserved power over corporations; it underlay the Supreme Court's language in the Falvey case; it was at the very heart of Justice Paine's analogy between railroad corporations and the federal government; it found expression in Governor Bashford's message to the special session of 1856 and in the words of Governor Barstow two years earlier; it formed the basis for legislative grants of special charters; and it was implicit in the grant of the power of eminent domain to private enterprise.[1]

But with the years Wisconsin lawmakers tended to forget this derivative nature of the railroad's power. As roads grew bigger and stronger and carved out large slices of what amounted to sovereign power, the law found it ever harder to reassert its control. This was particularly true of intercorporate and intracorporate affairs; the law paid little heed to the expansion and development of the corporate device that took place during this era. Even spokesmen for legal agencies voiced doubts whether those agencies had any power at all to impose their will on the roads. Astute railroad lawyers opened up the avenue of the contract clause and then, blocked by Judge Ryan, turned down the path of due process.

The legislature in general failed to establish its basic position of supremacy. In tinkering with the condemnation statutes, for instance, it became so preoccupied with detail that it all but forgot the quasi-sovereign basis for the grant of eminent domain. Nor did the mechanical way in which it ground out special charters show much perception of the fact that private companies were being granted portions of public authority.

When the legislature passed the general railroad act of 1872 it made the break almost complete. No longer must railroads come to the legislative body to obtain legal existence; if they complied with the very general terms of the statute, they needed only certification by the secretary of state. The change greatly lightened the load of the legislature and relieved it of much of the pressure to which it had been subjected by railroad promoters desiring special charters. But, by withholding from the secretary of state all substantive responsibility, the statute transformed the grant of corporateness into a mere ministerial act. A corporate charter, although it was a matter of public record, became in practice a semi-secret document likely to be known only to the company and the secretary of state.[2] It would probably have done no good to invest the secretary of state with authority to determine policy, for he was not, in this period of Wisconsin's history, equipped to make substantive decisions on the grant or denial of a charter. The fact remains, however, that the general corporation law, in effect, removed the railroad companies one more step from the status of quasi-public corporations. It was not the panacea that contemporary commentators said it was; there may have been a case for the special charter—to give form to what were, in fact, special situations.

Only once during these forty years did the law consciously and in a major way try to implement the public-utility concept of the railroad. This was through the Potter Law and its judicial sequel, the Railroad Companies case. Economic realities doomed the Potter Law to failure, but the principle of the injunction suits had lasting vitality. No one saw more clearly than Judge Ryan the essentially public nature of the railroads and none expressed this view so forcefully. Had nineteenth-century men of the law grasped the full import of his words concerning the similarity between public and private corporations, the history of corporate development might have been different. But only the basic and very general principle survived: that the state possessed a higher, more legitimate authority than the corporations it created.

Law and the Balance of Power.—Thus, shortly after the railroad came to Wisconsin, the law abandoned its concept of "delegation of power to private agency" and forfeited a clear claim to effective residual control. The role of legal supervision over the roads during these years, consequently, was a drab one. Only occasionally was there an attempt to use law to redress the balance of power. This is to say that, at this time and in this area of public concern, law was not used for what is one of its primary jobs: to keep account in the public interest of the over-all allocation of decision-making in the society and, when necessary, to correct dangerous imbalance by affirmative action. Ordinarily the law acts as umpire, arbitrating and administering disputes between two adverse parties presumed to have approximately equal power; only in making the final decision does it tip the scales in favor of one or the other. This is the classic pattern of the Anglo-American judicial process, and for ordinary matters it was equal to the task.

But sometimes it was not enough to be merely an umpire. New events, new institutions, new technology, and new concentrations of economic power presented certain challenges that could be met only by positive action. So it was with the railroad in Wisconsin. In their law, as in their business and social aspirations, the attitude of the people of Wisconsin toward the railroads was an ambivalent one. They wanted them intensely for the lasting prosperity they seemed to promise; at the same time there were those who saw in the growing power and independence of the roads a threat to the public welfare. Wisconsin law did not reflect this concern quite so clearly as Wisconsin politics did. In the formal pattern of its law Wisconsin rejected Taney's fears respecting the rise of corporations in favor of uncritical enthusiasm. Wisconsin politics, imbued with the antimonopoly sentiment of the times, railed constantly against the increasing number of consolidations and mergers. Yielding to the pressures thus created, Wisconsin law spoke through ineffectual statutes that permitted consolidations to go on apace. Neither law nor politics saw the problem as unique: that, given the economics of railroading, consolidation was inevitable and, with vigilant public regulation, would ultimately redound to the public good.

Men of law found it hard to meet, and sometimes even to see, the many new problems that the railroads ushered in. The concept of "property" represented by stock certificates did not fit neatly into an ancient law preoccupied by tradition and doctrine with land and cattle. The law failed, therefore, to refashion its control over property rights so as to surround these intangible interests with meaningful protection. In fact, the divergence between management and control that was taking place was uncurtailed, and indeed affirmatively aided, by agencies of law. In 1881, for instance, the legislature repealed a statute requiring the board of directors of the Milwaukee Road to obtain the approval of the stockholders in order to mortgage its lines.[3] When the law did step in to aid the stockholder, it spent all its energy in declaring policy and had none left for enforcement. The act of 1858, for instance, which came out of the legislative investigation did little to make the stockholder's position more secure.[4]

Nor did the law effectively counteract the power that the railroads exerted against official agencies. The anti-lobbying law of 1858 bristled with strong declarations, but it did not prevent the roads from dominating the Wisconsin legislature throughout most of the period from 1850 to 1890. To implement its policy the statute relied on the conventional sanctions of prosecution by the district attorney and fine and imprisonment. It ignored the fact that power had gone so far out of balance that the initiative and courage of isolated prosecutors and complainants would not suffice to bring declared policy to life.

Wisconsin law reflected little recognition of the industrial-urban-communication revolution that was running full course in the United States at this time. It failed to recognize the need for anything more than the time-tested techniques of an agricultural society. In this the law was not alone; it simply exemplified the limitations of imagination and will that characterized the society in which it worked.

To a degree at least, Wisconsin lawmakers saw the conflict of interest that has always accompanied creditor-debtor relationships in the United States. They responded to the cry against "Eastern capitalism" and "Wall Street," but theirs was a geographical analysis only. They did not see—and because they were too close to it, they could not see—that a molecularization of society into many interest groups, each with its own narrowly focused economic objective, was taking place throughout the land. Consequently they could not realize that this groupation process was creating more significant conflicts of interests than those born of mere geography.

And the law had its own inertia to overcome. Tough common-law doctrines did not yield easily to the rush of events: Wisconsin judges and legislators tusseled manfully with the fellow-servant rule before it finally yielded and then only in part; Chief Judge Ryan refused to accept the statutory abolition of contributory negligence under the fencing laws until the legislature had spelled it out in elaborate detail.[5]

The Relative Role of Court and Legislature.—By any test the major law-making job in these years was done by the courts. In grinding out decisions on a myriad of everyday controversies the courts fulfilled their proper function in society. In mid-nineteenth-century Wisconsin this work of the courts was important for another reason. A raw new state carved out of the frontier needed a legal system immediately; possessing the continuity of the common law and its tradition of judge-made policy, the courts were able to step in and fill the need. In so doing they gave legitimacy to government and built for themselves a position of prestige that other agencies of law could not match. And so the fate of legislative action—action relative to the farm-mortgage struggle, for instance, the local-aid controversies, the regulation of rates—depended ultimately on what the courts did. This was determined partly by the Wisconsin constitution and the American tradition of constitutionalism, but it is attributable no less to the superior prestige enjoyed by the judicial agency of law among Wisconsin citizens.

After they had shouldered the task of administering such law as there was, judges saw no reason why they should decide only routine and unspectacular disputes. Men enjoy responsibility with power once they have assumed it. It is hardly surprising then that the courts should have expressed policy boldly and balked at legislative attempts to abrogate sacred common-law doctrines. One can also understand how the Wisconsin Supreme Court could have decided a case involving illegal lobbying on common-law principles alone, completely ignoring a statute that covered the situation almost exactly.[6]

The legislature, on the other hand, was at low ebb during most of these years. On occasion it sallied forth to meet challenging problems of the railroad, as it did in passing the Potter Law, the land-grant statutes, and taxation and license-fee measures, but more often than not it sent a boy to do a man's job. In its handling of substantive legislation it often displayed ignorance of the exact nature of the problem, and in its enforcement provisions it demonstrated its incapacity to design sanctions adequate to implement its declared policy. There were many reasons for this failure of the legislature: its marked parochialism, stemming in part from the one-man geographic-district basis of representation; its susceptibility to friction and political in-fighting resulting from the two-house system; and its inadequate and inexpert staffing. Moreover, the change from annual to biennial sessions in 1881 was a further setback to continuity of policy. Yet even at its lowest depths the legislature showed a latent vitality in the exercise of its power of investigation; twice during this period it exposed land-grant scandals in the interest of the public good.

Little can be said for the executive. It was notoriously lacking in strong leadership. With the exception, perhaps, of Randall and Taylor, Wisconsin governors showed no appreciation of the potentialities of their office or of the public nature of the railroad problem. With the Potter Law came the crude beginnings of the administrative process—the Railroad Commission. But in a climate of opinion that depreciated the expert and failed to grasp the difficulty of the problem, no tradition of professional pride of office could grow. When the legislature emasculated the regulatory statute in 1876, it prevented the railroad commissioners from doing an effectual job thereafter. Nevertheless something was gained by the mere creation of the office; when the time came to revitalize it, as it did during the administration of Governor La Follette, there was a foundation, however shaky, on which to build.

Running through the entire period was that aspect of law called the Constitution. Its impact derived not so much from the formal amending process as from the idea of constitutionalism that was implicit in the work of other agencies of law. Federal and state constitutions were effective symbols in political and legal combat; an appeal to the constitution was likely to carry more weight than reliance on the merits. With its reserved power over corporations, its prohibition of direct state aid to railroads, and its provision requiring uniform taxation, the Wisconsin constitution prescribed limits to which other agencies of law had to conform.

Another characteristic of American ideas of law that manifested itself during this period was the tendency to seek a legal basis to justify group action. A classic example of lawmaking by private groups was the organization that the farm-mortgagors set up in their fight against foreclosure. Elaborate rules, implemented by more or less effective sanctions, governed the activities of these thousands of hapless farmers. Fifteen years later the Wisconsin Grange organized its members in similar tightly knit units to stage its campaign against the railroads.[7]

* * *

Who Made the Decisions?

IF THE record of formal agencies of law was not a noteworthy one, where did the real decision-making process go on? Presumably in the only place left: among the private groups and corporate enterprises that the law was trying to control. During the forty years from 1850 to 1890 the status of the railroad company developed from that of a creature of the state into that of a more or less autonomous maker and administrator of far-reaching economic policy. Virtually unhindered, it parcelled out segments of the economy and made good its claim that these segments were thereafter immune from governmental control. It stood up successfully to all agencies of law except the Supreme Court in the injunction suits. It perfected its own internal organization so as to center authority directly in management with little interference from ownership. It built financial structures almost beyond the comprehension, much less the control, of men of law.

The full story of this tremendous development cannot be told until corporate minute books, business records, and lawyers' files are opened up to historians. Generalizations, therefore, must be guarded; at best they can be no more than informed guesses respecting the details of this growth, development, and day-by-day operation of private government. It seems safe to say, however, that during this period of Wisconsin history the corporate community lived pretty much apart from formal agencies of law or that it found formal agencies of law to be useful tools in the pursuit of its own specific objectives.

Notes to the Text

I. WISCONSIN PURCHASE, 1856

[1] For general information on the economic development of Wisconsin at this stage of its history Frederick Merk's *The Economic History of Wisconsin during the Civil War Decade* (Madison, 1916) is still the best source. Also excellent for background material with specific reference to railroad development is Herbert W. Rice's manuscript dissertation, The Early History of the Chicago, Milwaukee, and St. Paul Railway Company, pages 1–36, in the library of the State University of Iowa.

[2] For a general discussion see Rice, *op. cit.*, 25–27.

[3] The Milwaukee and Waukesha charter is in *Laws of Wisconsin, Private and Local*, 1847, ch. 194. For general account see Rice, *op. cit.*, 12–14, and Balthasar H. Meyer, "A History of Early Railroad Legislation," in *Wisconsin Historical Collections*, 14:206 (1898).

[4] On early railroad construction see Rice, *op. cit.*, 46–85.

[5] On local aid to railroads see Balthasar H. Meyer, "Early General Railway Legislation in Wisconsin," in the *Transactions of the Wisconsin Academy of Sciences, Arts, and Letters*, 12:337, 354–364 (1898). On the farm mortgage scheme see pages 44–47 above and Merk, *op. cit.*, 238–270.

[6] On opposition to land grants see Rice, History of the Chicago, Milwaukee, and St. Paul (MS.), 153–154, and John M. Bernd, "The La Crosse and Milwaukee Railroad Land Grant, 1856," in the *Wisconsin Magazine of History*, 30:141 (December, 1946). On the reasons for the change in public opinion see John B. Sanborn, *Congressional Grants of Land in Aid of Railways* (*Bulletin of the University of Wisconsin*, no. 30, Madison, 1899), 54–55, and Lewis H. Haney, *A Congressional History of Railways in the United States, 1850–1887* (*Bulletin of the University of Wisconsin*, no. 342, Madison, 1910), 15–17. Typical memorials can be found in *General Laws of Wisconsin*, 1849, "Memorials," ch. 5, 6; 1850, ch. 4; 1851, ch. 14; 1852, ch. 23. Congressional action against land-grant bills is reported in the *Congressional Globe*, 31 Congress, 1 session (1850), 470–471, 494, 627, 845, 858–859, 1278, 1447, 1456, 1461, 1868; 32 Congress, 1 session (1851–52), 102, 107, 285, 673; 32 Congress, 2 session (1853), 313. The full-dress fight staged in 1854 is reported *ibid.*, 33 Congress, 1 session (1854), 88, 181, 350, 467–470, 498, 515, 626–630. The 1856 grant is in *United States Statutes at Large*, 11:20 (1856). See also the *Congressional Globe*, 34 Congress, 1 session (1856), 1259–1261, 1272–1273, 1316, 1333, 1338, 1344, 1384.

[7] The biographical account of Kilbourn which follows is based mainly on a sketch prepared under the Works Progress Administration as part of a projected dictionary of Wisconsin biography, now being revised in preparation for publication by the State Historical Society of Wisconsin. See also Milo M. Quaife, ed., *The Attainment of Statehood* (*Wisconsin Historical Collections*, Vol. 29: *Constitutional Series*, Vol. 4, Madison, 1928), 914, and Rice, History of the Chicago, Milwaukee, and St. Paul (MS.), 49–52.

[8] One historian states that the Constitutional Convention of 1846 "probably owed more to Mr. Strong's influence than to that of any other man." Milo M. Quaife, ed., *The Convention of 1846* (*Wisconsin Historical Collections,* Vol. 27: *Constitutional Series,* Vol. 2, Madison, 1919), 794. A recent biography of Strong is Kenneth W. Duckett's *Frontiersman of Fortune: Moses M. Strong of Mineral Point* (Madison, 1955). See also Milo M. Quaife, ed., *Strong and Woodman Manuscript Collections in the Wisconsin State Historical Library* (State Historical Society of Wisconsin, *Bulletin of Information,* no. 78, Madison, 1915), 4–11.

[9] See Rice, History of the Chicago, Milwaukee, and St. Paul (MS.), 60. The charter is chapter 198 of *General Laws of Wisconsin,* 1852.

[10] Rice, History of the Chicago, Milwaukee, and St. Paul (MS.), 150. The clause is found in *General Laws of Wisconsin,* 1852, ch. 198, sec. 12, and its repeal in ch. 487, sec. 3.

[11] "Make a death struggle for a grant, and secure it if in the bounds of possibility, as with it we will put to shame the other company [the Milwaukee and Mississippi] and oust the present board.—It can be done if you succeed, to a certainty almost, and perhaps it can if you do not, but it will be in that case more difficult. But you *must not fail* if possible to avoid it. Talk to the South about Pierce and King, and tell them they are gone if they do not do something for the west.—I believe, in fact, that Scott stands a full equal chance for Wisconsin, and the only way to prevent it is for the democrats to do something for us." Kilbourn to Strong, August 9, 1852, in the Moses M. Strong Railroad Papers, 1835–56, in the possession of the State Historical Society of Wisconsin.

[12] See Bernd, in the *Wisconsin Magazine of History,* 30:144–145.

[13] For the 1856 grant see *United States Statutes at Large,* 11:20, sec. 1 (1856).

[14] Testimony of Moses Strong in the *Report of the Joint Select Committee Appointed to Investigate into Alleged Frauds and Corruption in the Disposition of the Land Grant by the Legislature of 1856, and for Other Purposes,* in the Appendix to the *Wisconsin Assembly Journal,* 1858, pp. 38–43. This document is in two parts: the report proper of the investigating committee and the transcript of testimony heard by the committee.

[15] The account of Kilbourn's generalship from the Capital House is based on Testimony of Thomas Falvey, 59–60, in the *Report of the Joint Select Committee.* On the events that made Kilbourn change his strategy see above, pages 10–12.

[16] *Wisconsin Assembly Journal,* Adjourned Session, 1856, p. 857. The motions may be found both in the *Assembly Journal,* 1027, 1042, and in the *Senate Journal,* 1083–1084. See also Rice, History of the Chicago, Milwaukee, and St. Paul (MS.), 151–152.

[17] *Wisconsin Assembly Journal,* Adjourned Session, 1856, p. 852.

[18] On the competing requests of the railroads see the *Assembly Journal,* Adjourned Session, 1856, p. 869, and the *Senate Journal,* 955, 1009.

[19] The memorials are in the *Wisconsin Senate Journal,* Adjourned Session, 1856, pp. 928–931, and in the *Assembly Journal,* 869–873. Regarding the rivalry between Chicago and Milwaukee see the explanation Kilbourn gave at the investigation two years later. *Report of the Joint Select Committee,* 4–6.

[20] See pages 14–15.

[21] *Wisconsin Assembly Journal,* Adjourned Session, 1856, pp. 869–873, 893–902, 928–931; *Senate Journal,* 943, 973–982, 1005–1008.

[22] The consolidation act was chapter 517 of *Laws of Wisconsin,* 1856. See the *Report of the Joint Select Committee,* 27–28, and Rice, History of the Chicago, Milwaukee and St. Paul (MS.), 69.

[23] This arrangement occupied much of the 1858 investigating committee's attention. See the *Report of the Joint Select Committee,* 27–30. Much of the testimony taken by the committee was addressed to this point. See the testimony of Byron Kilbourn, Moses Kneeland, William A. Barstow, John Lockwood, Prentis Dow, and others. On the interview with Judge Smith, see page 22 below.

[24] See Testimony of Moses Strong, 38–42, in the *Report of the Joint Select Committee,* and, on the shift in strategy, pages 10–12 above.

[25] The path of the bill can be traced in the *Wisconsin Senate Journal,* Adjourned Session, 1856, pp. 1122, 1132, 1135, 1143. Bashford's veto message may be found on pages 1143–1148. George B. Smith, a leading Madison attorney and member of the legislature in 1856, made the following notations in his diary: '*Tuesday, October 7* [1856]. Bashford vetoed bill giving land grant to La Crosse Co. Reasons poor. . . . *Monday, October 13.* Land grant bill all signed. Bashford has disgraced himself in these matters." Diary of George B. Smith, 1856, in the George B. Smith Papers in the State Historical Society of Wisconsin.

[26] Bill 775A was introduced, read three times, passed by both houses, enrolled, signed by the speaker of the Assembly and president of the Senate, and sent to the governor—all in two days time (October 9 and 10). *Wisconsin Senate Journal,* Adjourned Session, 1856, pp. 1170, 1171, 1172, 1173, 1174, 1181–82, 1183; *Assembly Journal,* 1179.

[27] See Testimony of James Duane Doty, 170 ff., in the *Report of the Joint Select Committee,* and the statement of the committee, *ibid.,* 45–46.

[28] On Ogden see Thomas W. Goodspeed, *The University of Chicago Biographical Sketches,* 1:35 (1922).

[29] The account of the bribery is based on the *Report of the Joint Select Committee, passim.*

[30] *Ibid.,* 113–114. Cobb's inference that Alexander Mitchell was a prominent party to the bribery is not corroborated by other evidence. See also "The Question Box—Honest Amasa Cobb," in the *Wisconsin Magazine of History,* 5:208 (December, 1921).

[31] On the financial condition of the La Crosse and Milwaukee see the *Report of the Joint Select Committee,* 39–43.

[32] On Farwell's intervention see, in the *Report of the Joint Select Committee,* Testimony of Leonard J. Farwell, 155–156, and Testimony of Byron Kilbourn, 24 (denying that he gave Tenney ten thousand dollars in stocks and bonds for suppressing his report). See also Josiah A. Noonan, "A Reply to Byron Kilbourn," in the *Milwaukee Sentinel,* June 18, 1857 (asking for an investigation). On the two Eastern investigations see the *Report of the Joint Select Committee,* 41–43.

[33] *Wisconsin Assembly Journal,* 1857, pp. 214, 259, 573, 574–575, 576, 577, 578, 625–626 (minority report of Z. R. Mason of Sheboygan); *Senate Journal,* 361, 405–406, 433. See also Kilbourn's report to the legislature on the state of progress of the La Crosse and Milwaukee, *ibid.,* 94–99.

[34] *Report of the Joint Select Committee,* 47. See also *ibid.,* Testimony of Moses Strong, 46–47, of Thomas Falvey, 72, of Edwin H. Goodrich, 77, of H. L. Palmer, 108, and of Orrin T. Maxon, 149–151. There were strong rumors that another barrage of bribery had choked off an investigation. See *Facts for the People: Addressed to the Electors of Wisconsin* (1857), a pamphlet in the possession of the State Historical Society of Wisconsin.

[35] *General Laws of Wisconsin,* 1857, ch. 70.

[36] See Annual Message of Governor Alexander Randall in the *Wisconsin Senate Journal,* 1858, pp. 42–43, and Memorial of Citizens of Columbia County in the

Assembly Journal, 130. See also Rice, History of the Chicago, Milwaukee and St. Paul (MS.), 110.

[37] The governor's remarks are in the *Wisconsin Assembly Journal,* 1858, pp. 22–23, and the formation of the Joint Select Committee is recorded on pages 51, 52, 59, 77.

[38] Testimony of Moses Strong, 40–41, of James H. Earnest, 119–120, and of Moses Strong, 42, in the *Report of the Joint Select Committee.* Knowlton's identity with the "association" is shown in the *Wisconsin Assembly Journal,* Adjourned Session, 1865, pp. 1068, 1126, 1127.

[39] At least the converse is true. Kilbourn and Strong harbored a strong dislike for Knowlton. See Byron Kilbourn to Moses Strong, December 6, 1856, in the Moses M. Strong Railroad Papers. See also Byron Kilbourn, *Review of the Report of the Investigating Committee,* 46–55, a pamphlet in the possession of the State Historical Society of Wisconsin. Knowlton was the plaintiff in a famous taxpayer's suit challenging the constitutionality of an 1854 statute taxing railroads. See Willard Hurst and Betty R. Brown, "The Perils of the Test Case," in the *Wisconsin Law Review,* 1949, pp. 26, 49–51, and page 84 above. He was also champion of the oppressed farm mortgagors in their struggle with the Eastern mortgage-holders and later the candidate of the farmers for a place in the Supreme Court. See page 192, note below and pages 58–59 above.

[40] *Wisconsin Assembly Journal,* 1858, pp. 59, 102, 128–129, 185–186.

[41] In re Falvey, 7 Wis. 630 (1858). See page 20 above.

[42] *Wisconsin Assembly Journal,* 1858, pp. 170–172, 191–195. The recommended legislation became chapter 4 of *General Laws of Wisconsin,* 1858. See pages 24–25 above.

[43] *Annual Report of the La Crosse and Milwaukee Railroad Company,* 1858, Appendix, 13 ff. The applicable section of the land-grant act was chapter 43, section 4, of *United States Statutes at Large,* 11:20 (1856).

[44] Cleveland v. La Crosse and Milwaukee Railroad, 5 Fed. Cas. No. 2, 887 (D. Wis., 1859). See also Rice, History of the Chicago, Milwaukee, and St. Paul (MS.), 170–172.

[45] *Report of the Joint Select Committee,* 38–39. The lease is set out in Documentary Evidence, pp. 286–289, *ibid.* See also Testimony of Prentis Dow, pp. 165, 168–169, *ibid.*

[46] In re Falvey, 7 Wis. 630 (1858).

[47] On the proceedings in the Assembly see the *Wisconsin Assembly Journal,* 1859, pp. 320–333, 334–336, 339–344, 376–378 (Falvey) and 379–384, 418–420 (Kilbourn). The writ is described in In re Falvey, 7 Wis. 630, 640–642 (1858).

[48] *General Laws of Wisconsin,* 1858, ch. 4. This was the law that had been recommended by the investigating committee.

[49] In re Falvey, 7 Wis. 630 (1858).

[50] This was not the first instance of legislative investigating committees. The infamous 1856 legislature itself had conducted a probe of certain executive agencies. See the Appendix to the *Wisconsin Assembly Journal,* 1856, Vol. 2.

[51] In re Falvey, 7 Wis. 630 (1858). The Falvey case was one of the early state cases on this point and United States Supreme Court precedents were few. See C. S. Potts, "Power of Legislative Bodies to Punish for Contempt," in the *University of Pennsylvania Law Review,* 74·691, 780 (May, 1926), and Oren C. Herwitz, William G. Mulligan, Jr., and Samuel Seabury, "The Legislative Investigating Committee," in the *Columbia Law Review,* 33:1 (January, 1933).

[52] *Wisconsin Assembly Journal,* 1858, pp. 320–333 (description of procedure concerning Falvey). See also the copy of the subpoena served on Moses Strong

to give testimony concerning conduct of William Chappell and Strong's answers to interrogatories, in the Moses M. Strong Railroad Papers.

[53] Testimony of Byron Kilbourn, 3, in *Report of the Joint Select Committee.* As to the formality of interrogatories see those served on Strong in the Moses M. Strong Railroad Papers.

[54] On the reaction of the newspapers see August W. Derleth, *The Milwaukee Road: Its First Hundred Years* (New York, 1948), 85. The report submitted by the dissenting committee member can be found in the *Wisconsin Assembly Journal,* 1957, pp. 625–626. The *Wisconsin Revised Statutes* of 1849, ch. 136, sec. 8 and 9, provided for punishment of legislative, judicial, and executive officials convicted of taking bribes.

[55] *Report of the Joint Select Committee,* 23.

[56] Testimony of Abram D. Smith, 147–148, *ibid.*

[57] *Report of the Joint Select Committee,* 27.

[58] Rice, History of the Chicago, Milwaukee, and St. Paul (MS.), 152.

[59] *Report of the Joint Select Committee,* 25–26.

[60] The inference is strong that Barstow, as much as Kilbourn and Strong, was behind the extra-legal conveyance of the northern part of the northwest lands to the St. Croix and Superior Railroad. See the *Report of the Joint Select Committee,* 28–29, and Testimony of Moses Kneeland, 80–86, *ibid.* According to a contemporary commentator, it was a "mere toss of a copper" as between Barstow and Bashford. Alexander M. Thomson, *A Political History of Wisconsin* (Milwaukee, 1900), 129. For the citation of Barstow and his discharge from custody see the *Wisconsin Assembly Journal,* 1858, pp. 446–449, 461.

[61] *Wisconsin Assembly Journal,* 1858, pp. 495, 497, 534. For the votes of confidence, see *ibid.,* 59, 102, 128–129, 1186. Knowlton would almost always ask the witness whether he knew of any facts implicating James H. Knowlton—or sometimes more vaguely "anyone else"—in the affair. And, except for Strong and Falvey, the witnesses answered in the negative. See Testimony of Byron Kilbourn, 24–25, of A. Hyatt Smith, 57–58, and of Isaac Woodle, 58–59, in *Report of the Joint Select Committee.*

[62] For Strong's charges against Knowlton see Testimony of Moses Strong, 42–43. See also Petition of Moses Strong in the Moses M. Strong Railroad Papers. For Kilbourn's charges see his pamphlet *Review of the Report of the Investigating Committee.* He said the same thing in his letters to Strong of March 26 and December 6, 1858, in the Moses M. Strong Railroad Papers.

[63] On Strong's incarceration in jail see pages 27-28 above.

[64] Kilbourn seemed strangely cool toward Strong's plans for revenge. "I have no heart," he wrote, "to engage in the enterprise you propose, for the reason that those who ought to cooperate with us, only seek an opportunity to stab me, and will not sustain you. I would as soon trust Noonan, Randall, Knowlton et al. as Barstow, A. H. Smith and their peculiar friends." He went on to say that he would aid Strong behind the scenes, but he must not be expected "to take a leading part." Kilbourn to Strong, April 12, 18, 1858, in reply to Strong's letter of March 31, all in the Moses M. Strong Railroad Papers.

[65] After participating in the investigation, in the test taxpayer's suit, and in the farm-mortgage struggle Knowlton finally moved to Chicago in 1861. John R. Berryman, *History of the Bench and Bar in Wisconsin* (Chicago, 1898), 2:197.

[66] *General Laws of Wisconsin,* 1858, ch. 91. Governor Randall had called for it in his annual message (Appendix to the *Wisconsin Assembly Journal,* 1858, p. 24), and the investigating committee concluded its report with the recommendation. *Report of the Joint Select Committee,* 47–48. See also the "Report of the Select Committee to Investigate the Affairs of the Milwaukee and Superior Railway," in

the *Wisconsin Assembly Journal,* 1858, pp. 1831–43. The 1857 act concerning fraudulent stock transfers was of course directed toward the same general objective. See above, pages 48–49.

[67] *General Laws of Wisconsin,* 1858, ch. 91, sec. 1, 2.

[68] *Ibid.,* sec. 3.

[69] *Ibid.,* sec. 9.

[70] *Ibid.,* ch. 145, sec. 1, 2.

[71] See Rice, History of the Chicago, Milwaukee, and St. Paul (MS.), 151–152. On the La Crosse and Milwaukee securities see the *Report of the Joint Select Committee,* 41, and the Testimony of Prentis Dow, 164–165, *ibid.* Dow was New York financial agent for the La Crosse and Milwaukee Railroad.

[72] On the reaction in the East see the cartoon in the *Harper's Weekly,* reprinted in Derleth's *Milwaukee Road,* page 90, and above, facing page 19, depicting the purchase of legislators by the dozen.

[73] On the farm-mortgage device, see pages 44–46.

[74] *Wisconsin Assembly Journal,* 1858, pp. 2225–2226 (Index).

[75] The account of Strong's conflict with the committee is based on the *Wisconsin Assembly Journal,* 1858, pp. 1028–1031, 1034–1056, 1080, 1103, 1153, 1161, 1185, and Kilbourn's letter to Strong, March 26, 1858, in the Moses M. Strong Railroad Papers. Strong's petition—addressed to the committee on the judiciary—alleged that the Assembly had acted illegally. The judiciary committee admitted that the Assembly had been in error but nevertheless concluded that since the procedures were regular and Strong had been adjudged on the record before the Assembly, the citation for contempt must stand. Report of the Majority of the Judiciary Committee on Memorial of Moses Strong, in the Moses M. Strong Railroad Papers. A detailed account of the whole affair is given in Duckett's *Frontiersman of Fortune,* 136–140.

[76] See page 5 above.

[77] See, for example, the argument of land-grant congressmen that the question how the land granted should be given was a matter of state rather than federal policy. *Congressional Globe,* 33 Congress, 1 session (1854), 498. The large grants made to the transcontinental railroads in the sixties, however, by-passed the states. See Haney, *A Congressional History of Railways in the United States,* 19–20. The public domain was of course the exclusive estate of the federal government. *United States Constitution,* Art. IV, sec. 2(2). See Thomas C. Donaldson, *The Public Domain: Its History with Statistics* (Washington, 1884), 14.

[78] Jackson Hadley, Kilbourn's lieutenant, took $200,000 in land-grant bonds to use in getting a Minnesota land grant through Congress. *Report of the Joint Committee,* 21–23. See also Testimony of Moses Kneeland, 77–78, of Jackson Hadley, 126–130, and of Prentis Dow, 167, *ibid.* On the activity of Kilbourn and Strong see the discussion on pages 7-8 above. On Ogden and the Chicago promoters' activities, see Memorials from Mayor and Common Council of Oshkosh and of the Chicago, St. Paul and Fond du Lac Railroad, in the *Wisconsin Assembly Journal,* Adjourned Session, 1856, pp. 1014, 1119. See also Bernd, in the *Wisconsin Magazine of History,* 30:144–145.

[79] See the discussion on pages 82-83 above.

[80] *Wisconsin Constitution,* Art. XI, sec. 1, and *Wisconsin Revised Statutes,* 1849, ch. 54. For a general discussion see Meyer in *Wisconsin Historical Collections,* 14:261–300.

[81] *Ibid.,* 261, 284–292.

[82] *Ibid.,* 265–284, 292.

[83] See, for example, *Private and Local Laws of Wisconsin,* 1857, ch. 314 (an act amending the charter of the La Crosse and Milwaukee to provide for a change

in the time of meeting of the board of directors). A typical example is *General Laws of Wisconsin,* 1856, ch. 137 (charter of the Wisconsin and Superior).

[84] In 1853, for instance, twenty-five new charters and nineteen amendatory acts were passed. See the index to *Private and Local Laws of Wisconsin,* 1853. See also Rice, History of the Chicago, Milwaukee and St. Paul (MS.), 120.

[85] *Private and Local Laws of Wisconsin,* 1852, ch. 198, sec. 12; ch. 487, sec. 3.

[86] On the difficulties of the Wisconsin and Superior and the northeast portion of the land grant see the *Report of the Joint Select Committee,* 45–48, and Testimony on the Northeast Grant, 170–211, *ibid.* Examination of the testimony on the disposal of the northeast tract and of the various bills drafted to incorporate the recipient road leads to the conclusion that Bashford and key legislators insisted on controlling some members of the board of directors. See, for example, *General Laws of Wisconsin,* 1856, ch. 140 (amending the charter of the Wisconsin and Superior so as to give the governor power to appoint two directors) and Bills 776A and 431S (incorporating the Wisconsin and Superior), Session of 1856, in the possession of the State Historical Society of Wisconsin.

[87] For newspaper comments see the *Milwaukee Daily Sentinel,* February 12, 1852, quoted in Rice's manuscript History of the Chicago, Mliwaukee, and St. Paul, 120. See also the letter from "Badger" in the issue for February 14, 1857, likewise quoted by Rice, page 124: "The multiplication of charters and this mania for new schemes bids fair to upset public confidence, and run down all useful projects. Who will venture to send his capital to this state, for investment in the most promising road if every session of the legislature brings forth charters of new companies, to build rival roads and eat out its legitimate business? . . . No state equals Wisconsin, in the inducements offered for the investment of foreign capital. No state is more in danger of throwing away her peerless advantages." For the debate on the general incorporation bill, see the *Wisconsin Senate Journal,* 1853, p. 474, and the *Assembly Journal,* pp. 400, 406, 502, 503, 635, 717, 843. The bill was a long structure of forty-three sections: "Bill No. 275A—To Authorize the Formations of Railroad Corporations and to Regulate the Same" in the possession of the State Historical Society of Wisconsin. See also Meyer in the *Transactions of Wisconsin Academy of Sciences, Arts, and Letters,* 12:337, 342–345. Two other attempts were made during this period to introduce general railroad legislation, but they were unsuccessful. *Wisconsin Assembly Journal,* 1855, p. 270 (select committee recommended that general railroad bill be passed and grant of special charters be done away with) and *ibid.,* 1857, pp. 303, 328 (resolution as to desirability of general railroad incorporation defeated).

[88] The provision of the two acts are in *United States Statutes at Large,* 11:20 (1856), and *General Laws of Wisconsin,* 1856, ch. 122, sec. 4. On the wholesale mortgaging see the *Report of the Joint Select Committee,* 28–29.

[89] See the discussion on page 22 and the attendant documentation.

[90] The legislators from this area stacked the Wisconsin and Superior board of directors in favor of the Chicago, St. Paul and Fond du Lac. And Bashford himself was from Oshkosh. See Testimony on the Northeast Grant, 170–211, in *Report of the Joint Select Committee.*

[91] On the party line-up of the legislature see the *Milwaukee Daily Sentinel,* November 13, 1857, p. 1, col. 1. Moses Strong characterized the legislature as follows: "To that decision (of the people as to my motives) I am content to submit and I shall cheerfully acquiesce in the verdict of my fellow citizens, with a full consciousness that I have done no intentional wrong, and that my most serious error was intrusting to the justice of a Black Republican Legislature, to respect rights guaranteed to the humblest citizen of the state." Moses Strong's

"Appeal to the People," p. 5, in the Moses M. Strong Railroad Papers. On Randall's politics see A. M. Thomson, *A Political History of Wisconsin* (Milwaukee, 1900), 139. On the party line-up in the 1856 legislature see the *Milwaukee Daily Sentinel,* December 12, 1855, p. 2, col. 2. Compare *To the People of the 11th Senate District* (1859), a pamphlet in the possession of the State Historical Society of Wisconsin (labeling the "corruptionists of 1856" as Republican) with J. A. Noonan's letter in the *Milwaukee Weekly Sentinel,* September 1, 1858 ("Messrs. Kilbourn, Barstow & Co. have been mainly instrumental in bringing the unfortunate and disgraceful condition of affairs upon the Democratic Party in this state. . . . Another winter's investigation may be necessary to enable them definitely to make up their minds whether there is any immorality in bribing public officials, or in forging election returns.") The two parties both took a stand in their platforms. The Republicans "Resolved, That the corruption and abuses in National and State Governments, and municipal and other corporations, have been the chief cause of the destruction of public and private credit; that while we recognize the vast benefits flowing from railroads, and would be the first to extend all proper aid and encouragement to every enterprise of internal improvement, we hold it to be the right and duty of the Legislature in protecting the public, to investigate into all frauds and mismanagement of railroad and other corporations of the State, and to guard against the recurrence of like abuses by the most stringent laws." Resolutions of Republican State Convention, 1858, in Roy O. I. Holmes's unpublished bachelor's thesis, Wisconsin State Party Platforms, 1848–1865, p. 102, in the library of the State Historical Society of Wisconsin. The Democrats "Resolved, That the Democratic party of this State repudiate the idea of apologizing for, excusing, or in any manner justifying the frauds and corruptions of the legislature of 1856, in disposing of the Rail Road Land Grants, and that we discontinue and condemn all persons engaged in those frauds, and that we trust our State may never again be disgraced by corruption on the part of the Legislature or Executive." Resolutions of the Democratic State Convention, 1859, *ibid.,* 107.

[92] The year 1853 "seems to have been the first time that the legislature was systematically worked by a railroad lobby and the methods employed this winter were such as to scandalize many good citizens." Leroy J. N. Murat, The Administration of Governor Barstow, 11–12, a manuscript thesis in the library of the State Historical Society of Wisconsin. The "forty thieves" and "Monk's Hall" were epithets for the railroad lobbyists and their meeting place during the legislative session of 1853. *Ibid.* "Barstow and the balance" refers to a remark of a Madison publisher who, when Barstow was governor, said he would get the state printing contract even if he had to buy out "Barstow and the balance" (of the printing commissioners). Reuben G. Thwaites, *Wisconsin: The Americanization of a French Settlement* (Boston and New York, 1908), 306–307.

[93] Testimony of Byron Kilbourn, 9–10, in the *Report of the Joint Select Committee.*

[94] Testimony of Newcomb Cleveland, 122, 124–125 (regarding payments to Stephen Alden and Moses Kneeland) and of Selah Chamberlain, 130–133 (payments to Daniel Wells and Stephen Alden) in the *Report of the Joint Select Committee.*

[95] The committee concluded that the directors were guilty of a breach of trust when they resigned under such circumstances as were brought out with respect to the northeast grant. "It was a violation of a duty when done for a personal pecuniary consideration." *Report of the Joint Select Committee,* 46. See also Testimony of Eliphalet Cramer, 91–94, *ibid.* (offer of $10,000 to resign as a director of La Crosse and Milwaukee).

[96] On the eighty thousand-dollar payment to the directors see the *Report of the Joint Select Committee,* 30–31, and Testimony of Levi Burnell and of Newcomb Cleveland, 116–119, 120, *ibid.* But see also Testimony of Moses Kneeland, 71 (denial). The transfer of the school land is described on page 73 of the *Report* and in the Testimony of Newcomb Cleveland, 121. The officer was Levi Burnell. For the terms of the land transfer by the La Crosse and Milwaukee see page 124 of the *Report.*

[97] The existing statute was *Wisconsin Revised Statutes,* 1849, ch. 136. Mason of Sheboygan, dissenting from the majority report of the 1857 committee that recommended against an investigation, summed up the situation thus: "To leave these questions of fraud to the courts, is virtually abandoning the same, for a majority of the committee as well as this House must be aware that no prosecutions would ever take place under the statutes." *Wisconsin Assembly Journal,* 1857, pp. 625–626. On the anti-lobbying law that came out of the 1858 investigation see page 25 above and accompanying notes.

[98] Typical of this attitude are the remarks Kilbourn made in his 1857 report to the legislature, in which he urged that they hold off on an investigation. *Wisconsin Senate Journal,* 1857, p. 98 (the state's "inexhaustible resources").

[99] The population figure is from the *Seventh Census of the United States* (Washington, 1853), 918–924. On the hustling of stock agents, etc., see Rice, History of the Chicago, Milwaukee, and St. Paul (MS.), 86 ff.

[100] In re Falvey, 7 Wis. 630, 636 (1858).

[101] On a somewhat comparable situation in Pennsylvania see Louis Hartz, *Economic Policy and Democratic Thought: Pennsylvania, 1776–1860* (Cambridge, 1948), 129–180.

[102] "The state shall never contract any debt for works of internal improvement, or be a party in carrying on such works; but whenever grants of land or other property shall have been made to the state, especially dedicated by the grant to particular works of internal improvement, the state may carry on such particular works, and shall devote thereto the avails of such grants, and may pledge or appropriate the revenues derived from such works in aid of their completion." *Wisconsin Constitution,* Art. VIII, sec. 10. "Though the constitution was rejected by the people this section met with great and general approval. It was said by Mr. Estabrook to have been 'as the precious jewel in the head of the toad'." Jones v. Froelich, 115 Wis. 32, 38 (1902), quoted in Ray A. Brown, "The Making of the Wisconsin Constitution," in the *Wisconsin Law Review,* 1949, pp. 648, 675–676.

[103] For a recent unfortunate consequence of the provision see State ex rel. Martin v. Giessel, 252 Wis. 363 (1948), in which the Veteran's Housing law was held unconstitutional.

[104] *Congressional Globe,* 33 Congress, 1 session (1854), 510–512. On the tendency to promote monopoly see the remarks of Senator Letcher of Virginia concerning the Illinois Central land grant of 1850 and its ultimate effect of creating a monopoly in the hands of the Illinois Central. *Ibid.,* 513. Bashford's remarks are included in the *Wisconsin Assembly Journal,* Adjourned Session, 1856, pp. 850–851.

[105] See Rice, History of the Chicago, Milwaukee, and St. Paul (MS.), 86 ff.

[106] For the debates in Congress see the *Congressional Globe,* 33 Congress, 1 session (1854), 499, 510–514.

[107] The investigating committee's conclusion was that "The testimony presents a strong probability that the control of the Wisconsin Company [the Wisconsin & Superior] would not have passed into the hands of any other company, but for the action of P. H. Smith [legislator from Winnebago County], and the *repre-*

sentative directors, named by Senators already stated." *Report of the Joint Select Committee* 47 (italics in the original). See also Testimony of James D. Doty, 170–177, 179–180, of William Scott, 185–188, of Anson Ballard, 188–190, of Julius White, 191–192, 194–195, of Cyrus P. Hiller, 196–197, and of Nelson K. Wheeler, 197–204, in the *Report of the Joint Select Committee.* The two roads were formally consolidated in 1857. *General Laws of Wisconsin,* 1857, ch. 17. The La Crosse and Milwaukee interests were apparently also willing to make concessions. Moses Kneeland reputedly offered money to get members of the board of the Wisconsin and Superior to resign in favor of men picked by the La Crosse and Milwaukee. *Report of the Joint Select Committee,* 47. As to Kilbourn's and Ogden's main interest in the northwest line, see, respectively, Testimony of Byron Kilbourn, 9, and the Memorial of the Chicago, St. Paul and Fond du Lac Railroad in the *Wisconsin Assembly Journal,* Adjourned Session, 1856, p. 1014 (asking for northeast tract only).

[108] From the beginning of railroad construction, apparently, it was common practice for construction firms to take part of their pay in securities of the road they were building. See Harry H. Pierce, *Railroads of New York: A Study of Government Aid, 1826–1875* (Cambridge, 1953), 5.

[109] See excerpts of minutes reprinted in the Appendix to the *Wisconsin Assembly Journal,* 1858, p. 244 (charging large amounts as charter expenses to northwestern division) and p. 249 (payment of $5,000 to M. Shoeffler, newspaper editor, "in pursuance to promise made by the president of this company, and charged the same to charter expenses"; authorizing issuance of many stock certificates to Kilbourn for use of "benefit of company").

[110] See pages 46–47 above.

[111] The so-called "Albany Board" was in control of the La Crosse and Milwaukee from about the end of 1857. *Report of the Joint Select Committee,* 43–44.

[112] Vose, Livingston & Co., for instance, was a New York supplier of the La Crosse and Milwaukee. On Cleveland see Edmund J. Cleveland, *The Geneology of Cleveland and Cleveland Families* (Hartford, 1899), 1:694; on Chamberlain see *The Biographical Cyclopaedia . . . of Ohio* (Cincinnati, 1884), 2:382.

[113] For instance, it was not settled until 1840 that a railroad corporation in New York had authority to borrow money and mortgage its property as security. See Francis L. Stetson, "Preparation of Corporate Bonds, Mortgages, Collateral Trusts, and Debenture Indentures," in Francis L. Stetson and others, *Some Legal Phases of Corporate Financing, Reorganization and Regulation* (New York, 1930), 1–13.

II. EMBATTLED FARMERS AND A COMMON-LAW COURT

[1] See Merk, *Economic History of Wisconsin,* 238–270, and Rice, History of the Chicago, Milwaukee, and St. Paul (MS.), 95–97, 116–140, 149–163. Article VIII, section 10, of Wisconsin's constitution prohibited the state from giving direct aid for internal improvements.

[2] It is hard to ascertain just what the legal effect of this agreement was. The last two clauses seem flatly contradictory. See above, page 55, and accompanying notes. The documents pertaining to the transaction are set out in Clark v. Farrington, 11 Wis. 306, 207–213 (1860). See also Merk, *Economic History of Wisconsin,* 241–242; Rice, History of the Chicago, Milwaukee and St. Paul (MS.), 116–140; and John W. Cary, *Organization and History of the Chicago, Milwaukee, and St. Paul Railway Company* (Milwaukee, 1893), 17.

[3] Except where otherwise indicated the factual material on pages 45–46 is derived from Merk, *Economic History of Wisconsin,* 224–226, 242–249, 262–269.

[4] This was a Pyrrhic victory, however. The proceeds were dissipated shamelessly by incompetent and corrupt administration. Merk, *Economic History of Wisconsin,* 267–269. See page 51 below.

[5] Except in the populous regions around Milwaukee popular sentiment in the state was with the farm-mortgagors. Local communities that had saddled themselves with railroad securities rallied to the farmers' support, and widespread disgust over the land-grant scandal of 1856 helped the mortgagors' cause. The votes on controversial farm-mortgage bills in the legislature show how great the farmers' influence was. In 1863, for instance, the legislature passed such a measure over Governor Salomon's veto by a vote of 28 to 1 in the Senate and 85 to 2 in the Assembly. *General Laws of Wisconsin,* 1863, ch. 123.

[6] The statute was chapter 49 of *General Laws of Wisconsin,* 1858, as amended by chapter 149 of *General Laws,* 1859. That the draftsmen were somewhat self-conscious is indicated by the title: "An Act *Declaratory* of Rights and Defenses of Mortgagors in Certain Cases" (italics supplied).

[7] Cornell v. Hichens, 11 Wis. 353 (1860).

[8] *General Laws of Wisconsin,* 1860, ch. 231; 1863, ch. 305. The 1860 act did not limit its provisions to the so-called "railroad farm mortgages" as did the law of 1863. Yet it is hard to believe that it was passed for any other reason than to aid the farm-mortgagors. The 1863 act was more elaborate and, in addition to specifying the particular type of mortgages to which it applied, contained a section compelling production of records by the railroad on penalty of having judgment rendered against it (section 5) and another one (section 11) providing for jury trial of all issues of fact upon demand of either party.

[9] The fraud-defense section of the foreclosure stay law was chapter 88, section 5, of *General Laws of Wisconsin,* 1861. It provided that in cases where fraud was pleaded the presumption was that the holder took the instrument with notice of the fraud. The act vetoed by Governor Salomon was chapter 123 of *General Laws of Wisconsin,* 1863. The purpose of the statute is not clear: section 2 permitted the court to order a discharge of record on proof by affidavit or otherwise "that such mortgage has not been delivered to, or accepted, or used by such corporation, or that such mortgage has been surrendered to the mortgagor or to any person or persons interested in the premises." Ostensibly the law purported to apply to certain mortgages given to the La Crosse and Milwaukee. These mortgages, though recorded, were not accepted by the company. Some of them were returned to the mortgagors and others found their way into the hands of third parties. Since the La Crosse and Milwaukee was now defunct, it could not cancel the mortgages of record. Hence the necessity for this act. It seems hard to believe, however, that this was all the framers intended. As Governor Salomon was quick to see, the law left the door open for the worst sort of summary cancellation of mortgages without any notice whatsoever to the holders. He vetoed the law for that reason, and went on to say: "By confining the relief sought to the class last mentioned [mortgagors whose mortgages were returned to them], making proper provision for public notice, no objection would probably exist." *Wisconsin Assembly Journal,* 1863, p. 575. This law was repealed by chapter 205 of *Wisconsin Revised Statutes,* 1873.

[10] It may have felt that the moratory laws were unnecessary if the other farm-mortgage legislation was in effect. Yet no effort was made to re-enact these moratoria statutes after the other laws were declared invalid. The 1858 act was chapter 113 of *General Laws of Wisconsin,* 1858. It also provided, in section 3, that foreclosure sales which did not conform to exacting notice provisions were invalid. The Supreme Court upheld the law in Von Baumbach v. Bade, 9 Wis. 559 (1859). The reduction from six months to ninety days was effected by chap-

ter 220 of *General Laws of Wisconsin,* 1859. This law came before the courts only on the issue of its retroactive effect on actions begun under the 1858 law. Beebe v. O'Brien, 10 Wis. 481 (1860) and Cornell v. Skinner, *ibid.,* 487. The 1863 act was chapter 299 of *General Laws of Wisconsin,* 1863.

[11] Oatman v. Bond, 15 Wis. 20 (1862). The law, chapter 88 of *General Laws of Wisconsin,* 1861, was a labyrinthine structure of twenty-seven sections to which mortgagors' counsel—undoubtedly the draftsmen of the act—must have given unremitting toil.

[12] Truman v. McCollum, 20 Wis. 360 (1866), invalidating chapter 169 of *General Laws of Wisconsin,* 1864, and Callanan v. Judd, 23 Wis. 343 (1868), invalidating chapter 79 of *General Laws,* 1867. See the discussion on pages 56-58.

[13] The optional sinking-fund law provided an elaborate scheme of first-, second-, and third-priority liens arising from certain classes of stock issues. *General Laws of Wisconsin,* 1862, ch. 330. Despite the fact that compliance was voluntary, railroad officials had urged the governor to veto the bill, knowing that they would be subject to pressure from the mortgagors to abide by its terms. Letters in Railroad Farm-mortgage Papers, Miscellaneous Executive Documents, a collection in the possession of the State Historical Society of Wisconsin. The compulsory sinking-fund acts, chapters 224 and 232 of *General Laws of Wisconsin,* 1864, applied to any successor lines of the La Crosse and Milwaukee and the Milwaukee and Horicon railroads. When the railroads refused to make the contribution the governor simply did not appoint a receiver. See Rice, History of the Chicago, Milwaukee, and St. Paul (MS.), 133–134. These two laws were early instances of legislative grappling with the problem of railroad reorganization, yet they apparently had no subsequent impact. When, ten years later, federal sinking-fund legislation came before the United States Supreme Court, the court made no reference to the Wisconsin statutes. Sinking Fund cases, 99 U.S. 700, 727 (1878).

[14] *General Laws of Wisconsin,* 1864, ch. 241. For details on the settlements see Merk, *Economic History of Wisconsin,* 266–267.

[15] The congressional Act was *United States Statutes at Large,* 15:238 (1868). Senator Potter had suggested this legislation as early as 1858 and Governor Randall had urged it in 1860 and 1861. Merk, *Economic History of Wisconsin,* 250, 267. The scandal provoked another full-dress legislative investigation. *Wisconsin Assembly Journal,* 1883, Appendix 4, pp. 33–35. On the role of Philetus Sawyer in the scandal see Richard N. Current, *Pine Logs and Politics: A Life of Philetus Sawyer, 1816–1900* (Madison, 1950), 137–140. See also Merk, *Economic History of Wisconsin,* 268–269.

[16] On the various alternatives see Rice, History of the Chicago, Milwaukee, and St. Paul (MS.), 133–134.

[17] *Portage Register,* August 8, September 5, 1863, quoted in Merk, *Economic History of Wisconsin,* 256. See pages 249 and 255 of the latter for discussion of pressures against officials.

[18] Randall's denouncement is in the *Wisconsin Assembly Journal,* 1861, Appendix, p. 22. See also Merk, *Economic History of Wisconsin,* 267. Randall's conduct here is reminiscent of his behavior in the incident involving bribery of the legislature by Byron Kilbourn and the La Crosse and Milwaukee Railroad in 1856.

[19] Merk, *Economic History of Wisconsin,* p. 263, n. 1. The mortgagors' constitutional argument can be found in the *Hartford Home League,* August 18, 1860, p. 1, col. 2. The reserved power over corporations is stated in Article XI, Section 1, of the Wisconsin Constitution. See also the *Wisconsin Assembly Journal,* 1864, pp. 323–324.

[20] In Von Baumbach v. Bade, 9 Wis. 559 (1859) the trial court held the 1858 moratory law unconstitutional. In Crosby v. Roub, 16 Wis. 616 (1863) the foreclosing holder received judgment below. In Truman v. McCollum, 20 Wis. 360 (1866), involving the first jury-trial statue, the trial judge also gave judgment for the holders.

[21] Von Baumbach v. Bade, 9 Wis. 559 (1859). Compare Ogden v. Glidden, 9 Wis. 46 (1859), Weissner v. Wells, 9 Wis. 471 (1859), and Starkweather v. Hawes, 10 Wis. 125 (1859). In Von Baumbach v. Bade (pp. 578–583) the court reviewed the federal decisions on the question whether the remedy constituted part of the obligation of contract within the terms of Article I, Section 10, of the federal constitution. Speaking through Chief Justice Dixon, the court accepted the rationale of Bronson v. Kinzie, 1 How. 311 (U.S. 1843) and McCracken v. Hayward, 2 How. 608 (U.S. 1844), in which the United States Supreme Court had declared Illinois mortgage-redemption statutes unconstitutional. But Chief Justice Taney had said by way of dictum that although the remedy did constitute part of the obligation, legislators were free to modify it so long as they did not "impair the obligation of contract." In other words, he simply imposed a rule of reasonableness on moratory legislation. It was up to the court to draw the line. Chief Justice Dixon phrased it this way: "The only limit or qualification to its exercise [i.e., legislative power to modify the remedy] is that the legislature shall confine their action within the bounds of reason and justice, and that they shall not so prolong the time within which legal proceedings are to be had, as to render them futile and useless in the hands of a creditor, or seriously impair his rights or securities." 9 Wis. 559, 583 (1859). Justice Paine concurred specially. He rejected the middle ground Taney had taken in *Bronson v. Kinzie,* saying that either the remedy was part of the obligation or it was not. If it was, the legislature could not modify it at all. His own position was that the remedy was not part of the obligation and therefore legislators could go so far as to abolish it entirely without running afoul of the contract clause. *Ibid.,* 585–595. See A. H. Feller, "Moratory Legislation: A Comparative Study," in the *Harvard Law Review,* 46:1061, 1069–74, 1085 (May, 1933).

[22] Martineau v. McCollum, 3 Pinney 455 (Wis., 1852). See Fisher v. Otis, 3 Pinney 78, 88 (Wis., 1850). See also Cook v. Helms, 5 Wis. 107 (1856), Hilton v. Waring, 7 Wis. 492 (1858), and Croft v. Bunster, 9 Wis. 503 (1859). On the history of the doctrine as then rationalized, see Theophilus Parsons, *A Treatise on the Law of Promissory Notes and Bills of Exchange* (Philadelphia, 1863), 1:274–276.

[23] Clark v. Farrington, 11 Wis. 306 (1860); Blunt v. Walker, 11 Wis. 334 (1860); Cornell v. Hichens, 11 Wis 353 (1860). *Clark v. Farrington* was heard on February 23 and decided June 19; *Blunt v. Walker* was heard on March 21 and *Cornell v. Hichens* on March 17. In both the Clark and the Cornell case plaintiffs were foreclosing holders. In *Blunt v. Walker* plaintiff was a transferee from the mortgagor. Defendant had bought the mortgage from the Milwaukee and Mississippi Railroad on the securities market.

[24] This summary of the mortgagors' position is taken chiefly from the "Synopsis of Argument of Geo. B. Smith for Respondent," in *Cases and Briefs,* 29:3 ff. (Clark v. Farrington) in the Wisconsin State Law Library. George B. Smith was a prominent lawyer of Madison and later became one of Wisconsin's leading railroad attorneys. Presumably he presented the mortgagors' position as strongly as possible.

[25] Clark v. Farrington, 11 Wis. 306, 320 (1860). On this point the mortgagors had the better of it. Plaintiff knew very well the purpose of the note; it was written on the very face of the note.

[26] 11 Wis. 306, 319 (1860).

[27] 11 Wis. 334, 346–347 (1860). Mortgagors had also argued that taking a mortgage was "dealing in real estate," a practice expressly prohibited by the roads' charters. The court disposed of this contention by pointing out the security function of a mortgage and alluding to its common status in negotiation and trade as mere personalty. *Ibid.*, 346–348. Compare Clark v. Farrington, 11 Wis. 306, 332 (1860). But see also Waldo v. Chicago, St. P., & F. du L. R., 14 Wis. 575 (1861) (conveyance of warranty deed for stock subscription *was* dealing in real estate, particularly when land lay considerable distance from line).

[28] Cornell v. Hichens, 11 Wis. 353, 370–371 (1860).

[29] Clark v. Farrington, 11 Wis. 306, 333 (1860). Had cash-paying subscribers chosen to contest this practice, their position here would have been much stronger than that of the mortgagors. For the farm-mortgagors had received fully paid shares of stock without laying out one cent of cash.

[30] Crosby v. Roub, 16 Wis. 616 (1863). Speaking through Justice Paine, the court analogized the separate bond to the French *allonge* of the law merchant, to an endorsement without recourse, and to a guaranty of collection. All three of these operate to pass title free and clear of prior equities but do not necessarily impose on the company the liability of an indorser (pp. 654, 656–658). Actually the intent to pass the instruments free and clear of prior equities was stated explicitly in both the bond given to the plaintiff and the separate agreement between the defendant-mortgagor and the company.

[31] Downie v. Hoover, 12 Wis. 174 (1860) (corporation has implied power to assign stock subscriptions); Downie v. White, 12 Wis. 176 (1860) (oral evidence of secret agreement not admissible to avoid obligation of subscription); Lyon v. Ewings, 17 Wis. 61 (1863) (fraud and ultra vires not available as defense, citing earlier cases; nor was usury available: New York, place of payment, prohibited corporation from pleading usury, and under Wisconsin law the note was not usurious); Andrews v. Hart, 17 Wis. 297 (1863) ("money" does not necessarily mean cash; transaction not so irregular as to place plaintiff on notice, citing earlier opinions; James H. Knowlton, counsel for mortgagors); Howard v. Boorman, 17 Wis. 460 (1863) (prima facie presumption that note was given for authorized purpose); Western Bank of Scotland v. Tallman, 17 Wis. 530 (1863) (words in charter "to make all contracts and agreements which the execution and management of the works and the convenience and interests of the company may require" sufficiently broad to support power to take bond and mortgage for stock subscription; bond given by farmer instead of note permitted interposition of defense of fraud, but court overturned circuit court finding and held evidence to be sufficient); Burhop v. Milwaukee, 18 Wis. 431 (1864), 20 Wis. 338 (1866), and 21 Wis. 257 (1866) (not decided whether defense of fraud could be interposed against holders of notes and mortgages, who got them through alleged invalid transfer of municipal corporation); Curtis v. Mohr, 18 Wis. 615 (1864) (plaintiff need not allege mortgage held as collateral security only); Patterson v. Ball, 19 Wis. 243 (1865) (sufficient evidence shown of proper delivery of note and mortgage); Uncas National Bank v. Rith, 23 Wis. 339 (1868) (company has power to sell or pledge note and mortgage; language identical to that of Tallman case above); Bange v. Flint, 25 Wis. 544 (1870) (whole transfer constituted proper indorsement, affiming Crosby v. Roub); Kinney v. Kruse, 28 Wis. 183 (1871) (fraud not available as defense against bona fide purchaser); Murphy v. Dunning, 30 Wis. 296 (1872) (fraud and misrepresentation not available; indorsement sufficient to cut off equities, citing former cases). In all except the last two cases the trial court had decided in favor of the mortgagor.

[32] Stanley v. Goodrich, 18 Wis. 505 (1864) (granted petition to vacate judgment of foreclosure insofar as it affected rights of mortgagor's grantor); Leonard v. Rogan, 20 Wis. 540 (1866) (action for attorney's fees due for representing defendant in farm-mortgage case); Wicke v. Lake, 21 Wis. 410 (1867) (foreclosure decree set aside to adjudicate rights of impleaded party having title paramount to mortgagee); Rogers v. Wright, 21 Wis. 681 (1867) (defendant permitted to amend answer by setting up three new affirmative defenses); Smith v. Lewis, 20 Wis. 268 (1866) (purchaser at second-mortgage foreclosure sale could not acquire property free of first-mortgage lien merely by purchasing tax deed); State Bank of Wisconsin v. Abbot, 20 Wis. 570 (1866) (failure to serve holder of equity of redemption in foreclosure action); Hoppin v. Doty, 22 Wis. 621 (1868) and 25 Wis. 573 (1870) (failure to serve holder of second mortgage at first-mortgage foreclosure sale and mala fides of purchaser); Cleveland v. Southard, 25 Wis. 479 (1870) (collusion between purchaser and mortgagee at foreclosure sale); McClellan v. Sanford, 26 Wis. 595 (1870) (owner through various mesne conveyances could not assert that subordination (mortgage) clause was obtained by fraud).

[33] Oatman v. Bond, 15 Wis. 20, 28 (1862). See also Western Bank of Scotland v. Tallman, 15 Wis. 92 (1862). The merits of the latter case were decided a year later. See note 31 above.

[34] Wisconsin Constitution, Art. I, sec. 9, and Art. VII, sec. 19; Oatman v. Bond, 15 Wis. 27, 28 (1862). Actually the latter provision of the constitution simply required that testimony in equity causes be taken in the same manner as in actions at law. The court had previously held that this required examination of witnesses in open court. Brown v. Runals, 14 Wis. 693 (1861); Oatman v. Bond, 15 Wis. 20, 27 (1862). The court declared the statute invalid under the contract clauses of both the federal and the Wisconsin constitution. *Ibid.*, 28. The case came up on a procedural point: whether an order of the trial court was appealable. The order had stayed proceedings in accordance with the terms of the stay law until all the testimony had been taken by the person appointed by the court. A Wisconsin statute defined appealable orders as, *inter alia*, those involving the "merits of the action of some part thereof." *General Laws of Wisconsin*, 1860, ch. 264, sec. 10 (4). In deliberating on this point the court necessarily had to go to the merits of the stay law. Justice Paine concurred specially, disagreeing with the interpretation his colleagues placed on what he himself had said in Von Baumbach v. Bade. 15 Wis. 20, 29 (1862). See note 21 above.

[35] Truman v. McCollum, 20 Wis. 360 (1866). The statute involved was chapter 169 of *General Laws of Wisconsin*, 1864. The miscellaneous conditions were these: (a) that the defendant-mortagor get exactly the same type of stock certificate as a shareholder who had paid cash; (b) that the company raise one hundred thousand dollars in the region west of the Rock River; (c) that the company complete a road to Beaver Dam by January 1, 1856. None of these conditions had been fulfilled. It was the mortgagor's position—apparently—that the stock agent had taken the notes and mortgages in a fiduciary capacity to hold in trust until the conditions were met. Any delivery, then, prior to this time was in violation of his fiduciary duty. 20 Wis. 365–368. The trial court had found that the defendant had in effect waived fulfillment of any conditions by accepting without objection, two years after the original transaction, shares of stock differing from those received by cash subscribers. Furthermore, the defendant had known for from two to four years that the plaintiffs held these securities. He could hardly complain at this late date, then, that the securities had been wrongly delivered. So saying, the Supreme Court did not need to decide whether the manner of transferring the documents was so irregular as to put the plaintiff

on notice. The court also asserted that the plaintiff need not have alleged preliminary demand on the company inasmuch as the evidence showed that the railroad had defaulted on its interest coupons. The defect could have been cured by a mere amendment of the complaint. This was too technical an objection to justify reversal. *Ibid.*, 373.

[36] *Ibid.*, 374.

[37] Callanan v. Judd, 23 Wis. 343 (1868). The act was chapter 79 of the *General Laws of Wisconsin*, 1867. By abrogating the circuit court's power to dispense with jury findings the draftsmen of the act foreclosed the possibility of the Supreme Court's construing this act—as it had the one of 1864—as being discretionary only.

[38] Callanan v. Judd, 23 Wis. 343, 348 (1868). The provision guaranteeing jury trial is Article I, Section 5, of the Wisconsin constitution. The court also referred to Article VII, Section 2, which vests "judicial power as to matters of law and equity" in the various Wisconsin courts. "Judicial power" meant, *inter alia*, the chancellor's power to determine issues of fact because this had been part of equity procedure at the time the constitution was adopted. Callanan v. Judd, 23 Wis. 343, 349 (1868). The farm-mortgagors had argued that Article VII, Section 8, of the constitution permitted such legislative action: "the circuit court shall have original jurisdiction on all matters ... not excepted in this constitution, *and not hereafter prohibited by law*." (Italics supplied.)

[39] Unless otherwise indicated the account of the elections for the Supreme Court is derived from Merk, *Economic History of Wisconsin*, 258–261. Knowlton's attack on the court's decisions appeared in the *Hartford Home League*, September 8, 15, 1860, p. 1. He wrote the review primarily for lay consumption, but he stated the farmer's legal position as strongly as it could be presented. One purpose must have been to court the favor of the mortgagors; it established him as a militant champion of their cause and probably helped get him the nomination.

[40] Blunt v. Walker, 11 Wis. 334 (1860) and Cornell v. Hichens, 11 Wis. 353 (1860).

[41] Dixon was thirty-four when he first took office. Yet his youth was not atypical of judges at that time. Paine reached the bench when he was only thirty. See John B. Winslow, *The Story of a Great Court* (Chicago, 1912), 122, 155.

[42] Winslow states (*ibid.*, p. 178) that about five thousand Democrats persisted in voting for the Democratic candidate even after he withdrew. These votes, accordingly, could have cost the farmers the election. Strangely, Merk does not mention this in his account.

[43] State assumption of the debt, for instance, would probably have required a constitutional amendment. This expedient was suggested, but nothing came of it. Merk, *Economic History of Wisconsin*, 250.

[44] The Homestead Act was signed in 1862. How much direct effect it had, however, is questionable.

[45] The lawyers' fees are derived from Minutes of the Farmers' Home League of Monroe, January 26, February 9, 1861, in the possession of the State Historical Society of Wisconsin. The Monroe League subsequently offered to double this fee. The efforts to retain Carpenter are reported in the minutes for July 13, 1861. The League was apparently unable to retain Carpenter; consequently Bennett, Cassoday, and Gibbs argued the case. Oatman v. Bond, 15 Wis. 20, 21 (1862). Carpenter had been on the other side in one of the 1860 cases. Cornell v. Hichens, 11 Wis. 353, 355 (1860). In Monroe the farmers retained B. F. Dunwiddie and J. A. Sleeper. Minutes of the Monroe League, January 26, 1861. In Janesville they were represented by Bennett, Cassoday and Gibbs. See John R.

Berryman, *History of the Bench and Bar in Wisconsin* (Chicago, 1898), 1:231. George B. Smith, their attorney in Madison, was a luminary of the early Wisconsin bar. *Ibid.*, 2:377–381.

[46] Tweedy was chairman of a committee of nine stockholders who reported out the plan at a meeting early in 1850. Reply to the Address of the Farmers' General Home League, pages 43–45, pamphlet filed with Milwaukee and Mississippi Railroad Company Reports, 1849–61, in the library of the State Historical Society of Wisconsin. Merk credits Joseph Goodrich, president of the Milwaukee and Mississippi, with authorship of the plan. Merk, *Economic History of Wisconsin*, 241. On the pressures brought against local lawyers, see *ibid.*, 249.

[47] On Knowlton see Winslow, *Story of a Great Court*, 177. See also pages 23–24. The test case was Knowlton v. Board of Supervisors of Rock County, 9 Wis. 410 (1859). The evidence seems clear that Knowlton acquired the property in question for the sole purpose of bringing the suit. Hurst and Brown, in the *Wisconsin Law Review*, 1949, pp. 26, 41. On Cothren see Winslow, *Story of a Great Court*, 112–114.

[48] Fletcher v. Peck, 6 Cranch 87 (U.S., 1810); Dartmouth College v. Woodward, 4 Wheat 518 (U.S., 1819).

[49] 1 How. 311 (U.S., 1843).

[50] Ohio Life Ins. & Trust Co. v. Debolt, 16 How. 416, 435 (U.S., 1837). The classic example of Taney's mistrust is Charles River Bridge v. Warren Bridge, 11 Pet. 420 (U.S., 1837).

[51] *Hartford Home League*, September 15, 1860, p. 1.

[52] Clark v. Farrington, 11 Wis. 306, 321–322 (1860). Paine went on to say (pages 322–323): "There is a close relation between the principles applicable to the government of the United States and those applicable to a corporation. The former like the latter can exercise no powers except such as are delegated to it either expressly or implied as necessarily incident to those expressly delegated. The reasons for confining both within the limits of the delegated powers, are equally obvious and familiar, yet this being constantly conceded, it by no means follows, that either, within those limits, should be restricted with narrow and illiberal rigor in the choice of means adapted to the execution of their respective powers."

[53] See Delmar Karlen, *Cases and Materials on Trials and Appeals* (Madison, 1949), 26–55.

[54] Winslow, *Story of a Great Court*, 183.

[55] Merk, *Economic History of Wisconsin*, 261.

[56] Minutes of the Monroe League, July 13, 1861.

[57] Merk, *Economic History of Wisconsin*, 270.

[58] *Ibid.* On the threat of reprisals see *ibid.*, 252.

III. THE FORMATIVE PERIOD OF WISCONSIN RAILROAD LAW

[1] Actually the first period, 1858–63, includes six years.

[2] "In our youthful State, it becomes the duty of those having committed to their charge its interests, to foster, by all reasonable and proper means, those undertakings which will best tend to bring into use, our varied resources, and to be wary of throwing impediments in the way, which might deter capitalists from investing their means in such improvements, as are best calculated to effect that result." *Annual Message of Governor Barstow*, 1854, p. 14.

[3] Between 1858 and 1873 some forty-five cases arising out of railroad condemnation proceedings came up to the Supreme Court of Wisconsin.

[4] See, for example, *Private and Local Laws of Wisconsin,* 1847, ch. 194, sec. 10–12 (charter of the Milwaukee and Waukesha Railroad). On the appraisal procedures see, for example, *General Laws of Wisconsin,* 1852, ch. 149, sec. 11–13 (charter of the Madison and Prairie du Chien Railroad; arbitration by three "disinterested persons" appointed by the court); *ibid.,* ch. 198, sec. 11–13 (La Crosse and Milwaukee charter; each party to choose one arbitrator, the two arbitrators to choose the third). For a general discussion see Meyer, in *Wisconsin Historical Collections,* 14:206, 263–264.

[5] *General Laws of Wisconsin,* 1858, ch. 80. A typical charter provision merely stated that it should be lawful for the company "at any time to enter upon . . . and use such land . . . ; subject, however, to the payment of such compensation." *Ibid.,* 1852, ch. 198, sec. 11 (La Crosse and Milwaukee charter).

[6] *Ibid.,* 1859, ch. 168, sec. 2. The act was invalidated in Powers v. Bears, 12 Wis. 214 (1860). The court's opinion was possibly unnecessary. The legislature had repealed the act earlier the same year. *General Laws,* 1860, ch. 85.

[7] The Mill Dam Act appeared as chapter 56 in *Wisconsin Revised Statutes,* 1858. This was a re-enactment in 1857 of a law passed in 1840 and repealed in 1849. *General Laws,* 1857, ch. 62. See Daniel J. Dykstra, "Legislation and Change," in the *Wisconsin Law Review,* 1950, pp. 523, 626. The Supreme Court expressed its regrets about the Mill Dam Act as follows: "Setting to the one side the adjudications of this court upon the mill-dam law, so-called, which was sustained contrary to the individual convictions of all its present members, on the ground that the earlier decisions upon it had made it a rule of property which could not, with a due regard to individual interests, be departed from." Powers v. Bears, 12 Wis. 214, 221 (1860). See also Fisher v. Horicon Iron & Mfg. Co., 10 Wis. 351, 353–354 (1860) and Attorney General v. Eau Claire, 37 Wis. 400, 436 (1876) (opinion by Chief Justice Ryan).

[8] Powers v. Bears, 12 Wis. 214. This decision complemented an earlier one on almost the same point. In Shepardson v. Milwaukee & B.R., 6 Wis. 605 (1857), an amendment to the Milwaukee and Beloit charter was at issue. The provision permitted the company to enter on the lands for the purpose of constructing the right-of-way before making compensation to the owner. It went on to authorize the company to apply to a circuit judge for an appraisal of the value of the land taken. The Supreme Court, through Chief Justice Whiton, declared this procedure unconstitutional chiefly because it permitted only one party—the railroad—to make application to the court. Compare Power v. Bears, 12 Wis. 214, 219 (1860). The court felt that the constitutional section concerning "just compensation" was not complied with by puting on the owner the burden of suing out a writ of mandamus to compel the company to make the application to the court. Shepardson v. Milwaukee & B. R., 6 Wis. 605, 613 (1857).

[9] *General Laws,* 1861, ch. 175.

[10] Andrews v. Farmers' Loan & Trust Co., 22 Wis. 288 (1867). The challenge of constitutionality was made on a petition for a rehearing. Matthew H. Carpenter, a leading lawyer and later United States senator, was counsel for the owner. *Ibid.,* 294. No reason appears why the validity of the act was not attacked on the first hearing.

[11] Bohlman v. Green Bay & L. P. R., 30 Wis. 105, 109 (1872).

[12] *General Laws,* 1872, ch. 119, sec. 13–22.

[13] On the availability of injunctive provisions, compare Pettibone v. La Crosse & M. R., 14 Wis. 443 (1861) and Vilas v. Milwaukee & M. R., 15 Wis. 233 (1862) (injunction discretionary and available to volunteer) with Milwaukee v. Milwaukee & B. R., 7 Wis. 85 (1858) (injunction not available to city to prevent building track over street because city does not have the fee) and with Ford v.

Chicago & N. W. R., 14 Wis. 609 (1861) (injunction available to landowner to prevent building track in street because he has the fee subject to easement of city). Compare also Hegar v. Chicago & N. W. R., 26 Wis. 624 (1870) (damages for value of owner's half of street). See Wright v. Wisconsin C. R., 29 Wis. 341 (1872) (company permitted to drop proceedings upon discovering that defendant is not true owner). On the exclusiveness of remedy compare Burns v. Dodge, 9 Wis. 458 (1859) and Davis v. La Crosse & M. R., 12 Wis. 17 (1860) with Loop v. Chamberlain, 20 Wis. 135 (1865). On procedural matters relating to appraisal and award, see Burns v. Milwaukee & M. R., 9 Wis. 450 (1859) (appeal from commissioners' award); Neff v. Chicago & N. W. R., 14 Wis. 370 (1861) (regarding proper notice of appeal); Strang v. Beloit & M. R., 16 Wis. 635 (1863) (fact that two of commissioners were stockholders not grounds for quashing award when motion to quash is made by *company*); Pfeifer v. Sheboygan & F. du L. R., 18 Wis. 155 (1864) (judgment on commissioners' award good against successor company); Blake v. Chicago & N. W. R., 18 Wis. 208 (1864) (faulty notice not ground for dismissing appeal); Farrand v. Chicago & N. W. R., 21 Wis. 435 (1867) (whether award properly included value for side of street); Mason v. Nichols, 22 Wis. 376 (1867) (agreement not to appeal award upheld); Pomeroy v. Chicago & M. R., 25 Wis. 641 (1870) (right to damages remains in vendor when land is sold); Robbins v. Milwaukee & H. R., 6 Wis. 636 (1858) (measure of damages); Welch v. Milwaukee & St. P. R., 27 Wis. 108 (1870) (measure of damages); Bigelow v. West W. R., 27 Wis. 478 (1871) (measure of damages); Parks v. West W. R., 33 Wis. 413 (1873); Stoppelfield v. Milwaukee, M. & G. B. R., 29 Wis. 688 (1872) (unavailability of attorney was "excusable neglect" sufficient to permit new trial); Western U. R. v. Dickson, 30 Wis. 389 (1872) (authority of county judge to appoint commissioners). On construction of the 1872 act see Lee v. Northwestern U. R., 33 Wis. 222 (1872) (railroad as well as landowner may appeal from commissioners' award); Moore v. Superior & St. C. R., 34 Wis. 173 (1874) (regarding appointment of commissioners); and Chapman v. Oshkosh & M. Riv. R., 33 Wis. 629 (1873) (measure of damages).

[14] Bohlman v. Green Bay & L. P. R., 30 Wis. 105, 107 (1872).

[15] *Boundary disputes:* see, for example, Sanborn v. Chicago & N. W. R., 16 Wis. 20 (1862) (trespass); Weisbrod v. Chicago & N. W. R., 18 Wis. 35 (1864) (ejectment), 20 Wis. 419 (1866), and 21 Wis. 602 (1867) (ejectment). See also Welch v. Chicago & N. W. R., 34 Wis. 494 (1874) (ejectment coupled with prayer for damages). *Compensation for depreciation:* Snyder v. Western U. R., 25 Wis. 60 (1869) (compensation allowed for the portion of plaintiff's land not actually taken). *Injury to property by conduct of railroad:* Thompson v. Milwaukee & St. P. R., 27 Wis. 93 (1870) (damages for failure of railroad to build retaining wall); Price v. Milwaukee & St. P. R., 27 Wis. 98 (1870) (same); Young v. Chicago & N. W. R., 28 Wis. 171 (1871) (injunction against railroad's diversion of stream so as to injure plaintiff's land).

[16] The Illinois courts had held that the property owner must keep his property adjoining the railroad free of weeds or other combustible materials in order to avoid the defense of contributory negligence. The English courts had imposed no such obligation on the landowners. See Kellogg v. Chicago & N. W. R., 26 Wis. 223, 230–236 (1870); also Chapman v. Chicago & N. W. R., 26 Wis. 537 (1870); Ward and Butterfield v. Milwaukee & St. P. R., 29 Wis. 144 (1871); and Spaulding v. Chicago & N. W. R., 30 Wis. 111 (1872). Compare Spaulding v. Chicago & N. W. R., 33 Wis. 582 (1873) (fire caused by fireman's throwing burning stick on grass) and Martin v. Western U. R., 23 Wis. 437 (1868) (engine running at unlawful speed held to be cause of fire).

[17] *General Laws,* 1860, ch. 268. The provision in the land grant was chapter 122, section 15, of *General Laws of Wisconsin,* 1856. Construed in McCall v. Chamberlain, 13 Wis. 637 (1861).

[18] *General Laws,* 1872, ch. 119, sec. 30–35. The earlier law was chapter 97 of *General Laws,* 1867.

[19] Pritchard v. La Crosse & M. R., 7 Wis. 232 (1858) (railroad liable for gross negligence or wanton malfeasance for injury to horse, even if latter was trespasser); Stucke v. Milwaukee & M. R., 9 Wis. 202 (1859). In the latter case the Wisconsin court considered Butterfield v. Forrester, 11 East. 60 (K. B., 1809) and Davies v. Mann, 10 M. & W. Rep. 545 (Ex., 1842), both leading English cases on the issue of plaintiff's own misconduct as a bar to recovery. The former has come to be considered the original "contributory negligence" case and the latter the original "last clear chance" case, although the two phrases were not used either in the cases themselves or in the discussion in the Stucke case.

[20] Compare Chicago & N. W. R. v. Goss, 17 Wis. 428 (1863) and Dunnigan v. Chicago & N. W. R., 18 Wis. 28 (1864) (company liable where cattle guard was filled with snow); Galpin v. Chicago & N. W. R., 19 Wis. 604 (1865) (negligence of railroad must be proved where cattle are injured at public road crossing); Bennett v. Chicago & N. W. R., 19 Wis. 137 (1865) (no recovery if animal was on an area that the railroad was not required to fence); Blair v. Milwaukee & P. du C. R., 20 Wis. 254 (1866) (constitutionality of fencing statute upheld); Brown v. Milwaukee & P. du C. R., 21 Wis. 39 (1866) (liability absolute where railroad fails to maintain fence); Fisher v. Farmers' Loan & Trust Co., 21 Wis. 73 (1866) (where fences are kept up, cattle on track declared trespassers); Fowler v. Farmers' Loan & Trust Co., 21 Wis. 77 (1866) ("depot grounds" excepted from requirements); Sika v. Chicago & N. W. R., 21 Wis. 370 (1867) (liability absolute where fence was destroyed by fire); Antisdel v. Chicago & N. W. R., 26 Wis. 145 (1870) (daily patrol by railroad held to satisfy statutory requirement of diligence); Laude v. Chicago & N. W. R., 33 Wis. 640 (1873) (fact that third party let down fence not available to railroad as defense).

[21] Schmidt v. Milwaukee & St. P. R., 23 Wis. 186 (1868), Chief Justice Dixon dissenting without opinion. The court reasoned that protection of animals was not the only purpose of the 1860 fencing statute (pp. 192–193).

[22] *General Laws,* 1856, ch. 26, sec. 1–2; 1870, ch. 19.

[23] Butler v. Milwaukee & St. P. R., 28 Wis. 487, 492 (1871). Typical cases were Kinney v. Crocker, 18 Wis. 75 (1864); Butler v. Milwaukee & St. P. R., 28 Wis. 487 (1871); Duffy v. Chicago & N. W. R., 32 Wis. 269 (1873) and 34 Wis. 188 (1874); Delaney v. Milwaukee & St. P. R., 33 Wis. 67 (1873).

[24] Sir Frederick Pollock, *The Law of Torts* (14th edition, London, 1939), 55–56.

[25] *General Laws,* 1856, ch. 26, sec. 3; 1857, ch. 71.

[26] See, for example, Seaman v. Farmers' Loan & Trust Co., 15 Wis. 578 (1862); Langhoff v. Milwaukee & Prairie du C. R., 19 Wis. 489 (1865) and 23 Wis. 43 (1868); Rothe v. Milwaukee & St. P. R., 21 Wis. 256 (1866) and 25 Wis. 424 (1870); Woodward v. Chicago & N. W. R., 21 Wis. 309 (1867); Potter v. Chicago & N. W. R., 20 Wis. 533 (1866), 21 Wis. 372 (1867), and 22 Wis. 615 (1868).

[27] *General Laws,* 1864, ch. 390, requiring, *inter alia,* that railroads take all grain for shipment at the usual charges; *ibid.,* ch. 482, prohibiting a railroad director or officer from engaging in any shipping on the road with which he was connected and also requiring the railroads to transport firewood piled in accordance with certain directions. See note 56 below.

[28] On the law of bailments see Oliver Wendell Holmes, Jr., *The Common Law* (Boston, 1881), 180–205.

[29] Typical of cases involving the imposition of loss on carrier or shipper are the following: Curtis v. Chicago & N. W. R., 18 Wis. 312 (1864) (freezing); Candee v. Pennsylvania R., 21 Wis. 582 (1867) (robbery); and Parker v. Milwaukee & St. P. R., 30 Wis. 689 (1872) (fire). Compare Blade v. Chicago, St. P., & F. du L. R., 10 Wis. 4 (1859) (goods not in good condition when delivered to railroad); Farmers' & Millers' Bank v. Detroit & M. R., 17 Wis. 372 (1863) (shipper acquired goods illegally); and Ralph v. Chicago & N. W. R., 32 Wis. 177 (1873) (purchaser reshipped because of dissatisfaction). *Cases construing contractual provisions limiting liability:* Dimmick v. Milwaukee & St. P. R., 18 Wis. 471 (1864); Detroit & M. R. v. Farmers' & Millers' Bank, 20 Wis. 122 (1865); Betts v. Farmers' Loan & Trust Co., 21 Wis. 80 (1866); Strohn v. Detroit & M. R., 21 Wis. 554 and 23 Wis. 126 (1868). Compare Pierce v. Milwaukee & St. P. R., 23 Wis. 387 (1868) (whether customary to ship empty grain bags free). *Cases dealing with goods destroyed or damaged between time of delivery and time of pick-up:* Milwaukee & M. R. v. Fairchild, 6 Wis. 403 (1858) (goods called for by consignee morning after arrival); Nudd v. Wells, 11 Wis. 407 (1860) (undue delay); Wood v. Crocker, 18 Wis. 345 (1864) and Whitney v. Chicago & N. W. R., 27 Wis. 327 (1871) (goods destroyed by fire in warehouse night before consignee picked them up). *Cases involving wrongful delivery:* Sawyer v. Chicago & N. W. R., 22 Wis. 402 (1868); Congar v. Chicago & N. W. R., 24 Wis. 157 (1869); Meyer v. Chicago & N. W. R., 24 Wis. 566 (1869); Ela v. American Merchant Union Express Co., 29 Wis. 611 (1872). Compare Groves v. Smith, 14 Wis. 5 (1861) (action against warehousemen for failure to deliver to railroad) and Appleton v. Barrett, 22 Wis. 568 (1868) (replevin arising out of wrongful delivery). *Cases involving successive carriers:* Peet v. Chicago & N. W., 19 Wis. 118 (1865); McLaren v. Detroit & M. R., 23 Wis. 130 (1868); Schneider v. Evans, 25 Wis. 241 (1860); Parmelee v. Western Trans. Co., 26 Wis. 439 (1870); Wood v. Milwaukee & St. P. R., 27 Wis. 541 (1871) and 32 Wis. 398 (1873); Laughlin v. Chicago & N. W. R., 28 Wis. 204 (1871); Conkey v. Milwaukee & St. P. R., 31 Wis. 619 (1872). Compare Hooper v. Chicago & N. W. R., 27 Wis. 81 (1870) (whether it was custom of shippers to rely on directions given to carrier to deliver goods to next carrier).

[30] "The Court had told the jury in the general charge, that railroad companies were held to extraordinary diligence and care in the transportation of passengers and were liable for any injuries that might result from a want of such diligence and care." Spencer v. Milwaukee & P. du C. R., 17 Wis. 487, 492–493 (1863). For a general discussion see Isaac F. Redfield, *A Practical Treatise on the Law of Railways* (Boston, 1858), sec. 149.

[31] *Passenger in train at time of accident:* Spencer v. Milwaukee & P. du C. R., 17 Wis. 487 (1863) (plaintiff, with elbow out of window, not negligent as matter of law); Spicer v. Chicago & N. W. R., 29 Wis. 580 (1872) (negligence to uncouple train without blocking wheels). Compare Milwaukee & M. R. v. Finney, 10 Wis. 388 (1860) (plaintiff wrongfully put off train by conductor). *Boarding:* Detroit & M. R. v. Curtis, 23 Wis. 152 (1868) and 27 Wis. 158 (1870), *sub nom.* Curtis v. Bradford, 33 Wis. 190 (1873) (action against garnishee). *Alighting:* Davis v. Chicago & N. W. R., 18 Wis. 175 (1864); Imhoff v. Chicago & M. R., 20 Wis. 344 (1866) and 22 Wis. 681 (1868); Delamatyr v. Milwaukee & P. du C. R., 24 Wis. 578 (1869).

[32] Davis v. Chicago & N. W. R., 18 Wis. 175 (1864); Patten v. Chicago & N. W. R., 32 Wis. 524 (1873); Lucas v. Milwaukee & St. P. R., 33 Wis. 41 (1873).

[33] *General Laws,* 1872, ch. 119. The constitutional amendment was Article IV, sections 31 and 32, of the Wisconsin constitution, submitted to the people by chapter 122 of *General Laws,* 1871, and ratified at the general election on November 7, 1871. For typical governors' denunciations of the special charter see the

Annual Message of Governor Randall, 1860, p. 15; of Fairchild, 1867, p. 13; 1868, p. 6; 1870, p. 10; and 1871, p. 9; and of Washburne, 1872, pp. 10–11. In the *Synoptical Index of Laws* for the years 1836–73 railroad special charters, including amendments, occupied fifteen pages of small type. *Synoptical Index of Laws of Wisconsin, 1836–73* (Madison, 1873), 277–291. By way of comparison the number of pages devoted to certain other classifications may be cited: "Bridges," 10 pages; "Civil Actions," 7 pages; "Courts," 3 pages; "Ferries," 5 pages; "Governor," 4 pages; "Legislative Assembly," 1 page; "Milwaukee," 7 pages; "School Districts," 11 pages. During these years the listings under "Railroads" and "Railway Companies in the indices of the *Private & Local Laws of Wisconsin* are longer than those under any other topics. The existing constitutional provision was Article XI, section 1 ("Corporations without banking power or privileges may be formed under general laws, but shall not be created by special act, except for municipal purposes, and in cases where, in the judgment of the legislature, the objects of the corporation cannot be attained under general laws.") The existing statute was chapter 79 of *Wisconsin Revised Statutes,* 1858 ("Of Railroads").

[34] Justice Paine, in Racine C. Bank v. Ayres, 12 Wis. 512, 517–518 (1860) (whether noncompliance with certain conditions precedent in stock subscription permitted shareholder to avoid payment of remainder due on subscription). Compare Clark v. Janesville, 10 Wis. 135 (1859) (implicit that railroad under charter has authority to receive bonds of city in payment for stock subscription). See also the discussion of the leading farm-mortgage cases on pages 53–57 above.

[35] Fox River Valley R. v. Shoyer, 7 Wis. 365 (1858) (variance in pleadings and proof); Kimball v. Spicer, 12 Wis. 668 (1860) (turned on pleadings); Greenleaf v. Ludington, 15 Wis. 558 (1862) (stock certificates lost; res judicata); Kenosha R. & R. I. R. v. Marsh, 17 Wis. 13 (1863) (major alteration of route as ground for avoidance of payment of stock subscription); Noonan v. Isley, 17 Wis. 314 (1863) and 21 Wis. 138 (1866) (whether informal due bill constituted agreement to purchase).

[36] *General Laws,* 1858, ch. 91, discussed above, pp. 24-25; 1859, ch. 211, construed in In re Flemings Petition. 16 Wis. 70 (1862) (order directing meeting to be held was an "appealable order"); 1866, ch. 122. If the judge were a majority stockholder in a corporate litigant, for example, he presumably would not sit. The case in which Judge Downer disqualified himself was Langhoff v. Milwaukee & P. du C. R., 19 Wis. 489, 498 (1865).

[37] On the scope of officers' authority, see Walworth Co. Bank v. Farmers' Loan & Trust Co., 14 Wis. 325 (1861) and 16 Wis. 629 (1863) (president had no authority to negotiate sale of railroad ties); Jessop v. City Bank, 14 Wis. 331 (1861) and 15 Wis. 604 (1862) (president had no authority to execute mortgage with unusual covenant in it); Chicago & N. W. R. v. James, 22 Wis. 194 (1867) (vice-president had no authority to buy logs).

[38] On consolidations see Merk, *Economic History of Wisconsin,* 189–307, and Meyer in *Transactions of the Wisconsin Academy of Sciences, Arts, and Letters,* 12: 364–378. On the Milwaukee Road consolidations see Rice, History of the Chicago, Milwaukee, and St. Paul (MS), 169–226.

[39] Merk, *Economic History of Wisconsin,* 298–299. The general consolidation act was chapter 55 of *General Laws of Wisconsin,* 1857. See also Meyer in *Transactions of the Wisconsin Academy of Sciences, Arts, and Letters,* 12: 355–356. It was repealed by chapter 49 of the *General Laws* of 1864. See Meyer, *op. cit.,* 366–368, 372–373. The act prohibiting consolidation of the two roads was chapter 433 of *Private and Local Laws,* 1867.

[40] For instance, when the Milwaukee and St. Paul was unable to effect formal consolidation with the Milwaukee and Prairie du Chien, it entered into a pooling arrangement which failed to go into effect only because of the later formal consolidation. Merk, *Economic History of Wisconsin,* 292, 295, See also Meyer in *Transactions of the Wisconsin Academy of Sciences, Arts, and Letters,* 12: 376–377.

[41] On the development of sanctions during this period see pages 94–97.

[42] Among the members of the Wisconsin bar who appeared in these cases were Matthew H. Carpenter, John W. Cary, Edward G. Ryan, Harlow S. Orton, George B. Smith, and Joshua Stark.

[43] On the detailed proceedings involving the foreclosures of the La Crosse and Milwaukee mortgages, see John W. Cary, *Organization and History of the Chicago, Milwaukee and St. Paul, Railway Company* (Milwaukee, 1893), 30–43. The author was attorney for the road during this time. See also Rice, History of The Chicago, Milwaukee and St. Paul (MS.), 169–187. The incident resulting in the demise of the Milwaukee and Prairie du Chien Railroad occasioned much maneuvering. The Milwaukee and St. Paul, as part of its consolidation plans, wanted to get hold of the Milwaukee and Prairie du Chien Railroad, but the directors and stockholders would not sell. Meanwhile the New York brokerage firm of Henry Stimson and Company was quietly buying up a majority interest in Milwaukee and Prairie du Chien common stock. But Stimson and Company did not know of a peculiar provision in the railroad's charter which denied common stockholders the right to vote for directors. Thus the brokerage firm had no voice in management despite the fact that it held a majority of the common stock. It hired B. L. Hopkins, a shrewd Madison lawyer, to lobby a remedial amendment to the Milwaukee and Prairie du Chien charter through the legislature. Their strategy was masterful. They introduced the measure openly and overtly in the Senate. The lobbyists of the Milwaukee and Prairie du Chien Railroad discovered it immediately and saw to it that it was buried. But in the meantime Hopkins was quietly steering through the Assembly a bill permitting common stockholders to vote in all elections. The measure was drafted to apply to all corporations, but was represented to the legislators as intended to apply to a bankrupt petroleum company. It passed both houses and was signed by the governor as one of the many "petroleum" bills passed during the hectic last few days. Then Stimson and Company voted their shares, ousted the local directors, and replaced them with men of their choice. The new management quickly entered into a mutually advantageous agreement for the sale of the road to the Milwaukee and St. Paul. The consolidation occurred just before a pooling arrangement was being effected between the two roads. Merk, *Economic History of Wisconsin,* 292–295; Rice, History of the Chicago, Milwaukee, and St. Paul (MS.), 180–185. The interlocking directorates of the state's two big roads were consummated in 1868 when the stockholders of the Chicago and North Western voted to add four Milwaukee and St. Paul directors to their board, and the Milwaukee and St. Paul elected president Keep of the Chicago and North Western to its board. In 1869 Alexander Mitchell, president of the Milwaukee and St. Paul Railroad, was elected president of the North Western to fill the place of Keep who had recently died. Merk, *Economic History of Wisconsin,* 298.

[44] See Farmers' Loan & Trust Co. v. Commercial Bank, 11 Wis. 207 (1860); Dinsmore v. Racine & M. R., 12 Wis. 649 (1860); Farmers' Loan & Trust Co. v. Cary, 13 Wis. 110 (1860); Bean v. Fisher, 14 Wis. 57 (1861); and Farmers' Loan & Trust Co. v. Fisher, 17 Wis. 114 (1863) (all involving after-acquired property clauses in mortgages given by the Racine and Mississippi Railroad). See also Pierce v. Milwaukee & St. P. R., 24 Wis. 551 (1869).

[45] *General Laws,* 1859, ch. 10. Rice, History of the Chicago, Milwaukee, and St. Paul (MS.), 172.

[46] *General Laws,* 1859, ch. 34. Section 2 expressly excepted the Chicago, St. Paul, and Fond du Lac from the provisions of the act.

[47] See, for example, Milwaukee & M. R. v. Milwaukee & W. R., 20 Wis. 174 (1865) (whether right of action passes to purchaser under foreclosure sale); Board of Supervisors of Iowa Co. v. Mineral Point R., 24 Wis. 93 (1869) (leading case on res judicata). See also Mariner v. Crocker, 18 Wis. 251 (1864) and Mariner v. Chamberlain, 21 Wis. 251 (1886) (actions against receivers for rent); State *ex rel.* Pfeifer v. Taylor, 19 Wis. 567 (1865) (denial of mandamus against judge to vacate order in receivership proceedings). Compare Smith v. Chicago & N. W. R., 18 Wis. 17 (1864), 19 Wis. 90 (1865), and 19 Wis. 326 (1865) (suits growing out of reorganization of Chicago, St. Paul, and Fond du Lac and the ill-fated Wisconsin and Superior, chartered in 1856 as the recipient of the northeast land grant).

[48] See note 70 below.

[49] Wisconsin Constitution, Art. XI, sec. 1.

[50] *General Laws,* 1868, ch. 95, as amended by ch. 89 of *General Laws,* 1869. The acts giving the lands to the Wisconsin Central were Chapters 314 and 362 of *Private and Local Laws of Wisconsin,* 1864. See. Merk, *Economic History of Wisconsin,* 284–285. The congressional act was *United States Statutes at Large,* 13:66 (1864).

[51] "The adoption of this amendment [against local and special legislation] will diminish the legislation of the State more than one-half." *Annual Message of Governor Fairchild,* 1871, p. 9. The constitutional provision is Article IV, sections 31–32 and the general railroad law was chapter 119 of *General Laws of Wisconsin,* 1872. On the proposition that, in the main, applicants for special charters wanted only routine corporate powers, see George J. Kuehnl, The Wisconsin Business Corporation, 1800–1875, a manuscript dissertation in the Law Library of the University of Wisconsin.

[52] The law in question was chapter 74 of *General Laws,* 1854. It applied also to plank roads. The unreported case was Milwaukee & M. R. v. Board of Sup. of Waukesha County, 9 Wis. 431 (1859) (reporter's note only; the case had actually been decided in 1855). The test case invalidating the tax was Knowlton v. Board of Sup. of Rock County, 9 Wis. 410 (1859), discussed in detail by Hurst and Brown in the *Wisconsin Law Review,* 1949, pp. 26, 49–52. The third case was Attorney General v. Winnebago Lake & F. R. P. Co., 11 Wis. 35 (1860), and the final decision sustaining the tax was Kneeland v. Milwaukee, 15 Wis. 454 (1862) (first hearing), 15 Wis. 457 (1862) (grant of motion for rehearing), and 15 Wis. 691 (1862) (opinion on rehearing).

[53] *General Laws,* 1860, ch. 173–174; 1861, ch. 68; 1862, ch. 22 (increasing license fee to 3 per cent of gross revenue). See also *Annual Message of Governor Salomon,* 1863, pp. 9-10 (recommending that the legislature bring taxing of railroads into conformity with the Supreme Court's ideas of constitutionality). Compare *General Laws,* 1866, ch. 73 (extending tax exemption of land-grant lands to 1871); 1871, ch. 48, sec. 4–5 (increasing license fee to 5 per cent where railroad got help from local government, which 5 per cent was earmarked to pay interest on municipal bonds).

[54] Hurst and Brown, in the *Wisconsin Law Review,* 1949, pp. 45, 60.

[55] Brightman v. Kirner, 22 Wis. 54 (1867) (property exempt from special assessment by city of Milwaukee); Milwaukee & St. P. R. v. Board of Supervisors, 29 Wis. 116 (1871) (boarding and rooming houses used for railroad passengers); Milwaukee & St. P. R. v. Milwaukee, 34 Wis. 271 (1874) (elevators). See Merk, *Economic History of Wisconsin,* 308–343.

[56] For example, *General Laws*, 1859, ch. 58, prohibited a railroad from removing its tracks for the purpose of changing its route; *General Laws*, 1864, ch. 390, required all railroads to take all grain for shipment at the usual charges, and *General Laws*, 1864, ch. 482,prohibited directors or officers of a railroad from shipping goods over roads with which they were connected and required railroads to carry firewood if properly piled. These two provisions of the last-named act were all that was left after the railroad lobby got through with what started out to be a full-fledged regulatory statute. Merk, *Economic History of Wisconsin*, 341–342. See also *General Laws*, 1867, ch. 163 (prohibiting transportation of gunpowder); 1870, ch. 43 (prohibiting construction of railroad on Wisconsin Point in Lake Superior).

[57] For example, *General Laws of Wisconsin*, 1859, ch. 58, sec. 1 (any resident freeholder given power to enjoin); 1865, ch. 390, sec. 4 (informer technique); 1864, ch. 482 (no enforcement clauses whatsoever). On sanctions see pages 94–97 above.

[58] For Governor Fairchild's comments on discrimination see his *Annual Message*, 1867, pp. 11–12.

[59] State v. West Wisconsin R., 34 Wis. 197 (1874). Judge Ryan's opinion is found in 35 Wis. 425 (1874). See pages 112–122 above.

[60] See, for example, *Private and Local Laws of Wisconsin*, 1866, chs. 213, 226, 229, 262, 326, 338, 406, 408, 449, 460, 463, 471, 491, 547, 1216. See also *General Laws*, 1860, ch. 130 as amended by *General Laws*, 1862, ch. 1; *General Laws*, 1864, ch. 398, as amended by *General Laws*, 1868, ch. 73; *General Laws*, 1870, ch. 25.

[61] *General Laws*, 1870, ch. 24, as amended by *General Laws*, 1871, ch. 48.

[62] *General Laws*, 1872, ch. 182.

[63] See Breck P. McAllister, "Public Purpose in Taxation," in the *California Law Review*, 18:137, 241 (1930), and James M. Gray, *Limitations of the Taxing Power* (San Francisco, 1906), 123–227. In the Wisconsin cases the issue came up in one of two ways: a taxpayer's suit to enjoin the issuance of orders executing or delivering the bonds or as a defense to suits on the bonds (or their interest coupons) brought by the railroads.

[64] Whiting v. Sheboygan & Fond du L. R., 25 Wis. 167 (1870) (two hearings). Clark v. Janesville, 10 Wis. 135 (1859) had established the legality of tax levies for the servicing of bonds and had also determined that such activity by a city did not contravene the constitutional provision prohibiting the state from contracting debts to aid internal improvements. Compare Foster v. Kenosha, 12 Wis. 616 (1860) (amendment giving city unlimited power to levy taxes for *any* purpose invalid).

[65] McAllister, in the *California Law Review*, 18:142. The distinction was not too satisfactory to Chief Justice Dixon. In a later case he admitted that the majority of the court disapproved of aid of any sort but did not wish to overrule the older decisions. Phillips v. Albany, 28 Wis. 340, 357 (1871). In still another case, Rogan v. Watertown, 30 Wis. 259 (1872), he narrowed the holding of the Whiting case. See note 68 below. See also Charles Fairman, *Mr. Justice Miller and the Supreme Court, 1862–1890* (Cambridge, Massachusetts, 1939), 220–221.

[66] Whiting v. Sheboygan & F. du L. R., 25 Wis. 167, 182, 185–186, 189 (1870).

[67] *Ibid.*, 219–220.

[68] 16 Wall. 678 (U.S. 1873). The Wisconsin courts' partial retreat was in Rogan v. Watertown, 30 Wis. 259 (1872). In this case the court passed on a statute authorizing issuance of bonds in aid of a railroad as a "loan of the credit" of the city. The court found authority for the action in Article XI, section 3, of the state constitution, which provided for the organization of cities and incorporated

villages and made it the duty of the legislature to "restrict their power of taxation, assessment, borrowing money, contracting debts, and *loaning their credit*, so as to prevent abuses in assessments and taxation, and in contracting debts by such corporation." (italics supplied). *Ibid.*, 264. This, to the court, constituted a recognition of the power to do what the city had done here. Although the city could not "donate" the bonds to the road, under the Whiting rule, another statute gave the mayor and council unlimited discretion to fix the terms of the loan of credit. This statute, too, the court sustained. *Ibid.*, 266. In actual fact, the city in the Rogan case had given the bonds to the railroad. See also Lawson v. Milwaukee & N. R., 30 Wis. 597 (1872) (reaffirmance of power of legislature to authorize subscriptions to railroad stock by municipality).

[69] On matters of local aid see Clark v. Janesville, 13 Wis. 414 (1861) (vote to ratify bond issue must be taken after charter of railroad has been published); Rochester v. Alfred Bank, 13 Wis. 432 (1861) (same); Berliner v. Waterloo, 14 Wis. 378 (1861) (same situation as Clark and Rochester cases); Burhop v. Roosevelt, 20 Wis. 338 (1866) (jurisdiction); Mills v. Jefferson, 20 Wis. 51 (1865) (procedural and notice by publication); Paul v. Kenosha, 22 Wis. 266 (1867) (no authority to issue railroad bonds to third party); Wright v. Milwaukee & St. P. R., 25 Wis. 46 (1869) (liability of successor railroad company on guaranty given to city by original corporation); Sauerhering v. Iron Ridge & M. R., 25 Wis. 447 (1870) (technical requirements of notice of referendum); Knapp v. Grant, 27 Wis. 147 (1870) (validity of curative act legalizing unauthorized bond issue because of noncompliance with technicality); Phillips v. Albany, 28 Wis. 340 (1871) (validity of stock subscriptions where railroad failed to comply with conditions precedent relative to route of line); Lawson v. Schnellen, 33 Wis. 288 (1873) (same). See also Sheboygan v. Sheboygan F. du L. R., 21 Wis. 667 (1867), with which compare Janesville v. Milwaukee & M. R., 7 Wis. 484 (1859) (power of city to sue railroad for obstructing street); Chicago & N. R. v. Borough of Ft. Howard, 21 Wis. 44 (1866) (railroad's suit to enjoin dismissed).

[70] Cleveland v. Chamberlain, 1 Black 419 (U.S., 1861) (both creditors of La Crosse and Milwaukee; appeal dismissed because Chamberlain had bought out Cleveland's judgment and controlled both sides of the litigation); Bronson & Soutter v. La Crosse and M. R., 1 Wall. 405 (U.S., 1863) (motion for writ of prohibition against district court for exercising circuit court jurisdiction contrary to 1862 act of Congress); Bronson v. La Crosse & M. R., 2 Wall. 283 (U.S., 1863) (issues arising out of foreclosure sale of one of La Crosse and Milwaukee mortgages); Minnesota Co. v. St. Paul Co., 2 Wall. 609 (U.S., 1864) (issues arising out of foreclosure of another [Barnes] mortgage given by La Crosse and Milwaukee; contains tabulation of the various mortgages executed by the road) and 6 Wall. 742 (U.S., 1867) (whether mortgage covered all the rolling stock); Minnesota Co. v. Chamberlain, 3 Wall. 704 (U.S., 1865) whether chancery decree bound others than parties to original action); Crawshay v. Soutter & Knapp, 6 Wall. 739 (U.S., 1867) (validity of foreclosure sale of third La Crosse and Milwaukee mortgage); Fleming v. Soutter, 6 Wall. 747 (U.S., 1867) (regularity of clauses in decree for foreclosure sale); Railroad Co. v. Chamberlain, 6 Wall. 750 (U.S., 1867 (priority of Cleveland judgment lien in hands of assignee); James v. Railroad Co., 6 Wall. 752 (U.S., 1867) (invalidating the foreclosure sale under the Barnes mortgage as fraudulent); Railroad Co. v. Soutter, 13 Wall. 517 (U.S., 1871) (issues arising out of invalidation of Barnes mortgage-foreclosure sale). Compare Blossom v. Milwaukee & C. R., 1 Wall. 655 (U.S., 1863) (right of bidder at foreclosure sale to appeal even though he was not a party to the original foreclosure action).

[71] Moseley v. Chamberlain, 18 Wis. 700 (1861). Compare Kinney v. Crocker, 18

Wis. 74 (1864) (asserting jurisdiction of state court over personal-injury suit against receiver appointed by federal court).

[72] Milwaukee & St. P. R. v. Milwaukee & M. R., 20 Wis. 165 (1865). See page 88 above.

[73] Jackson v. Cleveland, 15 Wis. 107 (1862) and 19 Wis. 400 (1865) (construction of the contract: divisibility, certification, abandonment).

[74] Carney v. La Crosse & M. R., 15 Wis. 503 (1862) (action by subcontractor to enforce materialman's lien against railroad). See also Wells v. Milwaukee & St. P. R., 30 Wis. 605 (1872) (interpretation of contract for ballasting and grading).

[75] Jessup v. Stone, 13 Wis. 466 (1861) (priority between land mortgage and mechanic's lien); Hill v. La Crosse & M. R., 14 Wis. 291 (1861) (disposition of proceeds of execution sale); Farmers' Loan & Trust Co. v. Fisher, 17 Wis. 114 (1863) (between mortgagee asserting under after-acquired property clause and subsequent creditor); Smith v. Bouck, 33 Wis. 19 (1873) (conflict between mortgagee and purchaser of lands).

[76] Vilas v. Milwaukee & P. du C. R., 17 Wis. 497 (1863) (Milwaukee and Mississippi reorganization); Smith v. Chicago & N. W. R., 18 Wis. 17 (1864) (Chicago, St. Paul, and Fond du Lac reorganization), 19 Wis. 90 (1865) (action against creditors), 19 Wis. 326 (1865) and 23 Wis. 267 (1868) (assignment of claim). *Garnishment:* Prentiss v. Danaher, 20 Wis. 311 (1866); Graham v. O'Neil, 24 Wis. 34 (1869); Keyes v. Milwaukee & St. P. R., 25 Wis. 691 (1870); Winterfield v. Milwaukee & St. P. R. 29 Wis. 589 (1872); Ballot v. Scott, 32 Wis. 174 (1873). Compare Graham v. La Crosse & M. R., 10 Wis. 459 (1860) (creditor's bill); Osborne v. Farmers' Loan & Trust Co., 16 Wis. 35 (1862) (oral guaranty).

[77] Weymouth v. Chicago & N. W. R., 17 Wis. 550 (1863) (conversion); Chicago & N. W. R. v. James, 24 Wis. 388 (1869) (agent's authority to sell stumpage); Posey v. Rice & Halsted, 29 Wis. 93 (1871) (parol contract). Compare Menominee Locomotive Mfg. Co. v. Langworthy, 18 Wis 444 (1864) (reformation of bill of sale of machinery).

[78] *General Laws of Wisconsin,* 1863, ch. 120.

[79] The statutes were *General Laws of Wisconsin,* 1855, ch. 86; 1857, ch. 27; and 1860, ch. 353. The cases were Streubel v. Milwaukee & M. R., 12 Wis. 67 (1860); Jackson v. Cleveland, 15 Wis. 107 (1862); and Mundt v. Sheboygan & F. du L. R., 31 Wis. 451 (1872).

[80] Chamberlain v. Milwaukee & M. R., 7 Wis. 425 (1858) (first hearing), 11 Wis. 238 (1860) (first hearing on merits), overruled by Mosely v. Chamberlain, 18 Wis. 700 (1861). Compare Cooper v. Milwaukee & P. du C. R., 23 Wis. 660 (1868). See Willard Hurst and Lloyd K. Garrison, Material on Law in Society (mimeographed, Madison, 1940), 115–122.

[81] See Merk, *Economic History of Wisconsin,* 304–305.

[82] Whiting v. Sheboygan & F. du L. R., 25 Wis. 167, 180–182 (1870). The case involving the educational institution was Curtis v. Whipple, 24 Wis. 350 (1869).

[83] Hurst and Brown suggest that in this case the legislature might have been more aware of the uniqueness of the railroad-tax problem than the courts. Hurst and Brown, in the *Wisconsin Law Review,* 1949, pp. 45, 60. And at least one governor suggested that it would not do to return to piecemeal taxation of railroads by individual localities. *Annual Message of Governor Harvey,* 1862, p. 18.

[84] See, for example, Menominee Locomotive Mfg. Co. v. Langworthy, 18 Wis. 444 (1864) (instruments reformed to embody intent of parties). Phillips v. Albany, 28 Wis. 340 (1871) and Lawson v. Schnellen, 33 Wis. 288 (1873) (taxpayers' suits to enjoin local bodies from aiding railroads). Chicago & N. W. R. v. Ft. Howard,

21 Wis. 44 (1866) (stockholders' injunction against disposal of rolling stock denied); Sheboygan v. Sheboygan & F. du L. R., 21 Wis. 667 (1867) (injunction against railroad's obstruction of stream denied). State *ex rel.* Pfeiffer v. Taylor, 19 Wis. 567 (1865) (mandamus to vacate order staying proceedings denied). State v. West Wisconsin R., 34 Wis. 197 (1874) (original jurisdiction of Supreme Court in quo warranto affirmed). Welch v. Chicago & N. R., 34 Wis. 494 (1874) (ejectment for railroad entering on plaintiff's land).

[85] See, for example, Patten v. Chicago & Northwestern Ry. Co., 32 Wis. 524 (1873) (remittitur because of excessive damages). Spencer v. Milwaukee & Prairie du Chien Ry. Co.. 17 Wis. 487 (1863) (passenger with elbow out of window not negligent as a matter of law and issue must go to jury); Rothe v. Milwaukee & St. Paul Ry. Co., 21 Wis. 256 (1866) (plaintiff's failure to look out for train was negligence as matter of law and issue need not go to jury). Potter v. Chicago & N. Ry., 20 Wis. 533 (1866) and 21 Wis. 372 (1867) (contributory negligence); Kenosha R. & R. I. R. v. Marsh, 17 Wis. 13 (1863) (implying condition precedent in stock certificate).

[86] *Statutory construction:* Schmidt v. Milwaukee & St. P. R., 23 Wis. 186 (1868) (interpreting livestock-fencing statute to include protection of child); *semble:* Prentiss v. Danaher, 20 Wis. 311 (1866); Graham v. O'Neil, 24 Wis. 34 (1869); Keyes v. Milwaukee & St. P. R., 25 Wis. 691 (1870); Burlander v. Milwaukee & St. P. R., 26 Wis. 76 (1870); Winterfield v. Milwaukee & St. P. R., 29 Wis. 589 (1872) (all involving construction of garnishment statutes); see Smith v. Chicago & N. W. R., 19 Wis. 90 (1865) (court construed statute relating to appeal bonds to require by implication that sureties be residents of state). The court was not timid in using its power to declare laws unconstiuional. Compare Whiton v. Chicago & N. W. R., 25 Wis. 424 (1870) with Moseley v. Chamberlain, 18 Wis. 700 (1861) (court declared acts of Congress pertaining to diversity jurisdiction unconstitutional). With respect to matters of jurisdiction and procedure, see Milwaukee & St. P. R. v. Milwaukee & M. R., 20 Wis. 165 (1865) (closing doors of state court because federal court had already begun receivership proceedings); Mariner v. Milwaukee & St. P. R., 26 Wis. 84 (1870) (equitable defenses permitted in action for ejectment); see also Hegar v. Chicago & N. W. R., 26 Wis. 624 (1870) (reversed and remanded because lower court did not determine equitable issues in law action for damages). On use of presumptions, see, for example, Congar v. Galena & C. U. R., 17 Wis. 487 (1863) (presumption that plaintiff was owner of goods damaged); Mariner v. Crocker, 18 Wis. 251 (1864) (presumption that signature on bond was evidence of authority to execute); Laughlin v. Chicago & N. R., 28 Wis. 204 (1871) (presumption that box was opened by last carrier handling it); Martin v. Western U. R., 23 Wis. 437 (1868) (presumption that damages from sparks were caused by defendant's locomotive); Galpin v. Chicago & N. R., 19 Wis. 604 (1865) (presumption of negligence); McLaren v. Detroit & M. R., 23 Wis. 138 (1868) (presumption of liability of common carrier).

[87] See, for example, chapter 482 of *General Laws of Wisconsin,* 1864, which prohibited directors, officers, and employees from shipping on railroads with which they were affiliated, but contained no enforcement clause whatever. This was originally a general railroad-regulation bill, but it was ammended to death by railroad lobbyists. Merk, *Economic History of Wisconsin,* 341–342. See also *General Laws of Wisconsin,* 1870, ch. 43 (prohibition of railroad construction on Wisconsin Point in Lake Superior).

[88] *New causes of action: General Laws of Wisconsin,* 1867, ch. 97 (permitted adjoining landowner to repair railroad fence and recover amount expended from railroad in action for damages); *General Laws,* 1856, ch. 26 sec. 3, construed in

Langhoff v. Milwaukee & P. du C. R., 19 Wis. 489 (1865) (wrongful-death statute); *General Laws,* 1867, ch. 163 (prohibiting transportation of gunpowder and giving aggrieved party action in damages against officers of company). *Change in rules of liability: General Laws,* 1860, ch. 268 (absolute liability for damages to animals by trains until fences constructed); compare Sika v. Chicago & N. W. R., 21 Wis. 370 (1867) and Brown v. Milwaukee & P. du C. R., 21 Wis. 39 (1866) with Antisdel v. Chicago & N. W. R., 19 Wis. 145 (1865). *New forms of injunctive relief: General Laws,* 1859, ch. 59 (resident free holder could enjoin removal of tracks by railroad for purpose of changing route); *ibid.,* ch. 211 (stockholder given power to get decree compelling stockholders' meeting), construed in *In re* Fleming's Petition, 16 Wis. 70 (1862).

[89] *General Laws,* 1860, ch. 268, sec. 2, 3 (trackwalking and removal of fences); 1864, ch. 390 (accepting all grain for shipment).

[90] *General Laws,* 1867, ch. 163. The fine ranged from two hundred to a thousand dollars (section 1). The officer or agent knowingly permitting gunpowder to be carried was guilty of a misdemeanor and on conviction was subject to a fine of one hundred to five hundred dollars (section 2). In addition the act gave an aggrieved party an action in damages against the officers. See note 88 above. But imprisonment did not appear as an alternative sanction.

[91] *General Laws,* 1870, ch. 19, sec. 2. 3. The maximum fine was one thousand dollars and the maximum term of imprisonment one year (section 2).

[92] *General Laws,* 1872, ch. 119, sec. 54. See also *General Laws,* 1864, ch. 390, sec. 4.

[93] Apparently the attorney general was compelled to bring proceedings only upon order of the governor. *General Laws,* 1860, ch. 174, sec. 3. Forfeiture was to be effected "by the usual remedy." *Ibid.*

[94] *General Laws,* 1868, ch. 95, sec. 3. The act provided, in addition, for forfeiture of the charter.

[95] The river-ferry license act was chapter 185 of *General Laws of Wisconsin,* 1859.

[96] See the *Annual Message of Governor Randall,* 1859, pp. 16–18.

[97] *First Annual Message of Governor Taylor,* 1874, pp. 22–23. For the observations of other governors see the *Annual Message* of Governor Randall, 1859, pp. 18–20; 1860, pp. 15, 17–18; and 1861, pp. 10–11; of Governor Harvey. 1862, p. 18; of Governor Salomon, 1863, pp. 9–10; of Governor Fairchild, 1866, pp. 27–28; 1867, pp. 9–10, 11–12; 1868, pp. 6, 12; 1869, pp. 17–18; 1870, pp. 20, 22; and 1871, pp. 24–25; of Washburne, 1872, pp. 20–24, and 1873, pp. 25–29; of Taylor. 1874, pp. 20–24, and 1875, pp. 13, 14–15, 24, 25–32.

[98] See, for example, the *Wisconsin Senate Journal,* 1861, p. 854 (Randall's veto of a bill repealing the taxing section of the La Crosse and Milwaukee land grant; Randall realized that in all probability none of the land would ever pass to the road, but he felt that in the event it did the state would lose both land and money if this repealer were passed); *Wisconsin Assembly Journal,* 1863, p. 820 (Salomon's veto of an amendment to the mortgage stay law which, he claimed, did not meet the objections the Supreme Court had voiced in Oatman v. Bond); *ibid.,* 1873, pp. 919–25 (Washburne's veto of an act authorizing a bridge across the Mississippi on the grounds that it conflicted with the federal power over interstate commerce); *Wisconsin Senate Journal,* 1874, p. 602 (Taylor's veto of an act to legalize a lease taken by the Wisconsin Central Railroad on the grounds that it was a special law prohibited by the 1871 amendment of the constitution).

[99] See note 93 above.

IV. RAILROADS VERSUS THE STATE: THE IMPACT OF A JUDGE

[1] On the excesses of the railroads and the growing feeling against them see Solon J. Buck. *The Granger Movement* (Cambridge, Massachusetts, 1913), 12–14, 181.

[2] *Ibid.*, 181. On politics during this period see also Herman J. Deutsch, "Disintegrating Forces in Wisconsin Politics of the Early Seventies," in the *Wisconsin Magazine of History,* 15:169, 282, 391 (December, 1931; March and June, 1932). Contributing to the sentiment against the railroads was the fact that during the fall of 1873 they had been impolitic enough to raise freight rates for the transportation of agricultural products. Buck, *The Granger Movement,* 181.

[3] *Wisconsin Senate Journal,* 1874, p. 289. On the formation of the joint select committee, see the *Assembly Journal,* 1874, pp. 23, 34–35, 103, 125. Chairman of the commitee was F. W. Cotzhausen, a senator from Milwaukee.

[4] *Senate Journal,* 1874, pp. 289–290.

[5] Whether the railroad interests were behind the more radical Potter bill or not is a subject of dispute among scholars. Buck. *The Granger Movement,* 182–184, and Deutsch, in the *Wisconsin Magazine of History,* 15:393, 397, support the view that the Potter bill was railroad-sponsored. Robert T. Daland, in his article "Enactment of the Potter Law," in the *Wisconsin Magazine of History,* 33:53 (September, 1949) states that it was not so sponsored.

[6] *Laws of Wisconsin,* 1874, ch. 273. The four general classes of freight were to be classified by the railroad commissioners provided for in the act in accordance with the classification used by the Milwaukee and St. Paul Railroad as of June 15, 1872. The seven special classes of freight were defined in section 3 of the act: Class D, grain in carloads; Class E, flour in lots of 50 barrels or more and lime in lots of 24 barrels or more; Class F, salt in lots of 60 barrels or more, and cement, water lime, and stucco in lots of 24 barrels or more; Class G, lumber, lathes, and shingles in carloads; Class H, livestock in carloads; Class I, agricultural implements, furniture, and wagons; Class J, coil, brick, sandstone, and heavy fourth-class articles in carload lots. The maximum charges applicable to the special classes decreased as weight and mileage increased. For example, the rates for Class D were not to exceed six cents per 100 pounds for the first twenty-five miles, four cents per 100 pounds for the second twenty-five miles, and two cents per hundred pounds for each additional twenty-five miles or fractional part thereof unless the fraction was less than thirteen miles; if it was less than thirteen miles the rate was one cent for the fractional part, unless the whole distance was over two hundred miles, in which case the rate could not exceed one-half cent per hundred pounds for each twenty-five miles of that total distance. The remaining rate schedules for Classes E through J all followed the divisions set up for Class D, the only variation being in the amount per pound. To prevent the rate increases the railroads had announced for the next fall, June 1, 1873, was set as the effective date of the act. Buck, *The Granger Movement,* 185.

[7] *Laws of Wisconsin,* 1874, ch. 273, sec. 8. On the early efforts of state governments to set up railroad commissioners see the *First Annual Report of the Railroad Commissioners of the State of Wisconsin,* 1874, pp. 79–84.

[8] *Laws of Wisconsin,* 1874, ch. 273. sec. 9–13.

[9] *Ibid.*, sec. 16. The figure for Supreme Court salaries is from John B. Winslow, *The Story of a Great Court* (Chicago, 1912), 250.

[10] *Laws of Wisconsin,* ch. 273, sec. 6, 14. Violation of rates established by the commissioners was made a misdemeanor, subject to a fine of two hundred dollars. This section also gave the aggrieved party an action against the company for three times the overcharge.

[11] *Ibid.,* sec. 7. Presumably by conferring concurrent jurisdiction on justices of the peace the institution of actions against local agents would be facilitated. Such seemed to be the inference in Governor Taylor's Address to the People; see pp. 105–106. Sample complaint forms drawn up by the railroad commissioners are set out in a pamphlet entitled *The Railroad Law of 1874,* filed among Wisconsin Miscellaneous Pamphlets, 4:21–22) in the library of the State Historical Society of Wisconsin.

[12] Daland, in the *Wisconsin Magazine of History,* 33:48.

[13] On Osborn see Robert McCluggage, "Joseph H. Osborn, Granger Leader," in the *Wisconsin Magazine of History,* 35:178–184 (Spring, 1952); on Hoyt see Henry J. Peterson's biographical sketch in the *Dictionary of American Biography,* 9:321 (New York, 1932); on Paul see Frank A. Flower, *History of Milwaukee, Wisconsin* (Chicago, 1881), 629–630. Deutsch describes Paul as Taylor's "major domo" and "good man Friday." Deutsch, in the *Wisconsin Magazine of History,* 15:392. Publication of the act had been delayed a month to give the railroads time to comply. Joint Resolution No. 11, in *Laws of Wisconsin,* 1874, p. 773.

[14] The letters of Keep and Mitchell are reprinted in the *First Annual Report of the Railroad Commissioners,* 1–6. On the opinions of counsel received by the roads, see "The Railway War" in the *Daily Inter-Ocean* (Chicago), May 5, 1874. See also the *Fifiteenth Annual Report of the Chicago and North Western Railway Company for the Fiscal Year Ending May 31, 1874* (Chicago, 1874), 19.

[15] Taylor's proclamation is found in Wisconsin Miscellaneous Pamphlets, 4:1–4, a compilation in the library of the State Historical Society of Wisconsin.

[16] Carpenter's opinion appeared in the *Wisconsin State Journal* (Madison), May 15, 1874. For a general account of Carpenter's role see E. Bruce Thompson, *Matthew Hale Carpenter: Webster of the West* (Madison, 1954), 212–213, and Frank A. Flower, *Life of Matthew Hale Carpenter* (Madison, 1883), 156.

[17] "Address to the People," May 21, 1874. and "Opinion of Attorney General Sloan," in *The Railroad Law of 1874* (Cited in note 11 above) pp. 5–9, 10–16.

[18] *Ibid.,* 6–9.

[19] "Wisconsin, whose railroads more than all other enterprises, have enriched the state and developed its resources, passed an Act on the 11th of March last, known as the 'Potter Act,' which, if possible, exceeds in its oppressive provisions towards railroads all the unjust legislation of other states.... Commissioners are appointed under this monstrous act, who are authorized to still further reduce the tariffs at their discretion, and the attempt is thus made by the state to delegate to three persons, unfamiliar with and inexperienced in railway management, the power to prescribe the compensation which we may receive for our business." *Fifteenth Annual Report of the Chicago and North Western Railway Company,* 1874, pp. 18–19. See also the *Chicago Times,* May 18, 19, 1874, reviewing Carpenter's opinion on the constitutionality of the Potter Law. On the instructions to agents to collect the full fare see "The Railroads," in the *Milwaukee Daily Sentinel,* May 2, 1874 (the reporter rode from Fond du Lac to Milwaukee offering only the legal fare and reported the colloquy he had had with the conductor).

[20] Bondholders v. Railroad Commissioners, 3 Fed. Cas. 847, No. 1625 (C.C.D. Wis., 1874); Piek v. Chicago & North Western R., 19 Fed. Cas. 625, No. 11, 138 (C.C.D. Wis., 1874). The relationship between these two circuit court cases is not clear from the reports. The first case involved only "railroad bondholders," was brought solely against the railroad commissioners, and was tried before Judge Drummond alone. In the second suit (the Piek case) plaintiffs were foreign and domestic bondholders and the trustees under the mortgages securing the bonds. Defendants were the Chicago and North Western Railway Company, the railroad commissioners, and the attorney general. It was tried before a three-judge

court consisting of Drummond, Justice David Davis of the United States Supreme Court, and J. C. Hopkins, district judge. The facts and statement of the case are set out in greater detail in the Piek case, but the date for the decision of both cases is given as July 4. The two opinions are identical save that in the first (bondholder) opinion Judge Drummond made a final suggestion to the effect that while this suit was pending the state should drop its prosecutions under the misdemeanor clauses of the Potter Law. The railroad commissioners, however, said that this bit of advice had been penned by Mr. Justice Davis. *First Annual Report of the Railroad Commissioners,* 1874, p. 28. Affirmation by the United States Supreme Court was in Peik (*sic*) v. Chicago & N. W. R., 94 U. S. 164 (1876). Apparently it had been the railroads' strategy to seek a temporary injunction during the pendency of which the attorney general would presumably ask to prepare his case for trial, since he was expected to plead only to the jurisdiction. The state nonplussed both the railroads and the court by saying that if its motions as to the jurisdiction were overruled it was ready to go to trial at once. Out of this came a continuance during which time no injunction or stay of any kind was in effect. Hoyt to Paul, June 4, 5, 1874, in the George H. Paul Papers, in the possession of the State Historical Society of Wisconsin.

[21] B. C. Cook (general solicitor of the North Western) to George B. Smith, May 26. 1874, in the George B. Smith Papers. See also, in this collection, the telegram of Albert Keep, president of the North Western, to Smith, May 23, 1874, and letters and telegrams from various Wisconsin attorneys to Smith.

[22] "The business men of this place [Sparta] and the general feeling here among the residents is adverse to any proceedings being commenced. They think enough suits are pending to fully test the constitutionality of the law without any further trouble and expense either to the people or to the state." Tyler & Dickinson, Attorneys, to Smith, June 19, 1874, in the Smith Papers. By this time, it may be noted, the suit in the federal court had been commenced. On dissatisfaction with the state's role see "The Railroads," in the *Milwaukee Daily Sentinel,* May 2, 1874 (interview with Hoyt, one of the railroad commissioners). See also Hoyt to Paul, May 16, 1874, in the Paul Papers. "Inquiries made by and on behalf of 'the people' indicate a general misapprehension as to the terms of the law. They are wondering '*why the Commissioners do not move.*' Probably not one in twenty has read the law." (Italics in original.)

[23] State v. West W. R., 34 Wis. 197 (1874).

[24] There is no reported case on these quo warranto actions, since they were dropped later. The applications and petitions are reprinted in the *First Annual Report of the Railroad Commissioners,* 1874, pp. 17–26. The applications were dated as early as May 13 and May 16, 1874, but the petitions were not filed until June 2. *Ibid.* See also Attorney General v. Railroad Companies, 35 Wis. 425, 433 (1874). However, President Keep wrote Smith on May 18 to thank him for information about the quo warranto proceedings. The letter is in the Smith Papers.

[25] Presumably the situation was one for which either mandamus or injunction would lie. See note 41 below. Article VII, section 3, of the state constitution gave the Supreme Court original jurisdiction in mandamus. On mandamus against railroads see W. Francis Bailey, *A Treatise on the Law of Habeas Corpus and Special Remedies* (Chicago, 1913), Vol. 2, sec. 291.

[26] The reasons Dixon gave were financial; the salary at that time was $3500 a year. Winslow, *Story of a Great Court,* 303–304; John R. Berryman, *History of the Bench and Bar in Wisconsin* (Chicago, 1898), 1:123. Dixon had resigned once before because of insufficient salary, only to be immediately reappointed at a higher salary, the increase having meantime been passed by the legislature. Winslow, *op. cit.,* 250–252. Dixon's resignation was regarded by one of the rail-

road commissioners as coming at an "unfortunate time." Hoyt to Paul, June 5, 1874, in the Paul Papers. The state gained Dixon's services in another capacity, however, inasmuch as he promptly entered into the bondholders' suit in the federal court and into the forthcoming injunction suit as one of counsel for the state. Hoyt to Paul, June 10, 1874, in the Paul Papers.

[27] Taylor to Paul, June 9, 1874, in the Paul Papers.

[28] Taylor to Paul, June 11, 1874, in the Paul Papers.

[29] On the offer to Vilas see Horace S. Merrill, *William Freeman Vilas: Doctrinaire Democrat* (Madison, 1954), 19, 34. Both Vilas and his father felt that the bench was a blind alley. On Ryan's appointment see Winslow, *Story of a Great Court,* 305. Some contemporary commentators felt that Ryan was placed on the bench solely to render a decision favorable to the state. See Brooks Adams' "Letter" in the *New York Tribune* of December 28, 1874.

[30] On June 24 the officers of the two roads met in Milwaukee, presumably to discuss whether they would comply with the rates set up in the Potter Law. Burton C. Cook, for one, expressed some hope that the conference would result in the roads' yielding. But two days later he wrote to Smith: "Nothing could be done at Milwaukee. The earnings of both roads for June had fallen off so heavily that it took 77 per cent of the gross earnings to pay the operating expenses. It was idle to talk about reducing fare." Cook to George B. Smith, July 23, 25. 1874, in the Smith Papers. On the North Western's strategy see the numerous letters and telegrams exchanged between Cook and Smith, respectively its general solicitor and Madison counsel, in the Smith Papers. The procedural questions seemed to be whether constitutional points should be presented by way of plea to the jurisdiction, answer or demurrer. Smith's strategy seems to have prevailed, and the issue was joined by way of answer rather than by demurrer. Cook and other Chicago counsel were hesitant to mingle so many questions of law and fact in the answer, but at the same time they wanted to raise as many meritorious issues as they could, which they felt could best be presented by an answer. Unfortunately no record similar to the Cook-Smith correspondence is available with respect to counsel for the Milwaukee Road.

[31] The Attorney General v. The Chicago and North Western Railway Company, 35 Wis. 425, and The Attorney General v. The Chicago, Milwaukee and St. Paul Railway Company, 35 Wis. 425 (1874). The opinion of the Supreme Court is cited hereafter as Attorney General v. Railroad Companies or as Ryan's opinion.

[32] See Winslow, *Story of a Great Court,* 132–134, and Berryman, *History of the Bench and Bar of Wisconsin,* 2:523. On Ithamar C. Sloan see Parker M. Reed, *The Bench and Bar of Wisconsin* (Milwaukee, 1882), 156–157. A. Scott Sloan had been Dixon's opponent in a hotly contested election for the Supreme Court in 1862. Winslow, *op. cit.,* 132–133. The quo warranto action was State v. West W. R., 34 Wis. 197 (1874), although it was Sloan's predecessor as attorney general, S. S. Barlow, who had apparently initiated the action. Complaint, State v. West Wisconsin Railway Company, in *Cases and Briefs,* 1:17, in the Wisconsin State Law Library.

[33] Berryman, *History of the Bench and Bar in Wisconsin,* 1:131–230. During his last year on the Supreme Court bench Orton was chief justice. Berryman (2:525) states that Sloan did not argue orally in the Railroad Companies case. Dixon did not submit a brief, but apparently he did argue orally.

[34] On Cook see the *National Cyclopaedia of American Biography* (New York, 1906), 13:592. On Lawrence see *ibid.,* 5:437, and Arthur T. Hadley. *Railroad Transportation* (New York, 1885), 134. Thus, appearing as counsel in the injunction suits were former chief justices of both the Illinois and the Wisconsin Supreme Courts. On George B. Smith see Berryman, *History of the Bench and Bar*

in Wisconsin, 2:377–381. On Cary see *ibid.,* 1:482, and Cary's book on the *Organization and History of the Chicago, Milwaukee and St. Paul* (Milwaukee, 1893). On Philip Spooner see Berryman. *op. cit.,* 2:39–402.

[35] The best of the anecdotes about Ryan's frankness are collected in Winslow's *Story of a Great Court,* 305–308. Ryan appeared for the prosecution in the Hubbell impeachment trial even though Judge Hubbell had shown his hand in Ryan's favor during the murder trial out of which the incidents causing the impeachment arose. Ryan represented Coles Bashford in the disputed election contest with Governor Barstow, even though Ryan was a lifelong Democrat of deep conviction and a Barstow man himself. He took an unpopular position in the Sherman Booth case, in which he asserted the constitutionality of the fugitive slave law and the lack of power of a state court to declare it invalid. In the midst of the Civil War he delivered a speech—the famous "Ryan Address"—denouncing Lincoln's suspension of the writ of habeas corpus and other alleged infringements of the constitution; the address became the platform of Wisconsin Democrats. Though in other respects a political liberal, Ryan was a confirmed reactionary in his disapproval of women taking their place at the bar. *Ibid.* His remark that he despaired of ever going on the bench is quoted in Berryman, *History of the Bench and Bar in Wisconsin,* 1:182. Ryan's high place at the bar is attested to by Winslow, *op. cit.,* 305–353, 396–401; Berryman, *op. cit.,* 1:166–204; and Reed, *Bench and Bar of Wisconsin,* 55–65. See also the remarks of William F. Vilas, A. R. Butler, T. R. Hudd, E. E. Bryant, James G. Jenkins, and Justice Orsamus Cole upon the death of Judge Ryan in 50 Wis. 23 ff. (1880). See also Alfons J. Beitzinger's manuscript dissertation on Chief Justice Ryan of the Wisconsin Supreme Court in the Memorial Library of the University of Wisconsin and his articles on "Chief Justice Ryan and his Colleagues," in the *Wisconsin Law Review,* 1955, pp. 592–608, and "Edward George Ryan, 19th Century Lawyer," *ibid.,* 1956, pp. 248–282.

[36] Remarks of T. R. Hudd of the Brown County bar on the death of Chief Justice Ryan, 50 Wis. 35, 38 (1880). See also the remarks of William F. Vilas, *ibid.,* 31. Respecting his education Ryan wrote: "My mother's father was a very wealthy man who died while I was a mere youngster. He left an annuity to my mother for the purpose of educating her children. There was ten of us, and we all received an excellent education. I received mine at Clongowes Wood College, where I remained for seven years, from 1820 to 1827." Quoted in Winslow, *Story of a Great Court,* 307. Both the judicial and nonjudicial writings of Ryan contain liberal sprinklings of Latin that could not have been picked up in legal literature alone. The Railroad Companies case takes up 183 pages in volume 35 of the *Wisconsin Reports,* of which Ryan's opinion occupies 97 pages. The remainder consists of headnotes, statement of the case, lists of relevant statutes, and briefs of counsel. A search of the Wisconsin Attorney General's office has failed to locate any file on the case, nor has such a file been transferred to the State Historical Society. Presumably it was destroyed in the state capitol fire of 1904. Apparently the files in the general counsels' offices of both the Chicago, Milwaukee and St. Paul and the Chicago and North Western have all been destroyed also. Communications to the author from Messrs. A. N. Whitlock and Nye Morehouse, general counsellors for the Milwaukee Road and the North Western, respectively. Through the courtesy of Mr. Charles McLeod, clerk of the Supreme Court, the author was able to examine the files on the case, but they yielded nothing of additional significance.

[37] Wisconsin Constitution, Art. VII, sec. 3; Attorney General v. Railroad Companies, 35 Wis. 425, 512 (1874).

[38] 1 Wis. 317 (1853). This was. however, a quo warranto action and not a suit for injunction. See note 40 below.

[39] Argument of Smith & Lamb in Attorney General v. Railroad Companies, 35 Wis. 425, 486–489 (1874). Page citations to briefs of counsel, unless otherwise indicated, will be to the pages in the reported case. The briefs were abstracted *in extenso* and do not differ materially from the actual briefs on file.

[40] Attorney General v. Railroad Companies, 35 Wis. 425, 518 (1874). (References to the opinion of the court will hereafter be cited as "Ryan's opinion.") Ryan here relied on some language of Judge Smith's in *Attorney General v. Blossom,* in which the issue of original jurisdiction of the Supreme Court in the case of quo warranto was in issue. "And why was original jurisdiction given to the Supreme Court, of these high prerogative writs? Because these are the very armor of sovereignty. Because they are designed for the very purpose of protecting the sovereignty of its ordained officers from invasion or intrusion, and also to nerve its arm to protect its citizens in their liberties, and to guard its prerogatives and franchises against usurpation." Attorney General v. Blossom, 1 Wis. 317, 330 (1853).

[41] Ryan's opinion, 519–520. In his discussion of the analogy between these two writs Ryan indicated that mandamus would also have been proper here: "it may be that where defect and excess meet in a single case, the court might meet both, in its discretion, by one of the writs, without being driven to send out both, tied together with red tape, for a single purpose." *Ibid.* To make his argument stronger Ryan went on to show that in the history of chancery jurisdiction there were instances where the writ of injunction did rest on a jurisdiction of its own. *Ibid.*, 523.

[42] *Ibid.* Italics supplied.

[43] Ryan's opinion, 550. The statute simply gave the attorney general authority to file for an injunction in the circuit court against a corporation acting *ultra vires. Wisconsin Revised Statutes,* 1858, ch. 148, sec. 13–14. See also the argument of I. C. Sloan, p. 509.

[44] Ryan's opinion, 556–557, 593.

[45] "The Attorney General, by sec. 22 of chap. 79, R. S., 1858, is clothed with vesitorial [*sic*] power over all corporations in the state and it is his duty to bring proceedings in quo warranto and mandamus, and why not proceedings for injunction? There can be no question, if this is a proper proceeding in the circuit court, it is in the supreme court and it will admit of no further argument." Argument of H. S. Orton for Complainant, p. 7, Attorney General v. Railroad Companies, in *Cases and Briefs,* vol. 186.

[46] That American authority had been against Ryan was the considered judgment of a later distinguished justice of the Wisconsin Supreme Court, John D. Wickhem. See his article "The Power of Superintending Control of the Wisconsin Supreme Court," in the *Wisconsin Law Review,* 1941, p. 158. See also Roscoe Pound, "Visitatorial Jurisdiction over Corporations in Equity," in the *Harvard Law Review,* 49:377 (January, 1936). Contemporary writers also considered Ryan's opinion aberrational on this point. See James L. High, *A Treatise on the Law of Injunctions* (2d edition, Chicago, 1880), 1:18, n. 1. ("The case is believed to constitute the only precedent for the interference of equity to enforce by injunction obedience to a penal statute, and it certainly extends the jurisdiction by injunction to a point unsustained either by principle or authority.") Ryan's response to this array of authority was as follows: "Every person suffering or about to suffer their [i.e., the railroad corporations] oppression by a disregard of corporate duty, may have his injunction. When the oppression becomes public, it is the duty of the attorney general to apply for the writ on behalf of the public.

And in this country, where the judicial tone is less certain, it is refreshing to read the bold and true words of which English equity judges do not spare the utterance." He went on to say (pp. 533–534):

> "The United States decisions seem to establish the jurisdiction of courts of equity in this country, as conclusively as it is established in England, of private suits to restrain private wrong arising from excess or abuse of power by corporations.
>
> In such cases public wrong may be considered only as an aggregation of private wrongs. And the jurisdiction once established to enjoin private wrong, in each case, at the suit of the person wronged, it is almost a logical necessity to admit the other branch of the jurisdiction, to enjoin, at the suit of the state, such a general wrong common to the whole public, as interests the state, and could be remedied by private persons by a vast multitude of suits only, burthensome to each and impracticable for every number; more conveniently, effectively and properly represented by the attorney general as *parens patriae*. But jurisdiction of informations of this nature has sometimes been denied here, courts of equity in this country, singularly enough, being sometimes more timid to control corporate powers, and less willing to protect the public against corporate abuse than the English chancery. In both branches of the jurisdiction, it proceeds as for *quasi* nuisance; and it is difficult to understand why the jurisdiction should be asserted as to private nuisance and denied as to public nuisance; why, for the same cause, individuals should have a remedy denied to the aggregate of individuals, called the public. But as we remarked before, in this regard the judicial voice in America is less certain in tone than in England."

[47] Attorney General v. Utica Insurance Co., 2 Johns Ch. 371 (N.Y., 1817).

[48] Ryan's opinions, 530–531. The issue Kent had actually dealt with, therefore, had been the propriety of the exercise of jurisdiction in the particular case before him rather than the existence of jurisdiction itself. Yet Kent's dicta, said Ryan, had led American courts astray. "So mischievous is the sanction of a great name to error." *Ibid.*, 550.

[49] Ryan's opinion, 523–524, 552. Argument of B. C. Cook and C. B. Lawrence for the Chicago and North Western and of John W. Cary for the Chicago, Milwaukee and St. Paul, 476, 494–495.

[50] Ryan's opinion, 551. Argument of John W. Cary, 494. See also Cook to Smith, July 23, 1874, in the Smith Papers: "the act [*Wisconsin Revised Statutes,* 1858, ch. 148] is unconstitutional because it abridges the right of trial by jury which existed when the State constitution was adopted and which that Constitution says shall not be abridged, for the remedy for the usurpation of a franchise was then *quo warranto,* in which proceeding the party was entitled to a jury, and the party cannot be deprived of this right of trial by jury by changing the name of the proceedings by which his rights are to be affected."

[51] "The conscience of the court must be satisfied; and it may be satisfied or not, with or without averment. If an information should aver public mischief, where the court could see that there was none, the averment would go for nothing. So without averment, it suffices that the court can see the public injury. It was hardly questioned that, in these cases, a public injury is apparent in the acts charged against these defendants. Directly or indirectly, this injury reaches every inhabitant of the state, and affects the whole state in its corporate capacity. It was indeed, confidently foretold by the counsel for the defendants, that obedience to the law would work a still greater public injury. Upon that it is not for us to speculate.

And if we could, we cannot sit here to offset a speculative injury arising from obedience of law, against a positive injury arising from disobedience of law. In these days of self-judging insubordination, it would ill become this court to set so bad an example of compromise between right and wrong." Ryan's opinion, 552–553.

[52] 4 Wheat. 518 (U. S., 1819).

[53] Ryan's opinion, 563–568. Ryan was referring to Mr. Justice Daniel's opinion for the court in West River Bridge Co. v. Dix, 6 How. 507 (U. S., 1848).

[54] Ryan's opinion, 564–567, 569. It is unlikely, however, that Marshall would have followed Ryan on this argument. See Benjamin F. Wright, Jr., *The Contract Clause of the Constitution* (Cambridge, 1938), 42.

[55] Ryan's opinion, 567.

[56] *Ibid.*

[57] Wisconsin Constitution, Art. XI, sec. 1.

[58] Ryan's opinion, 569–574. This seemed to be the unanimous view. The opinions of Carpenter and Attorney General Sloan had pointed this out expressly. Carpenter's opinion, in the *Wisconsin State Journal,* May 15, 1874, pp. 8–10; opinion of Attorney General Sloan, in *The Railroad Law of 1874,* 10. Ryan himself had been a member of the Wisconsin Constitutional Convention, but in his opinion he did not cite any of the journals or debates. See Wright, *Contract Clause,* 84–86, 168–178.

[59] Ryan's opinion, 574. Ryan did not say, however, that a state could lift itself by its bootstraps out of the domain of federal law. "This is a question of state law, not of federal law. We give full scope to the federal constitution as interpreted by the federal courts, but we stand clearly outside of both. This question could be brought within the Dartmouth College rule, not by interpretation of the federal constitution, but by interpretation of the state constitution only. That is our function. We accept the construction of the federal constitution as the federal courts give it. But we give construction to our own constitution for ourselves. And there we might well rest." *Ibid.*

[60] Judge Lawrence's "due process" argument appears on pages 480–481. This portion of the argument was also made by Judge Lawrence in the Piek case in the federal courts. *Ibid.,* 478n. On the contributions to the "due process" concept made by lawyers in the Granger cases, see Benjamin R. Twiss, *Lawyers and the Constitution: How Laissez-Faire Came to the Supreme Court* (Princeton, 1942), 71–77. The expropriation rationale is set forth in the argument of John W. Cary, 499–500, and that of C. B. Lawrence and B. C. Cook, 479–482, 491–492. This was also the argument made by Evarts and Curtis. "The Railway War" in the *Daily Inter-Ocean* (Chicago), May 5, 1874.

[61] Ryan's opinion, 578.

[62] *Ibid.,* 579–580.

[63] *Ibid.,* 578–579; argument of C. B. Lawrence and B. C. Cook, 482–483.

[64] Ryan's opinion, 560–561; argument of C. B. Lawrence and B. C. Cook, 467–477.

[65] Ryan's opinion, 586–592, 596.

[66] Ryan's opinion on the motion to vacate in Attorney General v. Railroad Companies, 35 Wis. 425, 599–608 (1874). The attorney general moved to vacate that part of the order which exempted the portion of the Milwaukee Road that had formerly belonged to the Milwaukee and Prairie du Chien (successor to the Milwaukee and Waukesha). I. C. Sloan made the argument in support of the motion and John W. Cary the argument against it. *Ibid.,* 425, 597–598.

[67] Ryan's opinion, 585.

[68] Ryan's opinion, 554–555; arguments of P. L. Spooner and John W. Cary, 493, 502. The first law amended the general railroad act of 1872 by providing that "All existing railroad corporations within this state shall respectively have and possess all the powers and privileges contained in this act and in their respective charter, and they shall be subject to all the duties and liabilities." *Laws of Wisconsin,* 1874, ch. 292, sec. 2. Ryan pointed out that the intent of this provision was simply to insure that existing companies had the same powers under the general act that they had had under their special charters. It granted no new powers nor immunities to the companies. The other act stated that "if any railroad company organized or doing business within this state or, which may hereafter do business within this state, shall charge, collect, demand or recover *more than a fair and reasonable rate of compensation* upon any line or road within this state, which it has the right, license or permission to use, operate or control, the same shall be deemed guilty of extortion. and upon conviction thereof shall be fined...." *Laws of Wisconsin,* 1874, ch. 341, sec. 9 (italics supplied). Ryan pointed out three instances where this act could apply without conflicting with the rate provisions of the Potter Law: (1) maximum rates of the Potter Law which exceeded "reasonable" rates; (2) Class C rates which the Potter Law did not set out; and (3) rates for certain traffic on railroads which the Potter Law did not set out expressly and which the railroad commissioner had not yet prescribed. Ryan could not refrain from commenting, however, on the anomaly of this act juxtaposed to the Potter Law. "It must be admitted that this looks like careless and slovenly legislation." Ryan's opinion, 555.

[69] The injunctions prayed for had excluded all questions of interstate commerce. Ryan's opinion, 584. Lawrence and Cook had also argued that to permit railroad commissioners to fix rates was an unauthorized delegation of legislative power. Argument of C. B. Lawrence and B. C. Cook, 477. Ryan pointed out that since the only rates thus far established were those set out by the statute, the powers of the railroad commissioners were not in issue. Ryan's opinion, 553.

[70] Ryan's opinion, 516. See also the argument of Luther S. Dixon in Attorney General v. Eau Claire, 37 Wis. 400, 411 (1875): "It is not surprising that the court looked in vain to the bar for assistance in the argument of the *Railway Cases,* when we reflect that both court and bar had been wandering in utter darkness for a period of more than twenty-five years."

[71] Ryan's opinion, 522.

[72] Argument of Smith and Lamb, 485–487. Brief of Smith and Lamb for the Chicago and North Western Railway, 1–27, in *Cases and Briefs,* vol. 186; argument of John W. Cary, 502–503; brief of John W. Cary for the Chicago, Milwaukee and St. Paul Railway. Part I. With Ryan's opinion in the Railroad companies case should be read his opinion in Attorney General v. Eau Claire, 37 Wis. 400 (1875) (original jurisdiction of Supreme Court invoked to enjoin city from entering on proposed improvement of river dam; injunction granted, reaffirming principles of Railroad Companies case). See also his twenty-page dissent in In re Ida Louise Pierce, 44 Wis. 411 (1878). That suit—a habeas corpus proceeding—he asserted was not a proper controversy for the exercise of the original jurisdiction of the Supreme Court. The dissent complements the Railroad Companies and Eau Claire cases by suggesting limitations to the exercise of original jurisdiction.

[73] See Pound in the *Harvard Law Review,* 49:380.

[74] Typical of contemporary textbook discussion was Isaac F. Redfield's *Law of Railways* (5th edition, Boston, 1873), 2:309, n. 12.

[75] In Olcott v. Board of Supervisors, 16 Wall, 678, 694 (1873): "That the legislature may alter or repeal the charter granted to the Sheboygan & Fond du

Lac Railroad, is certain. This is a power reserved by the [state] constitution. The railroad can, therefore, be controlled and regulated by the state. Its use can be defined; its tolls and rates for transportation may be limited." Quoted in Ryan's opinion, 576. The facts that brought forth the Olcott decision are discussed above, pages 86–87. For contemporary law-review literature see Leonard A. Jones, ed., *Index to Legal Periodicals (to December 1, 1886)* (Boston, 1888), under heading "Railroads."

[76] Ryan's opinion, 594–595.

[77] High, *Law of Injunctions,* Vol. 1, sec. 11. Ryan, of course, was well aware of this. But he excepted this case from the general rule by emphasizing the public nature of the wrong committed and the manifest distinction between this and ordinary suits to restrain the commission of mere private wrongs. In cases where the matter was *publici juris,* Ryan said, issuance of the injunction was no longer a matter of discretion once the wrong had been proved. But in support of this dictum he could cite only Thomas Tapping, *The Law and Practice of the High Prerogative Writ of Mandamus* (1853), 287, and with respect to mandamus the statement was undoubtedly true. Ryan buttressed his position once more by pointing out the analogy between mandamus and injunction. Ryan's opinion, 554.

[78] Ryan's opinion, 595–596. Ryan felt that the attorney general must elect his remedy. If the court granted the injunction, the state must stipulate that it would discontinue its prosecutions under the quo warranto informations. Presumably Ryan saw that the two remedies were inconsistent, although he did not so state explicitly. Cook had written Smith of the importance of gaining time for the railroads to adjust their tariffs if the injunction was granted. Cook to Smith, September 12, 1874, in the Smith Papers. Presumably Smith made such a request to the court. In the event that this was not time enough Ryan gave defendants opportunity to move for more time upon showing proper proof of inability to prepare the new tariffs. Ryan's opinion, 596.

[79] Compare Morris R. Cohen's discussion of "Property and Sovereignty," in his *Law and the Social Order: Essays in Legal Philosophy* (New York, 1933), 41–68.

[80] "This very controversy may well bring about a better and more permanent understanding and relation between the state and its corporations. We say so much in deference to an earnest appeal from the bar to counsel modernation. But in the meantime, we cannot legislate for either party." Ryan's opinion, 582–583.

[81] See pages 114, 116 and 122 above.

[82] See, for example, his discussion of the historical jurisdiction of chancery over corporations and his remarks on the background and history of the contract clause. Ryan's opinion, 523–550, 562–574. His penchant for getting all the citations is revealed in a later case, where he added as a footnote some cases he had overlooked when he wrote the opinion. Attorney General v. West W. R., 36 Wis. 466, 487 (1874).

[83] "We are not considering the charter as a mere statute. We are considering it, in obedience to the Dartmouth college rule, as a contract. We are not giving our own views of its effect. We are looking at it in the mirage of federal construction. Considering this matter of purely state law and state policy, we are sitting *in vinculis,* bound by an interpretation of the prohibition in the federal constitution, on a subject with no federal relation, which we think it ought not to bear; and which, it is admitted it was not intended to bear; but which, while it stands, emasculates state authority over state corporations. We are sitting on this question of state law and state policy, not so much as the Supreme Court of Wisconsin, as an inferior federal court. And we are bound, on this subject to rule, not as we think, but as the federal supreme court thinks. The adjudications

of this court on state law and state policy have been frequently overruled by that court, without excuse found in the federal constitution. We do not mean to give an opportunity now, with excuse. On this point we admit and defer to their authority." Ryan's opinion, 590.

[84] Ryan's opinion, 544 (citation of concurring opinion in Missouri v. Saline County Court, 50 Mo. 350 [1873]). See his remark about "slovenly legislation" quoted in note 68 above and his rhetorical tirade against communism, page 120 above.

[85] Alexander Mitchell to Governor Taylor, September 26, 1874, in the *First Annual Report of the Railroad Commissioners,* 1874, 79–80. There would have been little point to an appeal inasmuch as the same questions were involved in the bondholders' suit which was up on appeal. Unless otherwise noted, discussion of the aftermath of the Potter Law and the Railroad Companies' case is based on Buck, *The Granger Movement,* 189–194.

[86] *Laws of Wisconsin,* 1875, ch. 113, 334.

[87] *Laws of Wisconsin,* 1876, ch. 57.

[88] See, for example, State *ex rel.* Wood v. Baker, 38 Wis. 71 (1875) (quo warranto involving county officers); Attorney General v. Eau Claire, 37 Wis. 400 1875), (cited in note 72 above; State *ex rel.* Cash v. Supervisors of Juneau County, 38 Wis. 554 (1875) (mandamus); State *ex rel.* Drake v. Doyle, 40 Wis. 175 (1876) *id. sub nom.* State *ex rel.* Continental Insurance Co. v. Doyle, 40 Wis. 220 (1876) (mandamus against secretary of state); In re Semler, 41 Wis. 517 (1877) (habeas corpus); In re Ida Louise Pierce, 44 Wis. 411 (1878) (habeas corpus; twenty-page dissent by Ryan). See John Varda's compilation, in manuscript, of Decisions of the Supreme Court of Wisconsin Rendered in the Exercise of Its Original Jurisdiction, in the possession of the Law Library of the University of Wisconsin.

[89] *Laws of Wisconsin,* 1874, ch. 273, sec. 8.

[90] See note 22 above.

[91] But compare Pound, in the *Harvard Law Review,* 49:394–395, to the effect that proper use of visitatorial power would be better than the administrative process.

[92] Munn v. Illinois, 94 U. S. 113, 134, (1876). Compare Brooks Adams' "Letter," in the *New York Times,* December 28, 1874 ("Where resistance should be made to the Potter law is at the polls.").

[93] Chicago, M. & St. P. R. v. Minnesota. 134 U. S. 418 (1890).

[94] It is interesting to note, however, that in 1873 Senator Matthew H. Carpenter delivered a twenty-nine page address in which he discussed the power of Congress to regulate railroads under the interstate commerce clause. Speech of Matthew H. Carpenter before the Agricultural Society of Winnebago County, Illinois (delivered at Rockford, September 18, 1873) in a manuscript collection of the Writings of Matthew H. Carpenter, 1865–80, in the possession of the State Historical Society of Wisconsin. See also Thompson, *Matthew Hale Carpenter,* 202–203.

[95] Cook to Smith, July 23, 1874, in the Smith Papers.

[96] When, in 1905, Wisconsin enacted another set of stringent regulatory laws, the states' mandate was obeyed without appeal to the courts. Gilbert E. Roe, ed., *Dixon, Luther S. and Ryan, Edward G.: Selected Opinions* (Chicago, 1907), 382.

[97] For another view of Taylor, see Deutsch in the *Wisconsin Magazine of History,* 15:396.

V. WISCONSIN RAILROAD LAW FROM 1875 TO 1890

[1] *Laws of Wisconsin,* 1883, ch. 276 (spur tracks and branch lines); 1891, ch. 282 (underpasses); 1877, ch. 205, amending section 16 of chapter 119 of the *General Laws* of 1872 (setting out period of delay); 1876, ch. 72, sec. 4 (authorizing Green Bay and Minnesota Railroad to condemn land in Minnesota in accordance with Minnesota laws, in order to construct a pontoon bridge over the Mississippi); 1889, ch. 255 (excepting land taken by eminent domain from general statute providing for recoverable damages).

[2] With respect to excess condemnation see Cornell University v. Wisconsin C. R., 49 Wis. 158 (1880) (Supreme Court affirmed overruling of motion to dismiss for lack of jurisdiction based on fact that land lay in county created after suit was begun). On the battle for the northern timberlands between Cornell University and the railroads see Paul W. Gates, *The Wisconsin Pine Lands of Cornell University: A Study in Land Policy and Absentee Ownership* (Ithaca, 1943), ch. 9. On depreciation in value see Neilson v. Chicago, M. & St. P. R., 58 Wis. 516 (1883); Weyer v. Chicago, W. & N. R., 68 Wis. 180 (1887); Heiss v. Milwaukee & L. W. R., 69 Wis. 555 (1887) (depreciation in value unaccompanied by physical invasion did not constitute a "taking"). Compare First Congregational Church v. Milwaukee & L. W. R., 77 Wis. 158 (1890) (expense of light gravel fill to restore street to former usefulness not recoverable) and Diedrich v. Northwestern U. R., 42 Wis. 248 (1877) and 47 Wis. 662 (1879) (no compensation to riparian owner for damages to breakwater constructed beyond river bank). See also State *ex rel.* Northwestern U. R. v. Small, 47 Wis. 436 (1879) (mandamus against circuit judge arising out of same circumstances). But compare Shealy v. Chicago M. & N. R., 72 Wis. 471 (1888) and 77 Wis. 653 (1890) (digging of lot in front of plantiff's lot was a "taking") and Buchner v. Chicago M. & St. P. R., 56 Wis. 403 (1882) and 60 Wis. 264 (1884) (no compensation in condemnation proceeding, but plaintiff could recover in action at law for damages).

[3] Bohlman v. Green Bay & M. R., 40 Wis. 157 (1876) (second hearing). On the first hearing the court had decided that under the 1861 law entry before compensation was permissible with the consent of the owner. See above, page 134. On the rehearing the decision construed the 1872 act as demanding appraisal and compensation first. Chief Judge Ryan administered the *coup de grace* in Sherman v. Milwaukee, L. S. & W. R., 40 Wis. 645 (1876), a case holding that the fee of a landowner in the public highway was protected just as much as the fee in his own land. "This case is governed by the constitution and statutes of this state, and the settled construction of them by this court. Upon open questions in this court, we listen always with interest and often with instruction to the decisions of courts elsewhere, upon kindred questions. But when the rules of decision in this court are settled, we cannot disregard them because different rules may prevail elsewhere. There must always come a time when questions settled by the decisions of this court cease to be open here." *Ibid.,* 649. See also Blesch v. Chicago & N. W. R., 43 Wis. 183 (1887), 44 Wis. 593 (1878), and 48 Wis. 168 (1879) (damages for land in public highway in which plaintiff had the fee).

[4] *Commissioners' awards and deeds of neighboring property inadmissible as evidence of value:* Munkwitz v. Chicago, M. & St. P. R., 64 Wis. 413 (1885); Seefeld v. Chicago, M. & St. P. R., 67 Wis. 96 (1896) (commissioners' awards); Esch v. Chicago, M. & St. P. R., 72 Wis. 229 (1888) (deeds of neighboring lands). Compare Neilson v. Chicago, M. & St. P. R., 58 Wis. 516 (1883) (propriety of a jury view of the premises). *Allowability of interest:* West v. Milwaukee, L. S. & W. R., 56 Wis. 318 (1882) (reversed for failure to instruct jury to allow interest); Uniake v. Chicago, M. & St. P. R., 67 Wis. 108 (1886) (general rule is to allow interest).

See also Seefeld v. Chicago, M. & St. P. R., 67 Wis. 96, 101 (1886) (following Uniake case). *Nominal damages:* Rusch v. Milwaukee, L. S. & W. R., 54 Wis. 136 (1882) (nominal damages only for feeholder of public street because six years earlier an amount had been paid into court for apportionment among several owners on joint award of compensation).

[5] *Proper to appraise the lands in gross:* Spaulding v. Milwaukee, L. S. & W. R., 57 Wis. 304 (1883); *accord:* Wooster v. Sugar R. V. R., 57 Wis. 311 (1883); Watson v. Milwaukee & M. R., 57 Wis. 332 (1883).

[6] *Jurisdiction:* Cornell University v. Wisconsin C. R., 49 Wis. 158 (1880), note 2 above; Wright v. Northwestern U. R., 37 Wis. 39 (1875) (Milwaukee County Court had power to enter order as of September term after first Monday in October). *Appellate procedure:* Weyer v. Milwaukee & L. W. R., 57 Wis. 329 (1883) (Supreme Court affirmed trial court's order denying motion of defendant-railroad that the appeal be dismissed because of plaintiff's failure to comply with certain procedural niceties regarding notice of appeal and posting of bond); Gill v. Milwaukee & L. W. R., 76 Wis. 293 (1890) (involving appeal from order appointing commissioners); Washburn v. Milwaukee & L. W. R., 59 Wis. 379 (1884) (separate appeals permitted); Larson v. Superior S. L. R., 64 Wis. 59 (1885) (single notice of several appeals permissible); Cornish v. Milwaukee & L. W. R., 60 Wis. 476 (1884) (general statute governing waiver of rights to cost where judgment is not perfected not applicable to condemnation proceedings). *Miscellaneous:* McVey v. Green Bay & M. R., 42 Wis. 532 (1877) and Lyon v. Green Bay & M. R., 42 Wis. 538 (1877) (legal status of conveyance to married women); Washburn v. Milwaukee & L. W. R., 58 Wis. 364 (1884) (many procedural points, none of which determinative of outcome).

[7] Typical cases were the following: Erd v. Chicago & N. W. R., 41 Wis. 65 (1876) and McHugh v. Chicago & N. W. R., 41 Wis. 112 (1876) (fences); Caswell v. Chicago & N. W. R., 42 Wis. 193 (1877) (barn); Abbott v. Gore, 74 Wis. 509 (1889) (hay); Mells v. Chicago, M. & St. P. R., 76 Wis. 422 (1890) and Moore v. Chicago, M. & St. P. R., 78 Wis. 120 (1890) (cranberry marshes). In Gibbons v. Wisconsin Valley R., 58 Wis. 335 (1885) the court adhered to its earlier rulings and held that it was not negligence per se for the defendant-railroad to fail to keep its right-of-way clear of combustible materials, citing Kellogg v. Chicago & N. W. R., 26 Wis. 223 (1870) discussed on pages 134–135 above. With respect to the relevance of out-of-state cases the court wrote: "We need not have gone outside of the decisions of this court for an authoritative decision of this question, but unfortunately it has been customary to cite other authorities in order to show that this court decided the question correctly." *Ibid.*, 342–343. On evidentiary questions see Brusberg v. Milwaukee, L. S. & W. R., 50 Wis. 231 (1880) and 55 Wis. 106 (1882) (evidence as to speed of locomotive does not necessarily have causal relation to fact of fire; also, proof by defendant of use of foolproof spark arrester not conclusive); Gibbons v. Wisconsin V. R.. 58 Wis. 335 (1883), 62 Wis. 546 (1885), and 66 Wis. 161 (1886) (evidence as to sparkproof equipment and frequent inspections); Allard v. Chicago & N. W. R., 73 Wis. 165 (1888) (evidence that other engines had caused other fires not admissible); Stacy v. Milwaukee, L. S. & W. R., 72 Wis. 331 (1888) (reversed because material testimony as to previous contradictory statement of witness had been excluded); Beggs v. Chicago, W. & M. R., 75 Wis. 444 (1890) (error in admission of evidence cured where evidence was withdrawn before closing argument of counsel). On the role of judge and jury, see Stertz v. Stewart, 74 Wis. 160 (1889) (damages to plaintiff's farm done by railroad engine a question for jury to decide); Clune v. Milwaukee & N. R., 75 Wis. 532 (1890) (issues of negligence and contributory negligence to be decided by jury); Murphy v. Chicago & N. W. R., 45 Wis. 222 (1878) (same); Reed

v. Chicago, M. & St. P. R., 71 Wis. 399 (1888) (Supreme Court affirmed order granting new trial where plaintiff had received only nominal damages).

[8] *Laws of Wisconsin,* 1882, ch. 286; Swarthout v. Chicago & N. W. R., 49 Wis. 625 (1880); Hustisferd Farmers' Mutual Ins. Co. v. Chicago, M. & St. P. R., 66 Wis. 58 (1886). The Wisconsin Supreme Court also followed precedent in other states by permitting the insurance company, on payment of the claim, to be subrogated to the property owner's cause of action. On these statutes and on subrogation in general see Harry Shulman and Fleming James, Jr., *Cases and Materials on the Law of Torts* (Brooklyn, 1942). 113–125.

[9] The statutes relating to clear rights-of-way applied to landowners as well as to railroads. *Laws of Wisconsin,* 1887, ch. 313, sec. 3, 6; 1889, ch. 512. The other statute gave plaintiffs injured by a railroad's interference with a navigable stream a chance to recover treble damages. *Wisconsin Revised Statutes,* 1878, sec. 1837; Sweeney v. Chicago, M. & St. P. R., 60 Wis. 60 (1884); Gates v. Chicago & N. W. R., 64 Wis. 64 (1885) (lumberman entitled to unrestricted right of passage on river). Compare Clark v. Chicago & N. W. R., 70 Wis. 593 (1888) (plaintiff must make a clear and unequivocal showing of damages in order to state a cause of action). See also Delaplaine v. Chicago & N. W. R., 42 Wis. 214 (1877) (court held damages recoverable against railroad for creating a stagnant pool interfering with drainage); O'Connor v. Fond du L.. A. & P. R., 52 Wis. 526 (1881) (damages allowed for the damming up of artificial ditch that drained water from plaintiff's premises); Denver v. Chicago, M. & St. P. R., 57 Wis. 218 (1883) (injunction would not lie in favor of naked possessor where railroad diverted stream on plaintiff's land; remedy was at law for abatement of nuisance or damages). Compare Carl v. Sheboygan & F. du L. R., 47 Wis. 59 (1879) (action for damages resulting when right-of-way cut off access to house; reversed by Supreme Court for improper admission of evidence). Many of the cases turned on procedural points alone. See, for example, Gilman v. Sheboygan & F. du L. R., 37 Wis. 317 (1875) (judgment against railroad enforceable in equity against successor in interest, even though no action at law would lie); Methodist Episcopal Church v. Northern P. R., 78 Wis. 131 (1890) (plaintiff denied recovery where he made out a case for damages but framed his complaint in ejectment).

[10] *Laws of Wisconsin,* 1875, ch. 248, sec. 1 (requiring fencing and construction of farm crossings and cattle guards; if company did not comply the owner, after giving notice, could recover ten dollars for each train that passed through); 1876, ch. 169 (amending the 1875 law by excluding the period between November and May from the six-month period); 1878, ch. 292, sec. 1 (excepting person driving from one part of his lands to another from sections of fencing laws prohibiting people from driving along track); 1878, ch. 328, sec. 2 (fence must be four and one-half feet high; railroad need not fence along rivers or other places where livestock were not likely to stray); 1879, ch. 153 (exempting Pine River Valley and Stevens Point railroads from fencing laws for ten years); 1881, ch. 119 (barbed-wire fence now defined as "legal-fence"); 1881, ch. 193, and 1882, ch. 201 (increased the number of barbs per foot).

[11] *Whether plaintiff came within the language of the statute:* Cook v. Milwaukee & St. P. R., 36 Wis. 45 (1874) (cattle injured where track traversed farm crossing rather than highway crossing; demurrer sustained); Bremer v. Green Bay, S. P. & N. R., 61 Wis. 114 (1884) (to recover the plaintiff must show that cow got on track at a point that defendant was compelled by statute to fence). A defense the railroads frequently raised was that the livestock were injured on "depot grounds," the fencing of which was not required by the statute. Peters v. Stewart, 72 Wis. 138 (1888) (directed verdict for defendant affirmed); McDonough v. Milwaukee & N. R., 73 Wis. 223 (1888) (verdict and judgment for

plaintiff affirmed); Jaeger v. Chicago, M. & St. P. R., 75 Wis. 130 (1889) (judgment for plaintiff affirmed—mere spur of track not "depot grounds"); Andersen v. Stewart, 76 Wis. 43 (1890) (judgment for plaintiff affirmed; evidence showed that location was not "depot grounds"). *Whether plaintiff sustained burden of proof as to negligence:* Among other cases, Goddard v. Chicago & N. W. R., 54 Wis. 548 (1882) (it was error to submit question of negligence to jury at all, since flood had washed fences away only eight days before the accident and it was not shown that defendant had had a chance to repair fences after storm blew them down). Compare Davenport v. Chicago, B. & N. R., 76 Wis. 399 (1890) (judgment on verdict for plaintiff reversed because evidence showed that horses got on track as a result of negligence of third party in leaving gate unlatched). *Whether plaintiff was contributorily negligent:* McCandless v. Chicago & N. W. R., 45 Wis. 365 (1878) (order directing nonsuit affirmed, plaintiff held guilty of "gross contributory negligence" in permitting cow to roam around railroad tracks); Williams v. Chicago, M. & St. P. R., 64 Wis. 1 (1886) (nonsuit affirmed, plaintiff contributorily negligent as matter of law—failed to exercise "ordinary vigilance"); Gunn v. Wisconsin & M. R., 70 Wis. 203 (1887) (Supreme Court reversed judgment on verdict, holding it to be contributory negligence as matter of law to leave horse and carriage to cross track alone). Richardson v. Chicago, M. & St. P. R., 56 Wis. 403 (1882) (negligence of minor in failing to keep gate locked imputed to plaintiff-father).

[12] See, for example, Blomberg v. Stewart, 67 Wis. 455 (1886); Dinwoodie v. Chicago, M. & St. P. R., 69 Wis. 454 (1887); Welch v. Abbot, 72 Wis. 512 (1888) (judgments on jury verdicts for plaintiff affirmed); Dean v. Chicago & N. W. R., 43 Wis. 431 (1877) (measure of damages).

[13] *General Laws of Wisconsin,* 1872, ch. 119, sec. 30.

[14] Brown v. Railway Co., 21 Wis. 39 (1866). See also McCall v. Chamberlain, 13 Wis. 637 (1861); Antisdel v. Railway Co., 26 Wis. 145 (1870); Sika v. Railway Co., 21 Wis. 370 (1867); Bennett v. Railway Co., 19 Wis. 145 (1865); Schmidt v. Railway Co., 23 Wis. 186 (1868); and Pitzner v. Shinnick, 39 Wis. 129 (1875) and 41 Wis. 676 (1877).

[15] Curry v. Chicago & N. W. R., 43 Wis. 665, 682–683 (1878). In the course of his opinion Ryan contrasted the fencing statute of 1872 imposing penal sanctions and the law of 1875 giving plaintiffs a civil right of action and said that the two sections were cumulative, not alternative. See also Lawrence v. Milwaukee. L. S. & W. R., 42 Wis. 322 (1877) (order directing nonsuit affirmed, opinion by Ryan).

[16] *Wisconsin Revised Statutes,* 1878, sec. 1810.

[17] Quackenbush v. Wisconsin & M. R., 62 Wis. 411 (1885) and 71 Wis. 472 (1888) (employee killed when thrown out of train as a result of its running over steer on track).

[18] *Laws of Wisconsin,* 1889, ch. 123 (guards and blocks) and ch. 516 (attendants at turntables).

[19] *Accidents at intersections:* Roberts v. Chicago & N. W. R., 35 Wis. 679 (1874) (plaintiff injured when defendant ran into buggy); Grasse v. Lake S. & W. R., 36 Wis. 582 (1875) (plaintiff and wife injured while going across "farm crossing"); Horn v. Chicago & N. W. R., 38 Wis. 613 (1875) (plaintiff thrown out of wagon when hit by defendant's cars); Gower v. Chicago, M. & St. P. R., 45 Wis. 182 (1878) (plaintiff injured while crossing public highway in Milwaukee); Urbanek v. Chicago, M. & St. P. R., 47 Wis. 59 (1879) (personal injury and damages to horses and wagon); Eilert v. Green Bay & M. R., 48 Wis. 606 (1879) (plaintiff injured when horse and wagon hit by train); Johnson v. Chicago & N. W. R., 49 Wis. 529 (1880) (child killed where railroad crossed city street); Russian v. Milwaukee,

L. S. & W. R., 56 Wis. 325 (1882) (plaintiff and son injured when train struck sleigh); Hoye v. Chicago & N. W. R., 62 Wis 667 (1885) (decedent killed at street crossing); Ferguson v. Wisconsin C. R., 63 Wis. 145 (1885) (plaintiff injured on crossing when struck by detached car as defendant was making running switch); Seefeld v. Chicago, M. & St. P. R., 70 Wis. 216 (1887) (injuries resulting from collision on railroad track); Duame v. Chicago & N. W. R., 72 Wis. 523 (1888) (decedent killed on crossing when train unexpectedly backed down); Abbott v. Dwinnell, 74 Wis. 514 (1889) (personal injuries received when thrown from wagon hit by train); Heddles v. Chicago & N. W. R., 74 Wis. 239 (1889) and 77 Wis. 228 (1890) (boy injured at crossing); Piper v. Chicago, M. & St. P. R., 77 Wis. 247 (1890) (personal injury suffered at town railroad crossing). Compare Winchell v. Abbot, 77 Wis. 371 (1890) (personal injury suffered where track crossed sidewalk); Hahn v. Chicago, M. & St. P. R., 78 Wis. 396 (1890) (personal injuries suffered at farm crossing); Winstanley v. Chicago, M. & St. P. R., 72 Wis. 375 (1888) (wrongful death at crossing of track and "private way"). *Accidents resulting from runaway horses:* Ransom v. Chicago, M. & St. P. R., 62 Wis. 178 (1885); McCandless v. Chicago & N. W. R., 71 Wis. 41 (1888); Abbott v. Kalbus, 74 Wis. 504 (1889) and 77 Wis. 621 (1890). *Accidents to pedestrians walking along the tracks:* Townley v. Chicago, M. & St. P. R., 53 Wis. 657 (1881); Davis v. Chicago & N. W. R., 50 Wis. 646 (1883); Hogan v. Chicago, M. & St. P. R., 59 Wis. 141 (1883); Burns v. North Chicago Rolling Mill Co., 60 Wis. 646 (1884) and 65 Wis. 451 (1886); Ewald v. Chicago & N. W. R., 70 Wis. 420 (1888); Schilling v. Chicago & N. W. R., 71 Wis. 255 (1888); Phillips v. Milwaukee & N. R., 77 Wis. 349 (1890). *Cf.* Ewen v. Chicago & N. W. R., 38 Wis. 613 (1875) (nine year old boy killed while playing on track); Haas v. Chicago & N. W. R., 41 Wis. 44 (1876) (10 year old boy killed by railroad passing through town at excessvie speed); Kearney v. Chicago, M. & St. P. R., 47 Wis. 144 (1879) (plaintiff killed running across tracks); Jucker v. Chicago & N. W. R., 52 Wis. 150 (1881) (child killed straying on tracks); Bohan v. Milwaukee, L. S. & W. R., 58 Wis. 30 (1883) and 61 Wis. 391 (1884) (child injured running across tracks near depot); Hoppe v. Chicago, M. & St. P. R., 61 Wis. 357 (1884) (child killed after crawling through hole in fence onto track); Kleinenhagen v. Chicago, M. & St. P. R., 65 Wis. 66 (1886) (plaintiff injured by door in stock car); Miller v. Chicago, M. & St. P. R., 68 Wis. 184 (1887) (decedent killed standing on track); McDonald v. Chicago, M. & St. P. R., 75 Wis. 121 (1889) (decedent killed driving horse and buggy along track); Hooker v. Chicago, M. & St. P. R., 76 Wis. 542 (1890) (decedent killed walking on bridge in town). *Accidents resulting from obstructions:* Washburn v. Chicago & N. W. R., 68 Wis. 474 (1887) (five-year-old boy fell into excavation); Goldstein v. Chicago, M. & St. P. R., 46 Wis. 404 (1879) (plaintiff in buggy thrown into canal because passage between canal and railroad was too narrow).

[20] The following wrongful-death cases came before the Supreme Court during this period: Ewen v. Chicago & N. W. R., 38 Wis. 613 (1875); Haas v. Chicago & N. W. R., 41 Wis. 44 (1876); Kearney v. Chicago, M. & St. P. R., 47 Wis. 144 (1879); Johnson v. Chicago & N. W. R., 49 Wis. 529 (1880), 56 Wis. 274 (1882), and 64 Wis. 425 (1885); Regan v. Chicago, M. & St. P. R., 51 Wis. 599 (1881); George v. Chicago, M. & St. P. R., 51 Wis. 603 (1881); Jucker v. Chicago & N. W. R., 52 Wis. 150 (1881); Schadewald v. Milwaukee, L. S. & W. R., 55 Wis. 569 (1882); Hoppe v. Chicago, M. & St. P. R., 61 Wis. 357 (1884); Hoye v. Chicago & N. W. R., 62 Wis. 667 (1885), 65 Wis. 243 (1886) and 67 Wis. 1 (1886); Leavitt v. Chicago & N. W. R., 64 Wis. 228 (1885); Schreier v. Milwaukee, L. S. & W. R., 65 Wis. 457 (1886); Miller v. Chicago, M. & St. P. R.. 68 Wis. 184 (1887); Schilling v. Chicago & N. W. R., 71 Wis. 255 (1888); Winstanley v. Chicago, M. & St. P. R., 72 Wis. 375 (1888); McDonald v. Chicago, M. & St. P. R., 75 Wis. 121 (1889); Hooker v. Chicago, M. & St. P. R., 76 Wis. 542 (1890); Phillips v. Milwaukee &

N. R., 77 Wis. 349 (1890); Tuteur v. Chicago & N. W. R., 77 Wis. 505 (1890). This list does not include wrongful-death actions in which railroad employees were killed. On these see the discussion on pages 153–157.

[21] On procedural points see, for example, Whalen v. Chicago & N. W. R., 75 Wis. 654 (1890) (issues of negligence for jury); Cheney v. Chicago, M. & N. R., 75 Wis. 223 (1889) (whether complaint was sufficiently definite and certain; Robert M. La Follette, counsel for plaintiff); Gonring v. Chicago, M. & St. P. R., 78 Wis. 16 (1890) (whether application for continuance was improperly denied when material witness was unavailable). Compare Lusted v. Chicago & N. W. R., 71 Wis. 391 (1888) (effect of release given by plaintiff in ignorance of contents).

[22] *Laws of Wisconsin,* 1875, ch. 207 (requiring construction and maintenance of warehouses), amended to include lumber, coal, and wool yards by chapter 370 of *Laws,* 1891; *Laws,* 1887, ch. 487 (requiring partitions in cars; when the partitions became loose the railroad was privileged to stop, unload the livestock, and replace or repair the partitions, for which it could charge the shipper five dollars a day); 1883, ch. 185 (giving railroad power to regulate time and manner of transportation).

[23] See, for example, Hickey v. Chicago. M. & St. P. R., 64 Wis. 649 (1885) (damage to carloads of potatoes); Blodgett v. Abbot, 72 Wis. 516 (1888) (damage to potatoes as result of delay); Morrison v. Phillips & Colby Construction Co., 44 Wis. 405 (1878) (injury to horses being shipped); Miltimore v. Chicago & N. W. R., 37 Wis. 190 (1875) (damage to wagon); Kirst v. Milwaukee, L. S. & W. R., 47 Wis. 489 (1879) (goods damaged while in custody of railroad); Thomas, Bradley & Wentworth Mfg. Co. v. Wabash, St. L. & P. R., 62 Wis. 642 (1885) (machine damaged en route); Wood v. Chicago, M. & St. P. R., 40 Wis. 582 (1876) and 51 Wis. 196 (1881) (goods in warehouse destroyed by fire); Lemke v. Chicago, M. & St. P. R., 39 Wis. 449 (1876) (same); Kronshage v. Chicago, M. & St. P. R., 45 Wis. 500 (1878) (same); Richardson v. Chicago & N. W. R., 58 Wis. 534 (1883) and 61 Wis. 596 (1884) (injury to livestock resulting from railroad's failure to furnish cars to transport with reasonable diligence); Ayres v. Chicago & N. W. R., 58 Wis. 537 (1883), 71 Wis. 372 (1888), and 75 Wis. 215 (1889) (same); Tolman v. Abbott, 78 Wis. 192 (1890) (damage to hack on Great Lakes steamer that connected with railroad); Morrison v. Phillips & Colby Construction Co., 44 Wis. 405 (1878) (injury to horses must be borne by owner because express language on receipt read "owner's risk"); compare Cream City R. v. Chicago. M. & St. P. R., 63 Wis. 93 (1885) (contractual limitation of liability signed by shipper not binding on consignee); Browning v. Goodrich Transportation Co., 78 Wis. 391 (1890) (successor carrier could not avail itself of exculpatory clause of original carrier). See comments on exculpatory clauses by Nils Haugen, railroad commissioner from 1882 to 1887: "No such contract and no agreement should have any binding force, and I suggest legislation to that effect." *Second Biennial Report of the Railroad Commissioner,* 1886, xiii.

[24] *Laws of Wisconsin,* 1876, ch. 57, sec. 11; 1883, ch. 129.

[25] *Laws of Wisconsin,* 1875, ch. 24 (requiring axe and saw); compare *Laws,* 1887, ch. 249, making it a felony to steal such axe or saw; 1878, ch. 292, sec. 2 (prohibiting locked doors); 1880, ch. 29 (giving conductor power to arrest passenger using profane language); 1875, ch. 119; 1876, ch. 167; 1880, ch. 29, sec. 2 (prohibition of gambling).

[26] *Passengers on train:* Bass v. Chicago & N. W. R., 36 Wis. 450 (1874) (plaintiff injured when ejected forcibly from "ladies car"; judgment for plaintiff reversed for erroneous instructions; opinion by Ryan), 39 Wis. 636 (1876) (reversed for excessive verdict), and 42 Wis. 654 (1877) (judgment for plaintiff affirmed on

basis of punitive damages, Ryan writing opinion and reluctantly bowing to Wisconsin precedent allowing punitive damages in tort); Craker v. Chicago & N. W. R., 36 Wis. 657 (1875) (lady assaulted by conductor, action mainly for mental suffering, judgment on verdict for $1000 affirmed; opinion by Ryan, elaborating at length his view of the basis of the doctrine of *respondeat superior*); Jenkins v. Chicago & N. W. R., 41 Wis. 112 (1876) (plaintiff injured when box car in which he was riding caught fire; judgment for plaintiff reversed because conductor at time had no knowledge of plaintiff's presence there and knowledge of original conductor was not imputable to successor); Yorton v. Milwaukee, L. S. & W. R., 54 Wis. 234 (1882) (action for ejection from train, verdict and judgment for plaintiff reversed because plaintiff had only "trip check" rather than "stop-over check" required by rules of company) and 62 Wis. 367 (1885) (reversed on measure of damages, holding that damages other than mere price of ticket were recoverable); Lawson v. Chicago, St. P., M. & O. R., 64 Wis. 447 (1885) (plaintiff's intestate killed while riding as passenger accompanying shipment of horses; verdict and judgment for plaintiff affirmed); Annas v. Milwaukee & N. R., 67 Wis. 46 (1886) (plaintiff's husband, riding on free pass in caboose, killed when rescue engine ran into caboose; judgment for plaintiff affirmed on ground that there was enough evidence to establish gross negligence); Abbot v. Tolliver, 71 Wis. 64 (1888) (plaintiff injured when thrown to floor after train was derailed; judgment for plaintiff reversed on grounds of excessive damages); Stutz v. Chicago & N. W. R., 73 Wis. 147 (1888) (court affirmed judgment for plaintiff injured by fall into excavation after conductor had ejected her from train); Kreuziger v. Chicago & N. W. R., 73 Wis. 154 (1888) (same facts as in Stutz case; reversed for error in admission of evidence and for failure to instruct jury properly as to proximate cause); Wightman v. Chicago & N. W. R., 73 Wis. 169 (1888) (plaintiff ejected and subjected to abusive language by conductor; judgment for plaintiff affirmed); Berry v. Chicago & N. W. R., 73 Wis. 197 (1888) (injuries to plaintiff-passenger; judgment on special verdict for defendant affirmed); Stimson v. Milwaukee, L. S. & W. R., 75 Wis. 381 (1890) (plaintiff injured when he stumbled on satchels in aisle; order sustaining nonsuit affirmed); Stewart v. Everts, 76 Wis. 35 (1890) (plaintiff injured when car was thrown as result of broken rail; judgment for plaintiff reversed because of admission of evidence as to other broken rails); Party v. Chicago, St. P., M., & O. R., 77 Wis. 218 (1890) (plaintiff put off train and forced to wait several hours without shelter because she had wrong ticket; judgment for plaintiff reversed for lack of evidence to support punitory [*sic*] damages or to show knowledge on part of brakeman that plaintiff had wrong ticket when she boarded train.) *Passengers on platform or depot grounds:* Patten v. Chicago & N. W. R., 36 Wis. 413 (1874) (plaintiff injured by fall in depot; judgment for plaintiff affirmed); Quaife v. Chicago, M. & St. P. R., 48 Wis. 513 (1879) (plaintiff injured in fall off station platform, much medical testimony at trial; judgment for plaintiff affirmed); Jewell v. Chicago, St. P. & M. R., 54 Wis. 610 (1882) (plaintiff injured when alighting from train; judgment for plaintiff reversed on grounds of contributory negligence); Kelly v. Chicago & N. W. R., 60 Wis. 480 (1884) (plaintiff injured when alighting from train; judgment for plaintiff reversed because of improper scope of pre-trial adverse examination); Griswold v. Chicago & N. W. R., 64 Wis. 652 (1885) (plaintiff, assisting wife, injured when alighting from train; judgment for plaintiff reversed on grounds that plaintiff himself was not a passenger); Bishop v. Chicago & N. W. R., 67 Wis. 610 (1887) (action against railroad for failure to provide lighted waiting room and for agent's use of insulting and abusive language to plaintiff;

judgment for plaintiff reversed for misjoinder of causes of action—tort and contract claims did not arise out of same transaction); Hemmingway v. Chicago. M. & St. P. R., 67 Wis. 668 (1887) (plaintiff injured in jumping from train to platform; judgment for plaintiff reversed because of error in submitting to jury certain issues regarding defendant's negligence) and 72 Wis. 42 (1888) (judgment for plaintiff affirmed); Fick v. Chicago & N. W. R., 68 Wis. 469 (1887) (plaintiff injured when assaulted by ticket agent; judgment for plaintiff affirmed). *Actions for damages due to delay or erroneous routing:* Walsh v. Chicago, M. & St. P. R., 42 Wis. 23 (1877) (action for damages suffered as result of failure of defendant to run train from Watertown to Madison; judgment for plaintiff reversed on measure of damages); Brown v. Chicago, M. & St. P. R., 54 Wis. 342 (1882) (action for damages resulting from wife's sickness caused by being put off train three miles from destination; judgment for plaintiff affirmed); Plott v. Chicago & N. W. R., 63 Wis. 511 (1885) (action for damages resulting from failure of railroad to stop at plaintiff's destination; judgment for plaintiff reversed on ground that defendant's only duty was to inform plaintiff well ahead of time so that she could get off at nearest station).

[27] Compare *Laws of Wisconsin,* 1883, ch. 118 (act amending general corporation law as to time when persons who have filed necessary papers officially become a corporate body).

[28] *Laws of Wisconsin,* 1875, ch. 25 (act amending the general law of 1872, to permit corporation to change name by vote of two-thirds of stockholders); 1875, ch. 29 (act authorizing Mineral Point Railroad to move station from Riverside to new point); 1876, ch. 66 (amending general law to permit railroads to extend lines from points named in charter to connect with other roads); 1878, ch. 328, sec. 1 (authorizing railroads organized under the general law of 1872 to amend articles by a two-thirds vote of directors for purpose of building new line in lieu of old line authorized by original articles); 1875. ch. 303 (act authorizing Green Bay and Minnesota Railroad to build bridge across the Mississippi); 1876, ch. 72 (same); 1880, ch. 228 (authorizing St. Paul & Chicago Short Line Railroad to construct bridge over Lake St Croix); 1883, ch. 129 (authorizing St. Paul Eastern Grand Trunk Railway to construct bridge over Wolf River); 1883, ch. 262 (authorizing the St. Cloud, Grantsburg & Ashland Railroad to construct bridge over St. Croix River); 1885, ch. 26–30 (acts authorizing bridges over the Kickapoo, Chippewa, Black, and Eau Claire rivers and over Lake St. Croix); 1882, ch. 159 (act amending portion of private law of 1870 authorizing Northwestern road to guarantee payment of bonds of other roads it had assumed and to hold stock in another road).

[29] *Laws of Wisconsin.* 1875, ch. 328 (providing in detail for election of directors of Chicago, Milwaukee & St. Paul Railroad); 1876, ch. 80 (providing for amendment of charter of Mineral Point Railroad with respect to election of new directors upon death of old ones); 1881, ch. 27 (general law permitting all railroad companies to provide for staggered terms of directors); 1881, ch. 49 (authorizing board to execute mortgages). This last act amended a provision of a previous law law requiring majority approval of stockholders. *Laws,* 1876, ch. 57, sec. 9 (prohibition of conflict of interest).

[30] *Laws of Wisconsin,* 1882, ch. 266.

[31] Doud v. Wisconsin, P. & S. R.. 65 Wis. 108 (1886).

[32] *Laws of Wisconsin,* 1876, ch. 57, sec. 8. Compare *Laws of Wisconsin,* 1876, ch. 66 (act amending section of general law permitting railroads to extend their lines to connect with other lines, stipulating, however, that nothing in the act should authorize competing roads to consolidate).

[33] *Laws of Wisconsin,* 1880, ch. 260; 1882, ch. 268; 1883, ch. 293. The 1876 act was chapter 57, section 8, of that year's *Laws.*

[34] *Laws of Wisconsin,* 1876, ch. 93; 1877, ch. 121; 1878, ch. 144.

[35] *Laws of Wisconsin,* 1876, ch. 57. The remarks Governor Taylor made in 1875 represented the views of an official who favored the Potter Law. After proclaiming the supremacy of law manifested by the Railway Company cases, he went on to say: "But I am not of the opinion that classifications of freight and rates of fare and freight can be expediently established by an iron bound and inflexible rule of law, with no power of revision and modification reserved. The best features of our law in respect to this branch of the subject, are exemplified in the establishment of maximum rates of fare, and its worst feature in the unyielding character of its limitation upon rates of freight." Second *Annual Message of Governor William R. Taylor,* 1875, pp. 26–32. The modifications in the Potter Law passed in 1875 were *Laws of Wisconsin,* 1875, ch. 113 (eliminating Class C lines and including them in Class B) and ch. 39 (changing effective date of appointing successor railroad commissioners). Compare *Laws of Wisconsin,* 1875, ch. 52 (appropriations to administer the law).

[36] *Annual Message of Harrison Ludington,* 1876. pp. 10–12.

[37] *Laws of Wisconsin,* 1876, ch. 57, sec. 4, 5, 11. The act also included (section 6) a provision making it the duty of every railroad to furnish suitable cars for transporting freight to all persons applying for them and to receive and transport the goods with reasonable dispatch.

[38] *Ibid.,* sec. 7. In the light of the Supreme Court's decision in Smith v. Chicago & N. W. R., cited in notes 40 and 116 below, it is questionable whether quo warranto would lie. See the discussion on pages 161-162.

[39] *Laws of Wisconsin.* 1876, ch. 57, sec. 13. Many such prosecutions under the Potter Law had reached the court before the 1876 act was passed. Ackley v. Chicago, M. & St. P. R., 36 Wis. 252 (1874) (involving a double charge by virtue of the transference of goods from the Northwestern to the Milwaukee Road; Supreme Court held that lawful charges for entire distance should be collected by one line and equitable apportionment between the two lines be made thereafter); State v. Stone, 37 Wis. 204 (1875) (Potter Law prosecution, judgment for state affirmed on basis of Railroad Companies case); *In re* Langley, 37 Wis. 377 (1875) (agent imprisoned and released on writ of habeas corpus by country court on grounds of unconstitutionality of Potter Law; reversed by Supreme Court on basis of Railroad Companies case); Hinckley v. Chicago, M. & St. P. R., 38 Wis. 194 (1875) (civil action for damages under Potter Law; judgment for plaintiff affirmed on grounds that constitutionality of Potter Law was no longer open to question); Streeter v. Chicago, M. & St. P. R., 40 Wis. 294 (1876) (civil action for damages; judgment for plaintiff reversed but only on point that plaintiff could not collect triple damages from both lines involved, citing Hinckley case, mentioned above).

[40] Rood v. Chicago, M. & St. P. R., 43 Wis. 146, 154 (1877). *Accord:* State v. Stone, 43 Wis. 481 (1878); Smith v. Chicago & N. W. R., 43 Wis. 686 (1878).

[41] Streeter v. Chicago, M. & St. P. R., 44 Wis. 383 (1878) (second appeal—see note 39 above; court reversed, saying there was no recovery unless plaintiff and amended complaint to make it a common-law action and declaring it unnecessary to determine here whether common-law action survived or was reborn with repeal of the statute); Smith v. Chicago & N. W. R., 49 Wis. 443 (1880) (second appeal—see note 40 above; Supreme Court affirmed denial of motion to strike amended complaint based on common-law action for excessive charges); Graham v. Chicago, M. & St.. P. R., 49 Wis. 532 (1880) (same situation as Smith case) and 53 Wis.

473 (1881) (Supreme Court affirmed judgment for treble damages for plaintiff, in long opinion by Judge Taylor dealing with the nature of the common-law right of action).

[42] *Second Annual Message of William E. Smith,* 1879, p. 12.

[43] *Second Annual Message of Jeremiah H. Rusk,* 1885, p. 17.

[44] *First Biennial Report of the Railroad Commissioner,* 1885, p. 22.

[45] *Eighth Annual Report of the Railroad Commissioner,* 1881, xliv–1.

[46] *Laws of Wisconsin,* 1876. ch. 97 (percentage changed to 4 per cent); 1883, ch. 353, and 1885, ch. 415 (including sleeping- and parlor-car companies), See *Second Annual Message of Jeremiah M. Rusk,* 1885, p. 17.

[47] State *ex rel.* Chicago, M. & St. P. R. v. McFetridge, 56 Wis. 256 (1882). Throughout this whole controversy the railroad commissioner appeared to stand on the sidelines. "I have no occasion to discuss the true meaning of the statutes or the justice of them, however they may be construed, but it seems to me very clear that they should be so amended that differences such as have arisen between the state officers and the railroad companies during the past year may be avoided in future." *Eighth Annual Report of the Railroad Commissioner* [Andrew J. Turner], 1881, xli.

[48] State v. Pullman's Palace Car Co., 64 Wis. 78 (1885).

[49] See *Fourth Biennial Report of the Railroad Commissioner* [Atley Peterson]. 1890, p. 12, and *First Biennial Report of the Railroad Commissioner* [Nils Haugen], 1885, p. 20.

[50] On the building of the northern Wisconsin railroads see William F. Raney, "The Building of Wisconsin's Railroads," in the *Wisconsin Magazine of History,* (1935), 19:399–403, and Richard L. Canuteson, Railway Development of Northern Wisconsin, a manuscript master's thesis in the Memorial Library of the University of Wisconsin. The various exemption statutes were the following: *Laws of Wisconsin,* 1875, ch. 278 (exempting the Wisconsin Valley Railroad from payment of license fees for three years); 1877, ch. 21 (extending time for exemption from assessment and taxation of certain lands granted to the Winnebago and Lake Superior Railroad and the Portage and Superior Railroad); 1878, ch. 229 (exempting certain lands of the North Wisconsin Railroad from taxation); 1880, ch. 290 (general act relieving from payment of license fee for ten years any railroad that might build line between certain points in northern Wisconsin); 1883, ch. 262 (declaring lands of the Chicago, St. Paul, Minneapolis & Omaha Railroad taxable and waiving forfeiture if company failed to build twenty miles during 1882 and 1883). Compare *Laws of Wisconsin,* 1878, ch. 39 (refunding overpayment of taxes to Mineral Point Railroad) and 1879. ch. 25 (providing for manner of collection and settlement of license fees due from railroad companies). The case sustaining the exemption acts was Wisconsin C. R. v. Taylor County, 52 Wis. 37 (1881). Compare State *ex rel.* Abbot v. McFetridge 64 Wis. 130 (1885) (construing the license-fee statute, holding that it was, in fact, a tax) and West Wisconsin R. v. Board of Supervisors, 35 Wis. 257 (1874) (act repealing former act exempting land-grant lands from taxation was upheld against challenge under the contract clause as legitimate exercise of the state's reserved power over corporations).

[51] State *ex rel.* Bell v. Harshaw, State Treasurer, 78 Wis. 230 (1890). The statute was *Laws of Wisconsin,* 1879, ch. 22, sec. 6–8.

[52] *Laws of Wisconsin.* 1879, ch. 7, sec. 5.

[53] *Ibid.,* 1876, ch. 223; 1877, ch. 208; 1878, ch. 213.

[54] *Ibid.,* 1881, ch. 186.

[55] *Ibid.,* 1882, ch. 10. See also *Laws,* 1883. ch. 29 (confirming the grant). The

grant to the Chicago and Northern Pacific Air Line Railway Company was chapter 126 of *Laws of Wisconsin,* 1874, and the time extension was chapter 229 of *laws,* 1878. By this time the road was called the Chicago, Portage and Lake Superior Railway Company. On the history of the Omaha see Raney in the *Wisconsin Magazine of History,* 19:387, 396–397. On the jobbery that accompanied the Omaha's acquisition of these land grants see Richard N. Current, *Pine Logs and Politics: A Life of Philetus Sawyer* (Madison, 1950), 140–143. The Omaha eventually became a part of the Chicago and North Western system.

[56] State *ex rel.* Peck v. Rusk, 55 Wis. 465 (1882). The statute involved was Chapter 267 of *Laws of Wisconsin,* 1882.

[57] On the theft of timber on the lands owned by Cornell University see Gates, *Wisconsin Pine Lands of Cornell University,* 200.

[58] *Laws of Wisconsin,* 1876, ch. 379 (assigning causes of action); 1876. ch. 75, 79 (authorizing appointment of timber agent and prescribing his location and duties and the requirements as to bond). Compare *Laws of Wisconsin,* 1876, ch. 339 (amending act of 1869 dealing with "protection" of timber lands) and ch. 308 (modifying common-law remedies). The law permitted the owner to get an injunction against the trespasser, and it also authorized a writ of attachment to issue against the trespasser's property.

[59] Sloan, Stevens, and Morris v. State, 51 Wis. 623 (1881). Plaintiffs had submitted their bill to the secretary of state, who had refused to audit it. Consequently the legislature failed to appropriate the money. Plaintiffs brought this suit in the Supreme Court to recover in *quantum meruit.* The Supreme Court dismissed the complaint. two justices dissenting, on the grounds that the proper remedy was by mandamus against the secretary of state.

[60] Andrews v. Powers, 35 Wis. 644 (1874); Pringle v. Dunn, 37 Wis. 449 (1875); Chipman v. Tucker, 38 Wis. 43 (1875); Roberts v. McGrath, 38 Wis. 52 (1875); Roberts v. Wood, 38 Wis. 60 (1875).

[61] *Laws of Wisconsin,* 1875, ch. 191, 208 (requiring the land company to keep duplicate lists of mortgagors and of lands held by the company); 1876, ch. 57; 1880. ch. 297; and 1881, ch. 113 (extending the time for filing claims); 1876, ch. 129 (imposing penalties for failure to comply with the provisions governing records and duplicate lists); 1876, ch. 227, and 1877, ch. 259 (providing for the recording of the lands with the registers of deeds of the several counties); 1877, ch. 84, and 1878, ch. 33 (extending the benefits of the act to certain other parties equitably entitled to them); 1882, ch. 235, and 1883, ch. 340 (authorizing the company to close up its business). The legislative investigation is reported in the *Wisconsin Assembly Journal,* 1883, Appendix 4, pp. 33–35. On certain aspects of this scandal see Current, *Pine Logs and Politics,* 137–140.

[62] *Laws of Wisconsin,* 1887, ch. 394. The act permitted them to build up to twenty-five miles and to condemn property. It required them to file a copy of their articles with the secretary of state, to appoint an agent to accept service of process, to file notice of acceptance of the act, to subject themselves to the same conditions and liabilities as domestic roads, to build their line within two years, and to agree not to remove to a federal court any action brought against them by a Wisconsin citizen. And the law specifically declared (section 3): "The legislature may at any time alter or repeal this act."

[63] *Laws of Wisconsin,* 1875, ch. 117 (narrow-gauge railroads). This law provided for municipal aid and also required roads to file their maximum rates, which might not exceed those established by law (presumably the Potter Act); 1875, ch. 329 (general law applying to all corporations and providing for service of process in actions begun by the attorney general to vacate the charter because

the company had exceeded its powers); 1876, ch. 333 (thirty miles of road to be constructed by the Milwaukee and Beloit Railroad west of Milwaukee by April, 1879); 1879, ch. 91 (extending the time to 1884 and reducing the required mileage to fifteen); 1880, ch. 193, and 1881, ch. 189 (acts requiring railroads to appoint resident attorneys to accept service of process and prescribing the penalties for failure to comply); 1883, ch. 241 (filing fees); 1885. ch. 23 (establishing southern terminus for the Omaha); 1887, ch. 552 (act to provide for more efficient service of process against railroads).

[64] State *ex rel.* Attorney General v. Milwaukee, L. S. & W. R., 45 Wis. 579 (1878) (defendant railroad, chartered in Wisconsin, kept records and "principal place of business" in New York; Supreme Court overruled defendant's demurrer).

[65] Chicago, M. & St. P. R. v. State, 53 Wis. 509 (1881). In addition there were two cases that were direct aftermaths of the Railroad Companies case: Attorney General v. West Wisconsin R.. 36 Wis. 466 (1874) (state's demurrer to answer sustained with leave to plead over) and Attorney General v. Chicago, M. & St. P. R., 38 Wis. 69 (1875) (same cause as was involved in the Railroad Companies case, coming up at this term from a judgment on original pleadings and proofs; but since rates had been changed by the 1875 amendments to the Potter Law, the cause was not now ripe for judgment; Ryan wrote the opinion, chiding the state for failing to modify the prayer for injunction to conform to the new rates).

[66] Chippewa Valley & S. R. v. Chicago, St. P., M. & O. R., 75 Wis. 224 (1890).

[67] *Laws of Wisconsin,* 1875, ch. 168. The law also placed a top limit on the tax equal to five per cent of the value of the total taxable property. Presumably this restriction was imposed to comply with the constitutional provision limiting municipal indebtedness.

[68] *Laws of Wisconsin,* 1875, ch. 117, sec. 2, 4, and 1877, ch. 4 (prescribing procedure for local aid to narrow-gauge railroads); 1876, ch. 66 (amending the general law of 1872 to permit local aid for connecting extension of railroads); 1876, ch. 128 (apportioning payment when territory was stricken from the rolls of one town and annexed by another).

[69] For example, *Laws of Wisconsin,* 1876, ch. 119 (authorizing counties, towns, cities, and villages to aid the Milwaukee, Lake Shore and Western Railway and prescribing the procedure therefor) and *Laws,* 1883, ch. 333 (amending the 1876 law by providing that thirty days' notice must be given instead of five days' notice); 1889, ch. 223 (authorizing towns, villages, and cities in Pierce, St. Croix, Douglas, Polk, and Burnett counties to aid the Duluth, Red Wing and Southern Railroad Company by issuing bonds); 1876, ch. 180 (amending laws of 1871 and 1867 regarding aid of towns and counties to Green Bay and Lake Pepin Railway); 1881, ch. 224 (authorizing Clark County to aid Black River Railroad by conveying lands); 1882, ch. 300 (authorizing Adams County to grant lands and certain other property in aid of Black River Railroad); 1889, ch. 356 (authorizing city of Berlin to aid Berlin and Green Lake Railroad by subscribing to stock paid for by bond issue). Compare *Laws of Wisconsin,* 1880, ch. 178 (authorizing the Iowa County Agricultural Society to donate a piece of land to the Mineral Point Railroad); 1881, ch. 284 (authorizing the Board of Managers of the Industrial School for Boys to settle with the Milwaukee and Madison Railway for a right-of-way); and 1885, ch. 143 (authorizing the Commissioners of School and University Lands to loan to ten towns in Polk County a portion of its trust funds to be used to secure rights-of-way and depots); 1875, ch. 72 (transferring local aid voted by town of Potosi to Grant County).

[70] See, for example, *Laws of Wisconsin,* 1881, ch. 169 (amending certain private and local laws relative to the railroad debt of Watertown); 1883, ch. 313 (same);

and 1887, ch. 271 (Jefferson). Compare *Laws of Wisconsin,* 1881, ch. 8 (relating to indebtednesses of municipalities). In general the cases arose in the same way as the earlier ones: by taxpayer's suit to enjoin collection of the necessary tax, by way of defense to suits on the bonds brought by the railroads, by actions in equity to cancel bonds, by suits to quiet title to land given to the road, and by suits against the road to enjoin further construction.

[71] Oleson v. Green Bay & L. P. R., 36 Wis. 383 (1874) (in affirming the judgment of the trial court upholding the validity of the bonds the Supreme Court stated that the constitutionality of local-aid statutes permitting subscriptions for capital stock of railroads and the issuance of bonds and levying of taxes to pay for the stock was no longer open to question); Ellis v. Northern P. R., 77 Wis. 114 (1890) (in action to quiet title Supreme Court declared that *donation* of land to road by county was void under the Whiting case and refused to re-examine the rule in the light of the decisions of the United States Supreme Court).

[72] Bound v. Wisconsin C. R., 45 Wis. 543, 579, 588–589 (1878).

[73] Noesen v. Port Washington, 37 Wis. 168 (1875) (taxpayer's action to restrain issuance of stock subscription on grounds of material change in route; court granted relief even though the action was brought before actual change had been effected); compare Board of Supervisors v. Walbridge, 38 Wis. 179 (1875) (court ordered rescission of agreement made by railroad with board on grounds that railroad did not construct line in accordance with agreement and that a subsequent agreement of the board assenting to the change was *ultra vires);* DeForth v. Wisconsin & M. R., 52 Wis. 320 (1881) (issuance of bonds enjoined because many names on petition were affixed on Sunday); State *ex rel.* Chicago, M. & St. P. R. v. Blackstone, 63 Wis. 362 (1885) (writ of mandamus to compel issuance of bonds denied because minors and incompetents had been counted in town's population); compare State *ex rel.* Pfister v. Mayor, 52 Wis. 423 (1881) (writ of mandamus to compel levy and collection of tax denied because relator had not first proved that he had clear legal right in ordinary action at law); State *ex rel.* Burnett v. Harshaw, 73 Wis. 211 (1888) (quashed alternative writ of mandamus to compel state treasurer to apply moneys paid by railroad to its indebtedness to Burnett County; new county had been created and court ordered rateable application); Perrin v. New London, 67 Wis. 416 (1886) (municipality acted in excess of its authority).

[74] Lackawanna Iron & Coal Co. v. Little Wolf, 38 Wis. 152 (1875) (court disallowed, as a defense to an action on bond coupons, that lack of certification of genuineness of signatures by town clerk voided the certificates); Single v. Supervisors, 38 Wis. 364 (1875) (validity of legalizing act concerning action of board of supervisors affirmed); State *ex rel.* Green Bay & M. R. v. Jennings. 48 Wis. 548 (1879) (court affirmed overruling of town's demurrer to application for writ of mandamus to compel issuance of bonds, holding that six years did not constitute laches as matter of law); Lynch v. Eastern, LaF. & M. R., 57 Wis. 430 (1883) (court affirmed dissolution of injunction, holding that town could not avoid obligation simply because assignee-railroad rather than original railroad passed through town). Compare Menasha v. Wisconsin C. R., 65 Wis. 502 (1886) (action for specific performance against railroad to perform its part of the contract denied).

[75] *Laws of Wisconsin,* 1887, ch. 493. Under the contract the railroad would construct the viaduct and the board would levy a tax to pay for it. *Ibid.,* 1891, ch. 467 (authorizing city to direct erection of gates).

[76] *Local taxation:* Chicago. M. & St. P. R. v. Board of Supervisors, 48 Wis. 666 (1880). This was another case involving taxation of the "Dousman House" in

Prairie du Chien, claimed to be exempt from the property. The case had been up once before. See above, p. 200 n. 55. In the present case the court reversed the dismissal of the complaint, holding that the hostelry was primarily for the use of railroad passengers rather than the general public—as had been true at the time of the first hearing—and therefore exempt from the general property tax. The railroads probably did not damage their cause by changing the name of the hotel from "Dousman House" to "Railway House." Compare Wisconsin C. R. v. Lincoln County, 57 Wis. 137 (1883) (Supreme Court reversed judgment for railroad, holding it liable for taxes on lands after exemption had expired and before it was renewed) and 67 Wis. 478 (1886) (judgment for county affirmed). Chicago & N. W. R. v. Oconto, 50 Wis. 189 (1880) (court reversed judgment for defendant-locality because property in question was not contiguous, and contiguity was held to be a *sine qua non* for the constitution of a "town"); Chicago & N. W. R., v. Langlade County, 56 Wis. 614 (1883) (affirmed judgment against plaintiff-railroad; involved change in town and country boundary lines); Wisconsin C. R. v. Price County, 64 Wis. 579 (1885) (reversed granting of perpetual injunction to restrain collection, holding that railroad's equitable interest in land-grant lands attached and was therefore subject to taxation). Chicago & N. W. R. v. Town of Langlade, 55 Wis. 116 (1882) (action for recovery of taxes alleged to have been unlawfully paid). *Actions to recover expenses from roads:* Oconto v. Chicago & N. W. R., 44 Wis. 231 (1878) (to recover expense of repairing streets; judgment for city affirmed); Jamestown v. Chicago, B. & N. R., 69 Wis. 648 (1887) (to compel railroad to put public highway in good shape; overruling of railroad's demurrer affirmed). Compare State *ex rel.* Milwaukee, L. S. & W. R. v. O'Connor, 78 Wis. 282 (1890) (certiorari to remove proceedings from board of supervisors to circuit court in order to review board's order laying out public highway across railroad's tracks). *Actions to enjoin construction:* Menasha v. Milwaukee & N. R., 52 Wis. 138 (1881), and 52 Wis. 414 (1881) (court reversed order granting injunction against railroad restraining them from building contemplated line, holding that charges of fraud had not been sustained). Compare Wisconsin C. R. v. Smith, 52 Wis. 140 (1881) (railroad got injunction against city restraining it from interfering with building of bridge, and city in turn sought injuncton to restrain road from constructing bridge; court held that mere bringing of injunction suit by city did not constitute disobedience of railroad injunctive order and hence did not subject city to contempt citation). *Adjudication of disputed ownership of stock:* City of Seymour v. Town of Seymour, 56 Wis. 314 (1882) (nonsuit sustained on ground that city was estopped from asserting that stock should not be apportioned).

[77] See, for example, *Laws of Wisconsin,* 1877, p. 635. Compare *Laws,* 1878, p. 711 (memorial to Congress for extension of time to complete Northern Pacific Railway).

[78] See *Laws of Wisconsin,* 1875, ch. 303, sec. 1 (bridge across Mississippi River); 1876, ch. 72 (same); and 1880, ch. 228 (bridge over Lake St. Croix to be constructed in accordance with plans approved by secretary of war). Congressional authorization derived from the Bridges Act of 1866. *United States Statutes at Large,* 14: 244–246 (1866).

[79] *Local aid cases:* Beckwith v. Racine, 7 Bissell 142 (C.C.E.D. Wis., 1876) (bonds enforceable against successor town after original town had been abolished by legislature); Preble v. Board of Supervisors, 8 Bissell 358 (C.C.W.D. Wis., 1878) (defenses of fraud, etc., not available against bona fide purchaser of interest coupons); Long v. New London, 5 Fed. 557 (C.C.E.D. Wis., 1880) (enabling act authorizing issuance of municipal railroad bonds valid, hence permitting en-

forcement by bondholder); Smith v. Fond du Lac, 8 Fed. 289 (C.C.E.D. Wis., 1881) (action by holders of interest coupons permitted as against defense of unconstitutionality of act authorizing local aid); Porter v. Janesville, 3 Fed. 617 (C.C.W.D. Wis., 1880) (assignee of railroad bond could sue for enforcement of obligation); Burton v. Koshkonong, 4 Fed. 373 (C.C.W.D. Wis., 1880) (action on interest coupons allowed as against defenses of statute of limitations, holding *inter alia,* that wiping out remedy impairs obligation of contract); Wadsworth v. St. Croix County, 4 Fed. 378 (C.C.W.D. Wis., 1880) (action for specific performance compelling board of supervisors to issue bonds denied on the grounds that, even after submission to vote, issuance was discretionary with board); Burleigh v. Rochester, 5 Fed. 667 (C.C.E.D. Wis., 1881) (authority to issue bonds presumed when bonds are signed by chairman of board of supervisors and countersigned by clerk); Worts v. Watertown, 16 Fed. 534 (C.C.W.D. Wis., 1883) (suit to recover on bonds turned on question of proper service of summons, the court holding that proper service had been made on city clerk and chairman of board of supervisors); Morgan v. Town of Waldwick, 17 Fed. 286 (C.C.W.D. Wis., 1883) (new town created after issuance of bonds by original town, liable for proportional share of obligation); Ferry v. Town of Merrimack, 18 Fed. 657 (C.C.W.D. Wis., 1833) (plaintiff could not remove to federal court after bringing suit originally in state court); Northern P. R. v. Roberts, 42 Fed. 734 (C.C.W.D. Wis., 1890) (authority of Douglas County to convey lands held under tax titles pursuant to local-aid statute; authority confirmed). *Receiverships and reorganizations:* Howard v. Milwaukee & St. P. R., 7 Bissell 73 (C.C.E.D. Wis., 1875) (priority of mortgages arising out of the La Crosse and Milwaukee foreclosures. involving Barnes and Bronson and Soutter mortgages); Barnes v. Chicago, M. & St. P. R., 8 Bissell 574 (C.C.E.D. Wis., 1879) (same; foreclosure of two Barnes's mortgages); Hiles v. Case, 9 Bissell 549 (C.C.E.D. Wis., 1880) (claim against receiver for damages to property caused by sparks from locomotive, involving question whether such claims are "operating expenses" and thus payable out of earnings of road); Kelly v. Receiver, 5 Fed. 846 (C.C.E.D. Wis., 1881) (lien of person making advancements to railroad not prior to lien of mortgages bondholders); Farmers' Loan & Trust Co. v. Green Bay & M. R.. 6 Fed. 100 (C.C.E.D. Wis., 1881) (priority of liens of first- and second-mortgage bondholders with respect to payments from foreclosure sale); Dexterville Mfg. & Boom Co. v. Case, 4 Fed. 873 (C.C.E.D. Wis., 1880) (claims resulting from destruction of timber and cranberry marshes not payable by receiver ahead of claims of mortgage bondholders); Farmers' Loan & Trust Co. v. Green Bay & M. R., 12 Fed. 773 (C.C.E.D. Wis., 1882) (same; damages recoverable even though company acquired title to lands for purposes foreign to object of creation); Peterson v. Case, 21 Fed. 885 (C.C.E.D. Wis., 1884) (liability of receiver operating road for damages resulting from delay in shipment); Farmers' Loan & Trust Co. v. Green Bay, W. & St. P. R.. 45 Fed. 664 (C.C.E.D. Wis., 1891) (claim against receiver for wrongful death not entitled to priority over claims of bondholders).

[80] *Condemnation:* Warren v. Wisconsin V. R., 6 Bissell 425 (C.C.W.D. Wis., 1875) (turned on permissibility of removal to federal court); Laflin v. Chicago, W. & N. R., 33 Fed. 415 (C.C.E.D. Wis., 1887) (damages for value of hotel property occasioned by proximity of railroad right-of-way) and 34 Fed. 859 (C.C.E.D. Wis., 1887) (admissibility of evidence). *Liability to shippers and passengers:* Halliwell v. Grand Trunk R. of Canada, 7 Fed. 68 (C.C.E.D. Wis., 1881) (liability of original carrier for damages to goods occasioned by delay of connecting carrier); Young v. Grand Trunk R. of Canada, 9 Fed. 348 (C.C.E.D. Wis., 1881) (same); Petersen v. Case, 21 Fed. 885 (C.C.E.D. Wis., 1884) (action against receiver for damages

resulting from delay of connecting carrier); Mauritz v. New York, L. E. & W. R., 23 Fed. 765 (C.C.E.D. Wis.. 1884) (liability of carrier for damage to passenger's baggage). *Title to land-grant lands:* North Wisconsin R. v. Board of Supervisors, 8 Bissell 414 (C.C.W.D. Wis., 1879) (after completion of requisite twenty miles and issuance of patent to road, title passed absolutely and hence land was subject to taxation); Farmers' Loan and Trust Co. v. Chicago, P. & S. R., 39 Fed. 143 (C.C.W.D. Wis., 1889) (act of legislature revoking grant to the Chicago, Portage and Superior Railroad and conferring it on the Omaha was valid, hence the Portage and Superior was divested of any interest in the lands; lobbying activities of the Omaha commented on); Angle v. Chicago, St. P., M. & O. R., 39 Fed. 912 (C.C.W.D. Wis., 1889) (same). *Controversies with suppliers:* Merchants' National Bank v. Chicago R. Equipment Co., 25 Fed. 809 (C.C.W.D. Wis., 1885) (negotiability of note given in payment for railroad freight cars).

[81] The Wisconsin statute was *Laws of Wisconsin,* 1887, ch. 394. See "Comment" in the *Yale Law Journal,* 59:737 (1950).

[82] Carton & Co. v. Illinois C. R., 59 Iowa 148 (1882 (rate-regulatory statute as affecting foreign corporations repugnant to commerce clause); People v. Wabash St. L. & P. R., 104 Ill. 476 (1882) (rate-regulatory statute governs foreign railroad corporations operating in Illinois and does not conflict with commerce clause).

[83] *Ninth Annual Report of the Railroad Commissioner,* 1882, xlv. See also the *First Biennial Report of the Railroad Commissioner.* 1885, p. 23 (Haugen suggested that no state legislation on rate discrimination would meet all requirements so long as there was no federal legislation of similar character).

[84] *First Annual Message of Jeremiah M. Rusk,* 1882, p. 17.

[85] *Laws of Wisconsin,* 1876, ch. 381. The act provided that the deed should be prima facie evidence of title and should inure to the benefit of both the railroad and persons claiming through it just as though the governor had granted the lands directly to the purchaser. The act extending the time allowing settlers to acquire title was *Laws,* 1876, ch. 392.

[86] *Rent:* Newell-House Stock Co. v. Flint & P. M. R.. 47 Wis. 516 (1879); Wittman v. Milwaukee, L. S. & W. R., 51 Wis. 89 (1881). *Ejectment:* Horner v. Chicago, M. & St. P. R., 38 Wis. 165 (1875) (condition of conveyance was that railroad would construct depot; road did not do so and court ordered ejectment, holding that railroad had committed breach of condition subsequent); Williams v. Western U. R., 58 Wis. 71 (1880) (ejectment against holders acquiring title through railroad because of "incurable uncertainty" in deed); Wisconsin Central R. v. Wisconsin River Land Co.. 71 Wis. 94 (1888) (plaintiff entitled to ejectment under color of compliance with land-grant terms against claim of defendant holding under tax deed); Wisconsin Central R. v. Comstock, 71 Wis. 88 (1888) (ejectment would not lie because plaintiff-railroad failed to comply with statute governing payment). *Foreclosure:* Aspinwall v. Chicago & N. W. R., 41 Wis. 474 (1877) (railroad impleaded as grantee of mortgagor; issue involved appraisal of value, court holding it proper to take into consideration increased value of land due to projected railroad). *Acquisition of right-of-way:* Hutchinson v. Chicago & N. W. R., 37 Wis. 582 (1875) and 41 Wis. 541 (1877) (conditions of contract was that vendor's grist mill be undamaged; case involved question of identification of the grist mills, and issues of title, deeds from co-tenants, and adverse possession).

[87] The central filing provision was *Laws of Wisconsin,* 1883, ch. 274. The legislature may have seen the futility of county filing. This appears to be one of the earliest examples of "central filing" of security instruments in the country. The act authorizing equipment trust certificates was *Laws of Wisconsin,* 1883, ch. 277.

[88] *General contract actions:* Gano v. Chicago & N. W. R., 49 Wis. 57 (1880), 60 Wis. 12 (1884), and 66 Wis. 1 (1886) (breach of contract for purchase of stone); Exhaust Ventilator Co. v. Chicago, M. & St. P. R., 66 Wis. 218 (1886) and 69 Wis. 454 (1887) (supplier of machinery). Compare Folger v. Dousman. 37 Wis. 620 (1875) (action on note given by defendant in payment of outstanding judgment against railroad and transferred to plaintiff by payee); United States Rolling Stock Co. v. Johnson, 67 Wis. 182 (1886) (action to recover for use of certain rolling stock). *Mechanics' liens:* West v. O'Hara, 55 Wis. 645 (1882) (action by merchants against railroad contractors on guarantees of payment for supplies bought by subcontractors); Vanderpool v. La Crosse & M. R., 44 Wis. 652 (1878) (action under mechanics'-lien statute by subcontractors); Purtell v. Chicago Forge & Bolt Co., 74 Wis. 132 (1889) (action by subcontractor under mechanics'-lien statute against both contractor and railroad). Compare Boorman v. Wisconsin Rotary Engine Co., 36 Wis. 207 (1874) (involved priority of liens against defendant-company which built foundry for Milwaukee Road); Edwards v. Remington, 51 Wis. 336 (1881) (action by six partners engaged in construction of Wisconsin Valley Railroad). *Garnishment:* Crerar v. Milwaukee & St. P. R., 35 Wis. 67 (1875); Lederer v. Chicago, M. & St. P. R.. 38 Wis. 244 (1875); Commercial National Bank v. Chicago, M. & St. P. R., 45 Wis. 172 (1878); Kentzler v. Chicago, M. & St. P. R., 47 Wis. 641 (1879); Bates v. Chicago, M. & St. P. R., 60 Wis. 296 (1884); St. Joseph Mfg. Co. v. Millers, 69 Wis. 389 (1887); Ingram v. Osborn. 70 Wis. 184 (1887). Compare Pierce v. Chicago & N. W. R., 36 Wis. 283 (1874) (direct suit for wages which defendant-company had previously paid out pursuant to garnishment); Drake v. Harrison, 69 Wis. 99 (1887) (garnishment of contractor by creditors of subcontractors).

[89] See the discussion on page 89 above.

[90] *Laws of Wisconsin,* 1875, ch. 173, sec. 1, 2. Upheld in Ditberner v. Chicago, M. & St. P. R.. 47 Wis. 138 (1879). See Gertrude Schmidt's manuscript dissertation. History of Labor Legislation in Wisconsin, 49, in the Memorial Library of the University of Wisconsin.

[91] *Laws of Wisconsin,* 1880, ch. 232. A loud cry had been raised that the 1875 act was "class legislation." See the *Sixth Annual Report of the Railroad Commissioner* [Andrew J. Turner], 1880, xxxiii. Undoubtedly the railroads had been active in seeking the repeal of the 1875 act ever since its passage. See Schmidt, History of Labor Legislation in Wisconsin (MS.), 50.

[92] *Laws of Wisconsin,* 1889. ch. 438.

[93] William L. Prosser, *Handbook of the Law of Torts* (2d edition, St. Paul, 1955), 378.

[94] Brabbits v. Chicago & N. W. R., 38 Wis. 289 (1875) (negligence of foreman not considered negligence of fellow servant because foreman was entrusted with authority and responsibility of employer.)

[95] *Coupling operations:* Brabbits v. Chicago & N. W. R., 38 Wis. 289 (1875) note 94 above; Wedgewood v. Chicago & N. W. R., 41 Wis. 478 (1877) (order sustaining motion to dismiss reversed, the court holding that plaintiff stated cause of action arising out of employer's duty to provide safe place to work) and 44 Wis. 44 (1878) (judgment for plaintiff affirmed against defenses of lack of primary negligence and contributory negligence); Smith v. Chicago, M. & St. P. R., 42 Wis. 520 (1877) (judgment for plaintiff on general and special verdict reversed, the court holding that there was no evidence to support jury finding of negligence based on inadequate inspection); Flanagan v. Chicago & N. W. R., 45 Wis. 98 (1878) (affirmed granting of defendant's motion for new trial on ground of erroneous instructions concerning defendant's duty in making repairs even though instruc-

tions were later corrected) and 50 Wis. 419 (1880) (judgment for plaintiff affirmed, turning on issues of instructions and sufficiency of evidence); Whitman v. Wisconsin & M. R., 58 Wis. 408 (1883) (judgment for plaintiff reversed—fellow-servant rule); Luebke v. Chicago, M. & St. P. R., 59 Wis. 127 (1883) (order granting nonsuit reversed on the ground that in the absence of contrary evidence it would be presumed that company did not take precautions, Justices Cassoday and Taylor dissenting on basis of fellow-servant rule) and 63 Wis. 91 (1885) (judgment for plaintiff reversed on basis of fellow-servant rule); Fowler v. Chicago & N. W. R., 61 Wis. 159 (1884) (order granting nonsuit affirmed—fellow-servant rule); Kelly v. Abbot, 63 Wis. 307 (1885) (judgment for defendant affirmed—fellow-servant rule—per Orton, J.: "It is very sad and pitiful that so many deaths and severe personal injuries result from coupling cars; but this part of the employment of brakeman is extremely dangerous and hazardous, and especially when it becomes necessary to couple together cars coming from different roads with dissimilar coupling appliances; and the care necessary to be used increases in proportion to such danger, and the law exacts its exercise, or it will refuse redress." *Ibid.*, 312); Pease v. Chicago & N. W. R., 61 Wis. 163 (1884) (order granting nonsuit affirmed—fellow-servant rule); Phillips v. Chicago. M. & St. P. R., 64 Wis. 475 (1885) (fellow-servant rule did not apply; signal watchers not properly fellow servants); Cole v. Chicago & N. W. R., 67 Wis. 272 (1886) (reversed order overruling demurrer: plaintiff need not allege ignorance of defects; burden on defendant to show knowledge) and 71 Wis. 114 (1888) (no recovery—assumption of risk and fellow-servant rule); Carey v. Chicago & N. W. R., 67 Wis. 608 (1887) (affirmed order denying defendant's motion to make more definite and certain); Kittner v. Milwaukee & N. R., 77 Wis. 1 (1890) (order granting new trial reversed, the court holding that it was an error to set aside special verdict for plaintiff when trial judge merely disagreed with finding).

Conduct on trains in motion: Dorsey v. Phillips & Colby Construction Co., 42 Wis. 583 (1877) (conductor injured in cattle chute; judgment for plaintiff affirmed, Supreme Court, through Chief Justice Ryan, discussing assumption ("acquiescence") of risk and contributory negligence); Cottril v. Chicago, M. & St. P. R., 47 Wis. 634 (1879) (engineer killed; judgment on special verdict for defendant reversed, the court holding that trial judge erroneously took certain issues from jury); Delie v. Chicago & N. W. R., 51 Wis. 400 (1881) (judgment for plaintiff-fireman affirmed; discussion confined to issues of damages); Hulehan v. Green Bay, W. & St. P. R., 58 Wis. 319 (1883) (brakeman injured stumbling over firewood; order overruling demurrer affirmed); Heine v. Chicago & N. W. R., 58 Wis. 525 (1883) (workman injured boarding train; judgment on directed verdict for defendant affirmed on ground of fellow-servant rule).

Work around yards, shops. and bridges: Shultz v. Chicago, M. & St. P. R., 40 Wis. 589 (1876) (plaintiff injured while working on pile driver; judgment for plaintiff reversed, the court holding that jury must determine whether plaintiff was working for an independent contractor) and 48 Wis. 575 (1879) (judgment for plaintiff affirmed); Schultz v. Chicago & N. W. R., 44 Wis. 638 (1878) (plaintiff injured while working in yards; judgment for plaintiff affirmed); Essex v. Chicago & N. W. R., 45 Wis. 477 1878) (plaintiff injured by falling into excavation; nonsuit reversed, the court holding issues should have gone to jury); *idem, sub nom.* Hartwig v. Chicago & N. W. R., 49 Wis. 358 (1880) ($100 judgment for original plaintiff's administrator affirmed); Steffen v. Chicago & N. W. R., 46 Wis. 259 (1879) (judgment for plaintiff, a section hand, reversed on grounds of unavoidable accident and assumption of risk—"occult risk incident to the employment"); Stetler v. Chicago v. Chicago & N. W. R., 46 Wis. 497 (1879) (plaintiff injured on spur track; judgment for plaintiff reversed on ground that trial court improperly took issue of causation from jury) and 49 Wis. 609 (1880) (judgment for plaintiff affirmed); Pool v. Chicago, M. & St. P. R., 53 Wis. 657 (1881) (plaintiff injured while riding on hand car; order overruling defendant's demurrer affirmed) and 56 Wis. 227 (1882) (judgment for plaintiff affirmed); Naylor v. Chicago & N. W. R., 53 Wis. 661 (1881) (plaintiff fell down embankment, recovery denied—assumption of risk); Howland v. Milwaukee, L. S. & W. R., 54 Wis. 226 (1882) (plaintiff injured when car overturned on him; order overruling defendant's demurrer reversed—assumption of risk); Murray v. Abbot, 61 Wis. 198 (1884) (plaintiff killed while repairing bridge; judgment on special verdict for plaintiff reversed because issues framed in special verdict not clear); Muster v. Milwaukee & St. P. R., 61 Wis. 325 (1884) (plaintiff injured by bag thrown out of train by postal clerk; judgment for defendant affirmed); Peschel v. Chicago, M. & St. P. R., 62 Wis. 338 (1885) (plaintiff-mason injured on watertank; recovery denied because scaffolding constructed by fellow servants was defective); Quackenbush v. Wisconsin & M. R., 62 Wis. 411 (1885) (employee killed because of railroad's failure to fence tracks; order overruling demurrer affirmed, the court holding liability of railroad absolute when it failed to fence) and 71 Wis. 472 (1888) (judgment for plaintiff affirmed; contributory negligence no defense in action based on fencing statute); Goltz v. Milwaukee, L. S. & W. R., 76 Wis. 137 (1890) (plaintiff injured in fall from scaffolding that broke as result of defective hook; judgment on special verdict for plaintiff reversed; fifth finding of special verdict was that owner could have observed defect in hook; this being so, Supreme Court said plaintiff also could have observed it and therefore he was contributorily negligent); Radmann v. Chicago, M. & St. P. R., 78 Wis. 22 (1890) (personal injuries from defective machinery; judgment on directed verdict for defendant affirmed on grounds of contributory negligence).

Other railroading operations: Anderson v. Milwaukee, & St. P. R., 37 Wis. 321 (1875) (plaintiff injured in Iowa where fellow-servant rule had been abolished by statute; order sustaining demurrer affirmed on ground that abrogation of fellow-servant rule was matter of remedy and governed by the *lex fori);* Ditberner v. Chicago, M. & St. P. R., 47 Wis. 138 (1879) (judgment on special verdict for plaintiff affirmed, the court upholding the 1875 act abrogating the fellow-servant rule); Kelley v. Chicago, M. & St. P. R., 50 Wis. 381 (1880) (wrongful death; order overruling demurrer sustained—issue of negligence must go to jury) and 53 Wis. 74 (1881) (judgment on special verdict for defendant affirmed; general verdict had been rendered for plaintiff, but court held that this applied only to amount of damages); Berg v. Chicago, M. & St. P. R., 50 Wis. 419 (1880) (judgment for plaintiff affirmed on the basis of the 1875 statute abrogating the fellow-servant rule); Ballou v. Chicago, M. & St. P. R., 54 Wis. 257 (1882) (wrongful death; order granting nonsuit affirmed—no negligence sufficient to go to jury had been shown and plaintiff had assumed the risk); McQuade v. Chicago & N. W. R., 68 Wis. 616 (1887) (plaintiff's appeal dismissed, the court holding that contributory negligence could be set up by way of answer).

[96] *Annual Message of Governor William R. Taylor,* 1875, pp. 13–14.

[97] *Seventh Annual Report of the Railroad Commissioner,* 1880, xxxii. Turner also stated that he would recommend re-enactment of the 1875 law were it not for the fact that a case on this point was pending in the Supreme Court. *Ibid.* Research has not yielded the name of the case to which he referred.

[98] *First Biennial Report of the Railroad Commissioner,* 1885, p. 10. The observations Haugen made in 1882 are found in the *Ninth Annual Report of the Railroad Commissioner,* 1882, xxx.

[99] *Ibid.,* xxxiii. He recommended a law similar to that of Massachusetts.

[100] *Third Biennial Report of the Railroad Commissioner,* 1888, xx–xxi.

[101] *First Biennial Report of the Railroad Commissioner,* 1885. pp. 8–9.

[102] *Wage claims:* Dougherty v. North Wisconsin R., 36 Wis. 402 (1874); Miller v. Chicago, M. & St. P. R., 58 Wis. 310 (1883); Nelsen v. Chicago, M. & St. P. R., 60 Wis. 320 (1884). Compare Redmond v. Galena & S. W. R., 39 Wis. 426 (1876) (employee of subcontractor; recovery affirmed) and O'Reilly v. Milwaukee & N. R., 68 Wis. 212 (1887) (action to enforce laborer's lien on cordwood, railroad garnished). *Liability for board:* Hall v. Chicago, M. & St. P. R., 48 Wis. 317 (1879). Compare Sterling v. Ryan, 72 Wis. 36 (1889) (action by boardinghouse keeper against contractor) and French v. Langdon, 76 Wis. 29 (1890) (action between contractors).

[103] *Laws of Wisconsin,* 1885, ch. 85 (charging successor railroad with liability for wages owing from predecessor for period of six months prior to succession); compare *Laws of Wisconsin,* 1878. ch. 316 (prescribing procedure for receiver of insolvent road to pay wage claims).

[104] *Second Biennial Message of Jeremiah M. Rusk,* 1887, p. 5. On organized labor at this stage of United States history, see Selig Perlman, *A History of Trade Unionism in the United States* (New York, 1923), ch. 4.

[105] *Annual Message of Governor William R. Taylor,* 1875, p. 28. See pages 28–30 of this message for his views on the essential identity of interests of farmer and railroad management.

[106] *Annual Message of William D. Hoard,* 1889, pp. 18–19.

[107] See, for example, Brabbits v. Chicago & N. W. R., 38 Wis. 289 (1875) (knowledge of foreman imputed to defendant-railroad, the court adopting the "vice-principal" rule); Luebke v. Chicago, M. & St. P. R., 59 Wis. 127 (1883) (in the absence of evidence to the contrary, it would be presumed that the railroad had failed to take necessary precautions); Phillips v. Chicago M. & St. P. R.. 64 Wis. 475 (1885) (signal-watchers held not to be "fellow servants").

[108] See page 142 above.

[109] For example, State *ex rel.* Chicago, M. & St. P. R. v. McFetridge, 56 Wis. 256 (1882) (mandamus to compel state treasurer to issue license).

[110] "It is a little singular that no application should have been made for a modification of the injunction; and that the defendant should remain apparently bound by rates changed by law some four months ago. But, whatever may be the reason of that, we certainly cannot decree perpetual injunction not to disregard statutory rates which have, at least in part, ceased to be obligatory, or obedience to a statute as originally passed, which has since been materially amended." Attorney-General v. Chicago, M. & St. P. R., 38 Wis. 69, 90 (1875).

[111] *Land-use programs: Laws of Wisconsin,* 1876, ch. 129 (amending Wisconsin Railroad Farm Mortgage Land Company act by adding penal section subjecting to a fifty-dollar fine any person who failed to comply with the provisions of the act); *Laws of Wisconsin,* 1889, ch. 512 (fine of one hundred dollars imposed on person failing to keep right-of-way cleared of brush; action to be brought on complaint of town board in justice court); *ibid.,* ch. 516 (fine of twenty-five dollars for failure to keep turntable attended or locked). *Disorderly behavior: Laws of Wisconsin.* ch. 119, sec. 1 (two-hundred-dollar fine against the railroad for permitting gambling on board the train), sec. 2 (five-hundred-dollar fine against person convicted of gambling), and sec. 3 (one-half the penalty to informer); 1876, ch. 167, and 1880, ch. 29, sec. 2 (conductors empowered to "arrest summarily and without due process" and then turn culprit over to town authorities). Compare *Laws,* 1887, ch. 258 (to protect their property railroad companies were authorized to appoint police officers with power to arrest without warrant). *Theft of railroad equipment: Laws of Wisconsin.* 1887, ch. 249 (fine and imprisonment for stealing axe or saw from railroad car).

[112] *Laws of Wisconsin,* 1875, ch. 248, sec. 2. The owner could recover ten dollars

for each train or locomotive thereafter passing through the premises. Such recovery, however, had to be effected "in an action of trespass against the railroad company so offending."

[113] *Ibid.,* 1881, ch. 189. See "Comment" in the *Yale Law Journal,* 59:745 (1950) and note 81 above.

[114] *Laws of Wisconsin.* 1882, ch. 266.

[115] *Ibid.,* 1876, ch. 57, sec. 8.

[116] Smith v. Chicago & N. W. R., 43 Wis. 686, 689–690 (1878). The statutes involved were *Laws of Wisconsin,* 1875, ch. 334, sec. 3. and 1876, ch. 57, sec. 8.

[117] *Second Annual Message of Governor William R. Taylor,* 1875, p. 14.

[118] See, for example, State v. Pullman's Palace Car Co., 64 Wis. 89 (1885) and State *ex rel.* Attorney-General v. Milwaukee. L. S. & W. R., 45 Wis. 579 (1878).

[119] *Biennial Message of Jeremiah M. Rusk,* 1895, p. 12.

[120] State v. Pullman's Palace Car Co., 64 Wis. 78 (1885). Nils Haugen had spotted the defect of divided responsibility between railroad commissioner and state treasurer. See page 144 above.

[121] *Laws of Wisconsin,* 1885, ch. 193.

[122] *Ibid.,* 1889, ch. 438.

[123] *Ibid.,* ch. 459.

[124] *Ibid.,* 1875. ch. 54 (authorizing appropriations from the general fund for expenses of the Potter Law); 1876, ch. 57, sec. 14 (salary and expense sections of 1876 act); 1883, ch. 43 (creating office of deputy railroad commissioner and appropriating money for his salary); 1882, ch. 161; 1883, ch. 258; 1887, ch. 22; 1889, ch. 373; and 1891. ch. 256, 447 (all dealing with appropriations for maps); 1881, ch. 224 (authorizing railroad commissioner to take an expert with him in examining bridges).

[125] *Laws of Wisconsin,* 1876, ch. 57, sec. 3 (requiring submission of data). Statutes limiting the length of reports were *Laws of Wisconsin,* 1885, ch. 303 (limiting report to 300 pages) and 1889, ch. 526 (200 pages, more on written request).

[126] "The Commissioner has considered his position that of a mediator and as disputes and misunderstandings will naturally arise in the details of a business so far-reaching and diversified as is that of railroads. he has acted in the spirit of arbitrator. whenever complaints have been lodged with him, deeming such a course the most beneficient to the community at large, as well as being the real spirit of the law establishing the office. In the matter of complaints he has given the law a liberal construction considering the substance of more importance than form. In no instance have the companies objected to their consideration for the reason that they were not in proper form." *Ninth Annual Report of the Railroad Commissioner* [Haugen], 1882, li.

[127] *First Biennial Report of the Railroad Commissioner,* 1885, pp. 12–13, 23.

[128] He thought the chief fault of the law was its failure to define the powers of the commissioner with enough precision. *Third Biennial Report of the Railroad Commissioner.* 1888, xli.

VI. WHO MADE THE DECISIONS?

[1] See pages 37, 193 n. 52, 10, and 193 n, 2 above.

[2] On this development see Adolph A. Berle Jr. and Gardner C. Means, *The Modern Corporation and Private Property* (New York, 1932), 130–138.

[3] See page 139 above.

[4] See pages 24–25 above.

[5] See pages 151–156 and 135–136 above.

[6] See page 147 above.

[7] See pages 46–47 and 99 above.

BIBLIOGRAPHIC COMMENT

Most of the material for this book has come from the Wisconsin statute books and from the pages of the Wisconsin Supreme Court reports. Here I shall cite only those secondary authorities and non-legal sources from which I have derived pertinent information.

Bibliographic Material

Anyone doing work in Wisconsin history should acquaint himself with the following bibliographic aids: Leroy Schlinkert, *Subject Bibliography of Wisconsin History* (Madison, 1947), incomplete but well arranged according to topics; *The Wisconsin Region; A Bibliography of Theses in the Social Sciences and the Humanities,* prepared under the auspices of the Committee on the Study of American Civilization and published by the University of Wisconsin Centennial Committee (mimeographed, Madison, 1949); *Guide to the Manuscripts of the Wisconsin Historical Society,* edited by Alice E. Smith (Madison, 1944), and *Supplement Number One,* edited by Josephine L. Harper and Sharon C. Smith (Madison, 1957); and Willard Hurst, ed., *A Digest of Regional Sources for the Study of the Economic and Political History of the Law* (mimeographed, Madison, 1941), an invaluable digest of the decisions of the Wisconsin Supreme Court, broken down according to economic and political contents. As guides to material in the executive branch of government two mimeographed publications of the Wisconsin Historical Records Survey are helpful, although sketchy on the early periods: *An Index to Governors' Messages* (mimeographed, Madison, 1941) and *An Index to Documents in the Secretary of State's Office* (mimeographed, Madison, 1942); both publications are arranged by subject matter rather than chronologically. Of general value, though not limited to Wisconsin, is Henrietta M. Larson's *Guide to Business History: Materials for the Study of American Business History and Suggestions for Their Use* (Cambridge, Massachusetts, 1948).

CHAPTER I. WISCONSIN PURCHASE, 1856

The most fruitful source of information on the legislative scandal of 1856 is of course the *Report of the Joint Select Committee Appointed to Investigate into Alleged Frauds and Corruption in the Disposition of the Land Grant by the Legislature of 1856, and for Other Purposes,* printed as an appendix to the *Wisconsin Assembly Journal* for 1858. Bessie S. Winn's master's thesis, The Wisconsin Railroad Scandal, 1856, a manuscript in the Memorial Library of the University of Wisconsin, is a narrative account, and John M. Bernd's "The La Crosse and Milwaukee Railroad Land Grant, 1856," in the *Wisconsin Magazine of History,* 30:141 (December, 1946), emphasizes the struggle of the rival roads for the grant. Short published accounts of the incident can also be found in August W. Derleth's *The Milwaukee Road: Its First Hundred Years* (New York, 1948), 81–85; Frederick L. Holmes's *Badger Saints and Sinners* (Milwaukee, 1939), 153–173; Frederick Merk's *The Economic History of Wisconsin during the Civil War Decade* (Madison, 1916), 280–282; Milo M. Quaife's *Wisconsin: Its History and Its People* (4 vols., Chicago, 1924), 1: 532–539; William F. Raney's *Wisconsin: A Story of Progress* (New York, 1940), 182–183; Bayrd Still's *Milwaukee: The History of a City* (Madison, 1948), 169–173; and Reuben G. Thwaites's *Wisconsin: The Americanization of a French Settlement* (Boston and New York, 1908), 302–304. Good accounts of the incident in unpublished materials are those of Herbert W. Rice in his Early History of the Chicago, Milwaukee, and St. Paul Railway Company, 149–163, a doctoral dissertation in the library of the State University of Iowa, and of Richard L. Canuteson, in his master's thesis, Railway Development of Northern Wisconsin, 8–40, a manuscript in the Memorial Library of the University of Wisconsin.

Rice's dissertation, cited above, also gives, on pages 1–36, a good account of the economic and social situation in Wisconsin at the time of the advent of the railroads. On early Wisconsin railroads Merk's *Economic History of Wisconsin,* pages 271–288, and Chapter 10 of Raney's *Wisconsin* give good general descriptions; Frederic L. Paxson's "The Railroads of the 'Old Northwest' before the Civil War," in the *Transactions of the Wisconsin Academy of Sciences, Arts, and Letters,* 1914, Part I, vol. 17, p. 243 contains excellent maps. On northern Wisconsin roads Canuteson's Railway

Development in Northern Wisconsin is valuable. John W. Rodewald's master's thesis, Railroad Development in Wisconsin, a manuscript in the Memorial Library of the University of Wisconsin, is incomplete and inadequate. Invaluable for the relationship between railroads and legislative activity are two articles by Balthasar H. Meyer: "A History of Early Railroad Legislation in Wisconsin," in *Wisconsin Historical Collections,* 14:206 (1898), and "Early General Railway Legislation in Wisconsin," in the *Transactions of the Wisconsin Academy of Sciences, Arts, and Letters,* 12:337 (1898).

On the La Crosse and Milwaukee Railroad (and its successor lines), the best secondary account is Rice's Early History of the Chicago, Milwaukee, and St. Paul; more popularly written is the "official" history, Derleth's *Milwaukee Road.* Absolutely essential, however, is John W. Cary's *Organization and History of the Chicago, Milwaukee, and St. Paul Railway Company* (Milwaukee, 1893), because the author, who was general counsel for the Milwaukee during much of its eventful early history, treats in detail the many legal problems that engulfed the road. The library of the State Historical Society of Wisconsin has on file, under the title "La Crosse and Milwaukee Railroad Co.: Miscelleanous Reports," a collection of various printed documents pertaining to the road, which contains much source material; besides the annual reports, the collection includes newspaper clippings and legal documents. The library of the Historical Society also has the annual reports of other early Wisconsin railroads.

Gordon O. Greiner's Wisconsin National Railroad Land Grants, an unpublished master's thesis in the Memorial Library of the University of Wisconsin, is helpful on the Wisconsin grants, and John B. Sanborn's *Congressional Grants of Land in Aid of Railways (Bulletin of the University of Wisconsin,* 1899, vol. 30, no. 54), although old, is still a valuable general discussion. Lewis H. Haney's *A Congressional History of Railways in the United States, 1850–87 (Bulletin of the University of Wisconsin,* no. 342, 1910) discusses on pages 15–33 the Wisconsin grants, and Bernd, in the *Wisconsin Magazine of History,* 30:141, deals with the 1856 grant in particular. Various treatises and monographs dealing with the national domain necessarily discuss the railroad land grants: Thomas C. Donaldson, *The Public Domain: Its History with Statistics* (Washington, 1884); Benjamin H. Hibbard, *A History of the Public Land Policies* (New

York, 1924); Robert T. Hill, *The Public Domain and Democracy* (New York, 1910); Roy M. Robbins, *Our Landed Heritage: The Public Domain, 1776–1836* (Princeton, 1942); and George M. Stephenson, *The Political History of the Public Lands from 1840 to 1862* (Boston, 1917). The history of the legislative pull and haul over passage of the Wisconsin land-grant act is scattered through the pages of the *Congressional Globe,* 31st, 32d, and 34th Congress (1852–56). The 1856 grant itself appears in the *United States Statutes at Large,* 11:20 (1856).

The most complete account of Byron Kilbourn is that compiled under the aegis of the Works Progress Administration as part of a larger project of Wisconsin biographies currently being prepared for publication; the manuscript is in the possession of the State Historical Society of Wisconsin. Other sketches may be found in Milo M. Quaife, ed., *The Attainment of Statement* (*Wisconsin Historical Collections,* vol. 29: *Constitutional Series,* vol. 4, Madison, 1928), 914; Still, *Milwaukee, passim*; and H. Russell Austin, *The Milwaukee Story* (Milwaukee, 1946), 38–44. Older local histories and biographies are entirely eulogistic; representative of these are Frank A. Flower's *History of Milwaukee, Wisconsin* (Chicago, 1881), 1173–1176, and James S. Buck's *Pioneer History of Milwaukee,* 233–234 (1876).

Kenneth W. Duckett's *Frontiersman of Fortune: Moses M. Strong of Mineral Point* (Madison, 1955) is a good contemporary biography. Other biographical sketches of Strong appear in two volumes edited by Milo M. Quaife: *The Convention of 1846* (*Wisconsin Historical Collections,* vol. 27: *Constitutional Series,* vol. 2, Madison, 1919), 794, and *The Strong and Woodman Manuscript Collections in the Wisconsin State Historical Library* (Wisconsin Historical Society, *Bulletin of Information,* no. 78, Madison, 1915) 4–11. John R. Berryman's *History of the Bench and Bar of Wisconsin,* 2:224–227 (Chicago, 1898), contains a conventional uncritical account. Apart from the *Report of the Joint Select Committee,* cited above the details of Kilbourn's and Strong's plotting to get the grant can be gleaned from correspondence in the Moses M. Strong Railroad Papers, 1835–56, manuscripts in the possession of the State Historical Society of Wisconsin.

For information on other important personages involved in the episode the Works Progress Administration collection, cited above, is valuable. For the greater number, however, one is dependent on the eulogies in local biographies and genealogies. Berryman's *History of the Bench and Bar in Wisconsin* (2 vols.) provides a source of information about members of the bar, although its tone also is eulogistic. Parker M. Reed, *The Bench and Bar of Wisconsin* (Milwaukee, 1882) is older, shorter, and even less critical. A sketch of James H. Knowlton is included in Berryman's *History of the Bench and Bar in Wisconsin,* vol. 2, and Willard Hurst and Betty R. Brown in their article "The Perils of the Test Case," in the *Wisconsin Law Review,* 1949, pp. 26, 49–51, tell of Knowlton's activity in a famous taxpayer's suit. A good account of Kilbourn's adversary, William B. Ogden, appears in Thomas W. Goodspeed's *The University of Chicago Biographical Sketches,* 1:35 (Chicago, 1922). Alice E. Smith's *James Duane Doty: Frontier Promoter* (Madison, 1954) provides insight into the activities of a prominent personage of the time. "Honest Amasa Cobb" (appearing in an editorial department, "The Question Box"), in the *Wisconsin Magazine of History,* 5:208 (December, 1921) merely recounts the famous story of the attempted bribery. On Alexander Mitchell see James D. Butler's "Alexander Mitchell the Financier," in *Wisconsin Historical Collections,* 11:435 (Madison, 1888). John B. Winslow's *The Story of a Great Court* (Chicago, 1912) contains short biographies of Wisconsin Supreme Court justices.

Accounts of the power of legislative investigating committees are those of C. S. Potts, "Power of Legislative Bodies to Punish for Contempt," in the *University of Pennsylvania Law Review,* 74:691, 780 (May, 1926) and of Orin S. Herwitz, William G. Mulligan, Jr., and Samuel Seabury, "The Legislative Investigating Committee" (growing out of the Seabury investigation in New York), in the *Columbia Law Review,* 33:1 (January, 1933). On matters of legislative procedure at this time the authoritative reference is Luther S. Cushing's *Elements of the Law and Practice of Legislative Assemblies* (9th edition, Boston, 1907); the original edition came out in 1856. On the origins of legislative procedures and practices then prevalent, see Ralph V. Harlow's *The History of Legislative Methods in the Period before 1825* (New Haven, 1917). Moses Strong's period of incarceration in the Dane County jail is poignantly described by Strong himself in the Moses M. Strong Railroad Papers, cited above, and also in Duckett's *Frontiersman of Fortune,* 135–141.

On the economics of railroads and railroading, perhaps the most helpful general treatments are William Z. Ripley, *Railroads: Finance and Organization* (New York, 1915); Frederick A. Cleveland and Fred W. Powell, *Railroad Finance* (New York, 1912) and *Railroad Promotion and Capitalization* (New York, 1909); and Emory A. Johnson and Thurman W. Van Metre, *Principles of Railway Transportation* (New York, 1922). Still helpful is Arthur T. Hadley's *Railroad Transportation* (New York, 1885). An excellent study of the legal techniques of early railroad finance is Francis L. Stetson's "Preparation of Corporate Bonds, Mortgages, Collateral Trusts and Debenture Indentures," in Stetson and others, *Some Legal Phases of Corporate Financing, Reorganization, and Regulation* (New York, 1930), 1–13. For a good general discussion of the origins, growth, and development of the corporate form of doing business see Adolf A. Berle and Gardiner C. Means, *The Modern Corporation and Private Property* (New York, 1932) and, for valuable historical material, Arthur S. Dewing's *The Financial Policy of Corporations* (2 vols., 4th edition, New York, 1941). The early legal history of corporations (mainly in the East) is exhaustively described in E. Merrick Dodd's *American Business Corporations until 1860* (Cambridge, 1954). Joseph S. Davis' *Essays in the Earlier History of American Corporations* (Cambridge, Massachusetts, 1917) is a scholarly study, and Shaw Livermore's *Early American Land Companies* (New York, 1939) sets forth the interesting thesis that modern corporate institutions owe much in the way of origins to the land companies. Bishop C. Hunt's *The Development of the Business Corporation in England, 1800–1867* (Cambridge, Massachusetts, 1936) is an account of British analogues. Leonard W. Levy's "Chief Justice Shaw and the Formative Period of American Railroad Law," in the *Columbia Law Review*, 51:327, 852 (March and November, 1951) is a study of early developments in Massachusetts.

Critical analyses of Wisconsin politics during this early period are lacking; there is almost no discussion either of party or of sectional alliances. Of the general works Raney's *Wisconsin*, 144–155, and Quaife's *Wisconsin*, vol. 1, chs. 20, 23, 25, present narrative accounts. Ralph G. Plumb's *Badger Politics, 1836–1930* (Manitowoc, 1930) is entirely anecdotal and very incomplete. Alexander M. Thomson's *A Political History of Wisconsin* (Milwaukee, 1900) is more valuable as source material than as secondary comment; the author, a leader in the Grange, was refreshingly frank in his appraisal of contemporary political leaders. Winslow's *Story of a Great Court* depicts well the role of the Supreme Court in the issues of the day. Roy O. I. Holmes's bachelor of arts thesis, Wisconsin State Party Platforms, 1848–1865, a manuscript in the library of the State Historical Society of Wisconsin, is useful solely as a compilation of party platforms, and Leroy J. N. Murat's bachelor of law thesis, The Administration of Governor Barstow, a manuscript in the same library, contains an interesting discussion of the "Old Lobby." Gladys Gerecke's bachelor of arts thesis, A Political History of Wisconsin, 1848–1868, a manuscript in the library of the State Historical Society of Wisconsin, deals almost entirely with the slavery issue, and Edward J. Henning's bachelor of law thesis, The Development of Political Parties in Wisconsin Territory, a manuscript in the same library, is superficially done.

The Wisconsin constitutional conventions have been covered exhaustively in the monumental four-volume work edited by Milo M. Quaife *(Wisconsin Historical Collections, Constitutional Series):* Vol. 1, *The Movement for Statehood* (1918); Vol. 2, *The Convention of 1846* (1919); Vol. 3, *The Struggle over Ratification* (1920); and Vol. 4, *The Attainment of Statehood* (1938). The works contain copious passages from the journals and debates of the constitutional convention, lists and biographical sketches of delegates, and tabulations of votes. Ray A. Brown's "The Making of the Wisconsin Constitution" in the *Wisconsin Law Review,* 1949, p. 648, is an excellent critical summary of the work of the 1846 convention.

Two first-rate discussions of the interplay of law and economics in other states during the nineteenth century are Louis Hartz's *Economic Policy and Democratic Thought: Pennsylvania, 1776–1860* (Cambridge, Massachusetts, 1948) and Oscar and Mary F. Handlin's *Commonwealth: Massachusetts, 1774–1861* (New York, 1947).

Chapter II. Embattled Farmers and a Common Law Court

Merk's *Economic History of Wisconsin* contains the definitive account of the farm-mortgage struggle. Winslow's *Story of a Great Court,* 167–179, treats the legal issues in greater detail. Rice's manuscript History of the Chicago, Milwaukee, and St. Paul Railroad, 116–140, also contains a good account. Cary's *Organization and History of the Chicago, Milwaukee, and St. Paul,* 13, 17, 201, 326 ff., gives the best description in lawyers' terminology, of the farm-mortgage device.

Much miscellaneous information can be gleaned from the Railroad Farm Mortgage Papers in the collection of Miscellaneous Executive Documents in the possession of the State Historical Society of Wisconsin. Similarly, the issues of the *Hartford Home League* for the period 1856–60 ("uncompromising foe of swindling corporations"), a weekly published by the Farm Mortgage Leagues, are devoted almost entirely to the farm-mortgage struggle. Its editor was Alexander M. Thomson; for this reason his *Political History of Wisconsin* is of particular interest. The workings of a local Farm Mortgage League are fascinatingly portrayed in the Minutes of the Farmer's Home League of Monroe, in the possession of the State Historical Society of Wisconsin. The information on various lawyers who were prominent in the struggle has been taken from Berryman's *History of the Bench and Bar of Wisconsin* and Winslow's *Story of a Great Court.*

Apart from the reported court cases, material on the legal controversy can be found in the respective briefs of counsel in *Cases and Briefs* in the Wisconsin State Law Library. Knowlton's review of the Supreme Court opinion appears in the *Hartford Home League,* September 8, 15, 1860.

The effect of the farm-mortgage cases on the law of negotiable instruments with respect to defenses available against a holder in due course is discussed in William Colebrooke's *A Treatise on the Law of Collateral Securities* (Chicago, 1883), sec. 161 and 165, and Theophilus Parson's *A Treatise on the Law of Notes and Bills of Exchange* (Philadelphia, 1871), 1:274–275.

The constitutional point surrounding the contract clause is discussed in Thomas M. Cooley's *Constitutional Limitations* (Boston, 1868), 289–290. Benjamin F. Wright's *The Contract Clause of the Constitution* (Cambridge, Massachusetts, 1938) is the most extensive treatment of the general subject. On foreclosure stay laws such as were involved here A. H. Feller's "Moratory Legislation: A Comparative Study," in the *Harvard Law Review,* 46:1061 (May, 1933) is an excellent survey and analysis.

On the authority of corporations to accept notes in payment for shares, the most complete treatment is William M. Fletcher's *Cyclopedia of the Law of Corporations* (revised edition, Chicago, 1932) vol. 11, sec. 5194–5196. See also Harry W. Ballantine, *Corporations* (Chicago, 1946), sec. 344–345, Robert S. Stevens, *Handbook of the Law of Private Corporations* (St. Paul, 1949), sec. 177, and Berle and

Means, *The Modern Corporation and Private Property,* 251–253. On overvaluation of property received for shares of stock, the classic study is David L. Dodd's *Stock Watering* (New York, 1930).

On the bit of equity procedure frozen into the Wisconsin Constitution by *Callanan v. Judd* see Delmar Karlen, *Cases and Materials on Trials and Appeals* (mimeographed, Madison, 1949), 26–55.

Chapter III. The Formative Period of Wisconsin Railroad Law, 1858–1874

In addition to the statutes and court decisions, the Governors' Messages and the Senate and Assembly Journals have furnished a good portion of the raw material for this chapter. Meyer, in *Wisconsin Historical Collections,* 14:206, 263–264, contains a good discussion of the condemnation and appraisal sections of the special charters. Daniel J. Dykstra's "Legislation and Change," in the *Wisconsin Law Review,* 1950, pp. 523, 526, deals with analogous condemnation proceedings under the Mill Dam Act.

The causal relationship between the railroad and the enactment of wrongful-death statutes in England is described in Sir Frederick Pollock's *The Law of Torts* (14th edition, London, 1939), 55–56. On the evolution of shippers' liability from principles in the law of bailments the classic treatment is that of Oliver W. Holmes, Jr., in his *The Common Law* (Boston, 1881), 180–205. Issac F. Redfield's *A Practical Treatise on the Law of Railways* (Boston, 1858) was the leading treatise on railroad law at the time, and was a cut above the usual paste-and-scissors job. On early treatises on corporation law see Charles E. Warren's *A History of the Harvard Law School* (3 vols., New York, 1908), 2:141–142. On the struggle of the Wisconsin Supreme Court with the fellow-servant rule see Willard Hurst and Lloyd K. Garrison, *Materials on Law in Society* (mimeographed, Madison, 1940), 115–122. Merk's *Economic History of Wisconsin,* 189–307, Meyer's "Early General Railway Legislation in Wisconsin," in *Transactions of the Wisconsin Academy of Sciences, Arts, and Letters,* 12 (1898):364–378, and Rice's manuscript History of the Chicago, Milwaukee, and St. Paul, 169–226, contain good accounts of railroad consolidations during this period. Cary's *The Organization and History of the Chicago, Milwaukee, and St. Paul,* 30–43, has a detailed description of the various foreclosures of the La Crosse and Milwaukee mortgages.

On the general problem of the relationship between business corporations and the state government during this period see George J. Kuehnl's manuscript dissertation, The Wisconsin Business Corporation, 1800–1875, in the Law Library of the University of Wisconsin. The railroad tax-uniformity case is treated exhaustively by Hurst and Brown in the *Wisconsin Law Review,* 1949, p. 26. See also the monograph of Guy E. Snider on *The Taxation of the Gross Receipts of Railways in Wisconsin* (New York, 1906). Raymond V. Phelan's *The Financial History of Wisconsin* (Madison, 1908), 373–398, also treats of railroad taxation. Breck P. McAllister, "Public Purpose in Taxation," in the California Law Review, 18:137, 241 (January, 1930), is a good general treatment of the constitutional question, and Harry H. Pierce's *Railroads of New York: A Study of Government Aid* (Cambridge, Massachusetts, 1953) treats the problem of local aid to New York railroads *in extenso.* James M. Gray's *Limitations on the Taxing Power* (San Francisco, 1906), 123–227, is older and more traditional. On events surrounding the Olcott case in the United States Supreme Court, see the discussion in Charles Fairman's *Mr. Justice Miller and the Supreme Court 1862–1890* (Cambridge, Massachusetts, 1939), 220–221.

On the subject of legislatively designed sanctions the best treatment is Ernst Freund's *Legislative Regulation* (New York, 1932), 302–338. James D. Barnett's article on "This History and the Office of Governor in Wisconsin," in the *Iowa Journal of History and Politics,* 3:226 (April, 1905) is entirely narrative but nevertheless useful.

Chapter iv. Railroads Versus the State: The Impact of a Judge

On the general problem of agrarian dissatisfaction leading to the passage of regulatory legislation, Solon J. Buck's *The Granger Movement* (Cambridge, Massachusetts, 1913) is still the authoritative treatise. His *The Agrarian Crusade* (New Haven, 1920) presents the subject in shorter form. Frederick Merk's "Eastern Antecedents of the Grangers," in *Agricultural History,* 23:1 (January, 1949), offers a new corollary on the origins of the movement. *The First Annual Report of the Railroad Commissioners of the State of Wisconsin, 1874* also contains much information on the causes of unrest and early attempts at regulation. Covering politics during this period are three good articles by Herman J. Deutsch on "Disintegrating Forces in Wisconsin Politics of the Early Seventies," in the *Wisconsin Magazine of History,* 15:169, 282, 391 (December, 1931; March, June, 1932).

The events leading up to the enactment of the Potter Law are described in Buck's *Granger Movement,* 184–185. A recent study by Robert T. Daland, "Enactment of the Potter Law," in the *Wisconsin Magazine of History,* 33:45 (September, 1949) takes issue with Buck on certain points. Emanuel L. Philipp's *Political Reform in Wisconsin* (Milwaukee, 1910), 202–203, is a political tract, but it contains a good discussion of the Cotzhausen minority report.

Polemic about the Potter Law was spirited both within and outside Wisconsin. Governor Taylor's and Attorney General Sloan's exhortations are presented in a pamphlet entitled *The Railroad Law of 1874,* filed among Wisconsin Miscellaneous Pamphlets, vol. 4, in the State Historical Society of Wisconsin. The letters of defiance written by the presidents of the Milwaukee and North Western are printed in "Executive and Legal Documents," 1–6, included in the 1874 *Report of the Railroad Commissioners.* Other philippics directed against the Potter Law by the roads can be found in the *Fifteenth Annual Report of the Chicago and North Western Railway Company,* 1874, pp. 17–21, and *Memorial of the Chicago and North Western and Chicago, Milwaukee and St. Paul Railway Companies to the Senate and Assembly of the State of Wisconsin* (1875), filed among Wisconsin Miscellaneous Pamphlets, vol. 4, in the State Historical Society of Wisconsin. Representative of comment in Wisconsin are two items published in the *Milwaukee Daily Sentinel:* an appeal for enforcement by Moses Strong, headed "Railway Legislation," in the issue of May 7, 1875, and a reporter's account entitled "The Railroads," in the issue of May 2, 1874. The opinions of William G. Evarts and Judge Curtis on the unconstitutionality of the law are printed in an article entitled "The Railway War," in the *Daily Inter-Ocean* (Chicago), May 5, 1874.

Carpenter's opinion asserting the constitutionality of the law was published in the *Wisconsin State Journal* of May 15, 1874. His opinion was vigorously denounced in the *Chicago Times* of May 18 and 19, 1874. The most recent biography of Carpenter is E. Bruce Thompson's *Matthew Hale Carpenter: Webster of the West* (Madison, 1954). Earlier speeches and writings of Carpenter are compiled and bound in a collection entitled Writings of Matthew Hale Carpenter, 1865–80, in the State Historical Society of Wisconsin. Frank A. Flower, *Life of Matthew Hale Carpenter* (Madison, 1883), 156, describes Elisha Keyes" trip to Washington to enlist Carpenter's support but Richard W. Hantke does not mention it in his doctoral thesis, The Life of Elisha William Keyes, a manuscript in the Library of the University of Wisconsin. Herman J. Deutsch's "Carpenter and the Senatorial Elections of 1875 in Wisconsin," in the *Wisconsin Magazine of History,* 16:26, 42 (September, 1932), points out that Carpenter's stand cost him the support of the railroad lobby in his campaign for re-election.

On the first three railroad commissioners see Robert McCluggage's article on "Joseph H. Osborn: Granger Leader," in the *Wisconsin Magazine of History,* 35:178–184 (Spring, 1952); Henry J. Peterson's biographical sketch of John W. Hoyt in the *Dictionary of American Biography,* 9:321 (New York, 1932); and Frank A. Flower's article on George H. Paul in his *History of Milwaukee, Wisconsin* (Chicago, 1881), 629–630. The George H. Paul Papers, in the possession of the State Historical Society of Wisconsin, contain a wealth of information, mainly in the form of correspondence, about the administration of the Potter Law and the political atmosphere surrounding the appointment of Ryan to the bench. Horace S. Merrill's *William Freeman Vilas: Doctrinaire Democrat* (Madison, 1954) discusses the offer of the chief justiceship to Vilas.

On the personalities involved in the injunction suits see, on A. Scott Sloan, Winslow's *Story of a Great Court,* 132–134, and Dodge County Bar Association, *Memorial Addresses on the Life and Character of Judge A. Scott Sloan;* on Luther S. Dixon see Winslow, *op. cit.,* 122–128, 144–153, 289–304, and Berryman, *History of the Bench and Bar of Wisconsin,* 1:125; on Ithamar C. Sloan: Reed, *The Bench and Bar of Wisconsin* (Milwaukee, 1882), 156–157; on Harlow S. Orton: Berryman, *op. cit.,* 213–230; on Burton C. Cook: *National Cyclopaedia of American Biography,* 13:592 (New York, 1906); on Charles B. Lawrence: *ibid.,* 5:437; on George B. Smith: Berryman, *op. cit.,* 2:377–381; on John W. Cary: *ibid.,* 1:476–482. A detailed picture of the tactics of the North Western in the various enforcement suits under the Potter Law is presented in the almost complete file of correspondence from Lawrence and Cook, general solicitors of the North Western, to George B. Smith, Madison counsel, in the

George B. Smith Papers in the State Historical Society of Wisconsin.

As yet there is no published biography of Edward G. Ryan, although there is an exhaustive treatment of him in manuscript: Alfons J. Beitzinger's doctoral dissertation, Chief Justice Ryan of the Wisconsin Supreme Court, in the Memorial Library of the University of Wisconsin. Two Chapters of this study have been published: "Chief Justice Ryan and His Colleagues," in the *Wisconsin Law Review,* 1955, pp. 592–608, and "Edward George Ryan—19th Century Lawyer," *ibid.,* 1956, pp. 248-282. Apart from these, Winslow's *Story of a Great Court,* 305–353, is the best account in print. Other brief sketches appear in Berryman's *History of the Bench and Bar of Wisconsin,* 166–204, and Reed's *Bench and Bar of Wisconsin,* 55–65. Eulogies of Ryan by various members of the bench and bar are printed in 50 Wis. 23 ff. (1880). Ryan's address to the Law School class of 1873 was published, with an address of Matthew H. Carpenter, in a pamphlet that can be found in the Wisconsin Law School Library, and his eulogy of Judge Dunn, replete with evidence of his classical training, is printed in 30 Wis. 29 (1872). Some of his famous opinions have been collected and published, under the editorship of Gilbert E. Roe, in *Dixon, Luther S. and Ryan, Edward G.: Selected Opinions* (Chicago, 1907).

The original jurisdiction of the Supreme Court placed in issue in the Railroad Companies case is ably discussed in John D. Wickhem's "The Power of Superintending Control of the Wisconsin Supreme Court," in the *Wisconsin Law Review,* 1941, p. 153. A complete catalog of the cases, in manuscript, compiled by John Varda under title Decisions of the Supreme Court of Wisconsin Rendered in the Exercise of Its Original Jurisdiction, is in the Law Library of the University of Wisconsin. John E. Mulder's, "Case Comment," in the *Wisconsin Law Review,* 6:101 (February, 1931), discusses the application of Ryan's notion of *publici juris.* The standard treatise of the time on the law of injunction was James L. High's *A Treatise on the Law of Injunctions* (2d edition, Chicago, 1880). On the use of mandamus see W. Francis Bailey's *A Treatise on the Law of Habeas Corpus and Special Remedies* (Chicago, 1913).

The classic treatment of the power of equity courts over corporations is Roscoe Pound's "Visitatorial Jurisdiction over Corporations in Equity," in the *Harvard Law Review,* 49:369 (January, 1936). Joseph K. Angell and Samuel Ames, *Corporations* (11th edition, Boston, 1882), 723–740, and Redfield, *Railways,* vol. 2, sec. 205

(5th edition, Boston, 1873) represent legal opinion of the time on the issue. Fletcher's *Corporations,* vol. 12, sec. 4855 (revised edition, 1945) and Ballantine's *Corporations,* 66, state the present-day view. Chancellor Kent's opinion in *Attorney-General v. Utica Insurance Co.* is described by John T. Horton in his *James Kent: A Study in Conservatism,* 1763–1847 (New York, 1939), 206, as one of Kent's few deviations from English equity precedents.

The issue of constitutionality provoked most of the comments at the time. Representative samples are the following: Cooley, *Constitutional Limitations* (4th edition, 1878), 720–721; F. L. Wells, "Legislative Control of Railroads," in *Western Jurist,* 12:17–22 (January, 1878); S. S. Wallace, "Railroad Laws, or Legislative Control of Railroads," in the *Southern Law Review,* 3:656 (October, 1874); John W. Smith, "State Regulation of Railway Corporations as to Rates," in the *Central Law Journal,* 23:101 (July, 1886); Charles C. Savage, "State Legislation Regulating Railroad Traffic," in the *American Law Register,* N.S., 23:81 (February, 1884). Out-of-state comment on the injunction suits is illustrated by Brooks Adams' "Letter" in the *New York Tribune,* December 28, 1874, and the "Reply," *ibid.,* January 12, 1875.

Benjamin R. Twiss, *Lawyers and the Constitution: How Laissez-Faire Came to the Supreme Court* (Princeton, 1942), 71–77, discusses the lawyers' contribution to the "due process" concept in the Granger cases, although he does not mention Lawrence's brief. The quasi-sovereign power of private corporations is discussed in the chapter on "Property and Sovereignty," in Morris R. Cohen's *Law and the Social Order* (New York, 1933), 41–68, but Ryan's opinion is not cited.

Chapter v. Wisconsin Railroad Law from 1875 to 1890

To the Wisconsin statutes, the reports of the Supreme Court and the *Executive Documents* are added, now, with the creation of the Railroad Commission, the reports of the Wisconsin Railroad Commissioners as rich source material.

Chapter 9 of Paul W. Gates's *The Wisconsin Pine Lands of Cornell University: A Study in Land Policy and Absentee Ownership* (Ithaca, 1943) describes the battle between Ezra Cornell and the railroads for the rich pinelands. Richard N. Current's *Pine Logs and Politics* (Madison, 1950), 140–143, a biography of Philetus Sawyer, contains a vivid account of the political machinations that accompanied the land grant to the Chicago, St. Paul, Minneapolis and Omaha Railroad. William F. Raney, in his articles on "The Building of Wisconsin's Railroads," in the *Wisconsin Magazine of History,* 19:387 (June, 1936), 399–403, describes the building of the northern roads, as does Canuteson in his manuscript history of Railway Development of Northern Wisconsin. On the "insurable interest" and subrogation statutes a good general discussion with a representative selection of cases is included in Harry Shulman and Fleming James, Jr., *Cases and Materials on the Law of Torts* (Brooklyn, 1942), 113–125. William L. Prosser's *Law of Torts* (2d edition, St. Paul, 1955), 378–382, contains an excellent discussion of the three common-law defenses of contributory negligence, assumption of risk, and the fellow-servant rule.

Berle and Means discuss corporate growth and development during this period in their work on *The Modern Corporation and Private Property,* 127–287. Snider, in his *The Taxation of the Gross Receipts of Railways in Wisconsin,* 52–54, comments on the 1876 railroad-tax act. On the legal difficulties involved in attempts to confine national businesses to state boundary lines a studied analysis is presented in the "Comment" section of the *Yale Law Journal,* 59:737 (March, 1950). Gertrude Schmidt, in a manuscript dissertation on the History of Labor Legislation in Wisconsin, 48–50, in the Memorial Library of the University of Wisconsin, discusses legislative wrestling with the fellow-servant rule. Chapter 4 of Selig Perlman's *A History of Trade Unionism in the United States* (New York, 1923) describes union activities during this period.

TABLE OF AUTHORITIES

CONSTITUTIONAL PROVISIONS

STATUTES

Federal

Wisconsin

CASES

Davis v. La Crosse & M. R.
12 Wis. 17 (1860) 195 n.13
Dean v. Chicago & N. W. R.
43 Wis. 431 (1877) 220 n.12
De Forth v. Wisconsin & M. R.
52 Wis. 320 (1881) 229 n.73
Delamatyr v. Milwaukee & P. du C. R.
24 Wis. 578 (1869) 197 n.31
Delaney v. Milwaukee & St. P. R.
33 Wis. 67 (1873) 196 n.23
Delaplaine v. Chicago & N. W. R.
42 Wis. 214 (1877) 219 n.9
Delie v. Chicago & N. W. R.
51 Wis. 400 (1881) 234 n.95
Denver v. Chicago, M. & St. P. R.
57 Wis. 218 (1883) 219 n.9
Detroit & M. R. v. Curtis
23 Wis. 152 (1868) 197 n.31
27 Wis. 158 (1870) 197 n.31
Detroit & M. R. v. Farmers' & Millers' Bank
20 Wis. 122 (1865) 197 n.29
Dexterville Mfg. & Boom Co. v. Case
4 Fed. 873 (C.C.E.D. Wis., 1880) 230 n.79
Diedrich v. Northwestern Union R.
42 Wis. 248 (1877) 217 n.2
47 Wis. 662 (1879) 217 n.2
Dimmick v. Milwaukee & St. P. R.
18 Wis. 471 (1864) 197 n.29
Dinsmore v. Racine & M. R.
12 Wis. 649 (1860) 199 n.44
Dinwoodie v. Chicago, M. & St. P. R.
69 Wis. 454 (1887) 220 n.12
Ditberner v. Chicago, M. & St. P. R.
47 Wis. 138 (1879) 233 n.90, 235 n.95
Dorsey v. Phillips & Colby Construction Co.
42 Wis. 583 (1877) 234 n.95
Doud v. Wisconsin, P. & S. R.
65 Wis. 108 (1886) 224 n.31
Dougherty v. North Wisconsin R.
36 Wis. 402 (1874) 235 n.102
Downie v. Hoover
12 Wis. 174 (1860) 190 n.31
Downie v. White
12 Wis. 176 (1860) 190 n.31
Drake v. Harrison
69 Wis. 99 (1887) 233 n.88

Piek v. Chicago & N. W. R.
19 Fed. Cas. 625, No. 11,138 (C.C.D. Wis., 1874) 207 n.20
94 U.S. 164 (1876) 208 n.20
Pierce v. Chicago & N. W. R.
36 Wis. 283 (1874) 233 n.88
Pierce v. Milwaukee & St. P. R.
23 Wis. 387 (1868) 197 n.29
24 Wis. 551 (1869) 199 n.44
Piper v. Chicago, M. & St. P. R.
77 Wis. 247 (1890) 221 n.19
Pitzner v. Shinnick
39 Wis. 129 (1875) 220 n.14
41 Wis. 676 (1877) 220 n.14
Plott v. Chicago & N. W. R.
63 Wis. 511 (1885) 224 n.26
Pomeroy v. Chicago & M. R.
25 Wis. 641 (1870) 195 n.13
Pool v. Chicago, M. & St. P. R.
53 Wis. 657 (1881) 234 n.95
56 Wis. 227 (1882) 234 n.95
Porter v. Janesville
3 Fed. 617 (C.C.W.D. Wis., 1880) 230 n.79
Posey v. Rice & Halsted
29 Wis. 93 (1871) 203 n.77
Potter v. Chicago & N. W. R.
20 Wis. 533 (1866) 196 n.26, 204 n.85
21 Wis. 372 (1867) 196 n.26, 204 n.85
22 Wis. 615 (1868) 196 n.26
Powers v. Bears
12 Wis. 214 (1860) 194 nn.6,7,8
Preble v. Board of Supervisors
8 Bissell 358 (C.C.W.D. Wis., 1878) 230 n.79
Prentiss v. Danahar
20 Wis. 311 (1866) 203 n.76, 204 n.86
Price v. Milwaukee & St. P. R.
27 Wis. 98 (1870) 195 n.15
Pringle v. Dunn
37 Wis. 449 (1875) 227 n.60
Pritchard v. La Crosse & M. R.
7 Wis. 232 (1858) 196 n.19
Purtell v. Chicago Forge & Bolt Co.
74 Wis. 132 (1889) 233 n.88
Quackenbush v. Wisconsin & M. R.
62 Wis. 411 (1885) 220 n.17, 235 n.95
71 Wis. 472 (1888) 220 n.17, 235 n.95
Quaife v. Chicago, M. & St. P. R.
48 Wis. 513 (1879) 223 n.26

Index